Psychoeducational Development of Gifted and Talented Learners

Donald F. Sellin, Ed.D.

Western Michigan University

and

Jack W. Birch, Ph.D.

University of Pittsburgh

AN ASPEN PUBLICATION
Aspen Systems Corporation
Rockville, Maryland
London
1981

Library of Congress Cataloging in Publication Data

Sellin, Donald F., 1934-
Psychoeducational development of gifted and talented
learners.

Bibliography: p. 295.
Includes index.
1. Gifted children—Education—United States.
2. Gifted children—United States—Psychology.
3. Talented students—United States. I. Birch, Jack W.
II. Title.
LC3993.9.S4   371.95   81-3467
ISBN: 0-89443-362-8   AACR2

Library of Congress Catalog Card Number: 81-3467
ISBN: 0-89443-362-8

Printed in the United States of America

1 2 3 4 5

To our wives, *Lucy* and *Jane,* whose encouragement and patience made our efforts possible. We also acknowledge the lessons learned from our own children, *Andrew, Dee Ann, Elizabeth Ann, John, Mike,* and *Philip,* and grandchildren, *Andrew Tim* and *Martha Jane.*

Table of Contents

Overview .... **xi**

UNIT 1—UNDERSTANDING AND DESCRIBING HUMAN
      ABILITIES.. **1**

    Synopsis 1
    Key Ideas 1
    A Prototype... 3

Chapter 1—Understanding Human Abilities as Performance and
      Operations... **5**

      Human Abilities as Performance: Bloom........................ 6
      Human Abilities as Operations: Guilford 18

Chapter 2—Understanding Human Abilities as Adaptation **27**

      Intelligence as Adaptation: Piaget 27
      A View from the Top... 33

Chapter 3—Describing Gifted and Talented Persons........................ **39**

      Identifying Dimensions 39
      Defining Gifted and Talented.. 43
      Defining Human Ability as Adaptive Behavior 46
        Summing Up.. 49
          Understanding Human Abilities as
            Performance and Operations 49

Understanding Human Abilities as Adaptation   49
Describing Gifted and Talented Persons   50
Enrichment   50
Understanding Human Abilities as
    Performance and Operations   50
Understanding Human Abilities as Adaptation   51
Describing Gifted and Talented Persons   51

UNIT II—UNDERSTANDING THE SOCIAL CONTEXT OF
HUMAN ABILITIES   53

Synopsis   53
Key Ideas   53
A Prototype..   54

Chapter 4—Understanding Life's Sequence of Tasks   57

Early Childhood   59
Childhood   60
Adolescence   61
Young Adulthood   62
Middle and Full Adulthood....................................   62

Chapter 5—Understanding Family and Social Influences   65

Family Influences   65
Concerns of the Family   67
The Social Context of Performance   71
The Concept of Underachievement.............................   76
Levels and Forms of Underachievement........................   77

Chapter 6—Widening the Social Context of Opportunity   83

Human Ability, Culture, Language, and Poverty   83
The Gifted Handicapped...   90
Respecting Variations   97
    Summing Up..   101
        Understanding Life's Sequence of Tasks......   101
        Understanding Family and Social Influences   102
        Widening the Social Context of Opportunity   102
    Enrichment   102
        Understanding Life's Sequence of Tasks......   102

Understanding Family and Social Influences 103
Widening the Social Context of Opportunity 103

**UNIT III—UNDERSTANDING NEEDS AND PRIORITIES OF
GIFTED AND TALENTED LEARNERS** **105**

Synopsis 105
Key Ideas 105
A Prototype.. 106

Chapter 7—Identifying Gifted and Talented Learners..................... **109**

A Leadership Perspective... 109
A Case History Perspective....................................... 118
Strengthening Identification Procedures..................... 121

Chapter 8—Using and Adapting the Curriculum **125**

Selection of Curriculum Goals..................................... 125
Appraising the Structure of Curriculum..................... 128
Selecting Content by Brainstorming........................... 136

Chapter 9—Matching Learner and the Curriculum **139**

Understanding the Preferences of Consumers............. 139
Understanding the Sufficient Conditions of Learning. 145
Decisions Regarding Matching.................................... 148
Elements of Planning.. 150

Chapter 10—Managing and Maintaining the Match........................ **153**

Using Needs Assessment.. 153
Translating Needs Assessment 158
Understanding Education Programming..................... 161
Summing Up.. 166
Identifying Gifted and Talented Learners.... 167
Using and Adapting the Curriculum........... 167
Matching Learner and Curriculum.............. 168
Managing and Maintaining the Match........ 169
Enrichment 170
Identifying Gifted and Talented Learners.... 170
Using and Adapting the Curriculum........... 170

Matching Learner and Curriculum 171
Managing and Maintaining the Match 171

UNIT IV—DESCRIBING QUALITY EDUCATION 173

Synopsis 173
Key Ideas 173
A Prototype... 174

Chapter 11—Defining the Educational Context of Quality 177

The Meanings of Education 177
The Substance of Quality 179
A Framework for Quality Education 181
A Range of Options 182
Understanding the Attributes of Quality Teachers 183

Chapter 12—Developing High-Quality Programs 189

Common Questions about Starting Programs 189
Organizing for Innovation 190
Understanding the Tactics of Innovation.................... 193

Chapter 13—Developing a Confederacy for the Gifted and Talented   201

An Open System... 201
Support Systems 202
Building Program and Budget............................. 206

Chapter 14—Understanding the Impact of Quality Programs 213

The Nature of Evaluation 213
A Model for Evaluation.................................. 215
Accountability and Evaluation.............................. 218
Summing Up... 221
Defining the Educational Context of Quality   221
Developing High-Quality Programs 224
Developing a Confederacy for the Gifted and
Talented...................................... 224
Understanding the Impact of Quality Programs 225
Enrichment 225
Defining the Educational Context of Quality   225

Developing High-Quality Programs   226
Developing a Confederacy for the Gifted and
    Talented...   226
Understanding the Impact of Quality Programs   227

**UNIT V—UNDERSTANDING AND USING INDIVIDUALIZED
EDUCATION PROGRAMS.....................................**   **229**

Synopsis   229
Key Ideas...   230
A Prototype..   231
Education Program Components   231
Pupil Activities   235
Staff and Responsibilities   235

**Chapter 15—Providing a Rational for Individualized Educational
Planning**...   **239**

The Precedent of Pub.L. 94-142   239
Prior Conditions for Individualized Programs.............   240
Conditions for Preparing IEPs   246
The IEP As Public Policy...   249

**Chapter 16—Specifying the Content of an Individualized Education
Program**...   **251**

The Scope of the Individualized Education Program..   251
Preparing Goals and Objectives for Gifted and Talented
    Pupils   254
Services...   256
Instructional Dimensions...   259

Chapter 17—Assembling and Assessing Information.......................   **261**

Preferred Practices   261
Understanding and Interpreting Data   263
Understanding Aptitude/Treatment Interaction   268
Performance Assessment...   272

Chapter 18—Understanding the Key Role of Teachers **281**

Competencies for Individualized Programs   281
Teachers As Parent Consultants   282

The Teacher As a Resource for Quality 284
Toward a Common Core of Practice........................... 285
Summing Up... 288
Providing a Rationale for Individualized
Education Programs.................................... 288
Specifying the Content of an Individualized
Education Program 289
Assembling and Assessing Information........ 290
Understanding the Key Role of Teachers..... 290
Enrichment 291
Providing a Rationale for Individualized
Education Programs.................................... 291
Specifying the Content of an Individualized
Education Program 291
Assembling and Assessing Information........ 291
Understanding the Key Role of Teachers..... 292

Epilogue... 293

References.. 295

Index 305

Overview

Do gifted and talented children and youth need special attention? Some say they definitely do, because bright, creative children, as a group, do relatively poorly in school and society. Others argue that these children already receive enough special attention because they often win the highest school grades, the top honors, the major scholarships, the most desirable jobs, and the approval of society. There is some truth in both points of view. In the resolution of that puzzling paradox is the rationale for the authors' view that special attention to giftedness and talent is very much needed.

Today's theories of child psychology and today's elementary and secondary schools do appear to be oriented toward the most able. Child development specialists emphasize "wellness." Favorable attention is drawn to early attainment of mental and physical milestones. Parents are advised to stimulate social and language development in young children. Teachers praise those who earn high grades. A member of the fastest moving school group has a great deal of prestige. Privileges, formal and informal, are reserved for high achievers. Recognition (plaudits from grandparents, honor rolls, dean's lists) and material help (awards, scholarships) go to those with the top test scores and grade point averages. In short, home and school reward systems tilt toward the achievers.

School curricular and cocurricular structures show the same bias. Prestige-laden secondary school courses are for the college-bound. Counselors direct the students with the highest grades into low-enrollment honors classes and seminars that are taught by the most scholarly teachers. Librarians happily give individual attention to the quietly thoughtful and studious Clubs organized for such activities as forensics, dramatics, student newspaper and yearbook, chess, magic, and photography draw leading teachers as advisors and leading students as major participants. Adults held up as models by school staff and parents are those who exemplify the enormous value of "going on" to higher and higher education. From kindergarten to the valedictorian's address, the most able seem to be the most valued and the most honored.

Yet a wave of protest rose during the 1960s and 1970s, and the nation's families and schools were challenged to improve opportunities for gifted and talented children and youth. Strong charges were lodged, alleging neglectful practices with these young citizens. For example, a major national study concluded that gifted and talented children are disadvantaged and handicapped in the usual school situation. In fact, it has been observed that, when mental age and chronological age are compared, the gifted are the most retarded group in the schools (U.S. Office of Education, 1972). A few years later a leading scholar said:

> For decades, information has been amassed which depicted clearly the extent to which the gifted are retarded in light of their respective capacities. No condition is more clearly recognized by those conversant with the field of the gifted . . . (Newland, 1976, p. 333)

The indictment was repeated more recently by specialists in underachievement:

> Gifted children are the most misunderstood and educationally neglected group in American schools today. No other group of American children, except the Blacks, has suffered so much from misunderstanding of their needs, from lack of interest in them as persons, and from exploitation under great pressure to perform for the benefit of society. (Whitmore, 1980, pp. 3 and 7)

Why do esteemed educational and social psychologists, as well as other professionals and scientists, make accusations like these?

Some facts refute and some support the position. Today's homes and schools have many positive conditions that nurture gifted and talented students. Most parents and teachers enjoy many of the qualities of bright children. Also, *some* such students receive very high-quality education. At the same time, many negative conditions crop up in almost all schools. It is these unsatisfactory conditions, which have been linked to maladjustment, underachievement, and excessive dropout rates among the most able young people, that are being challenged. It is these conditions that Whitmore (1980) speaks of when she says:

> Gifted children, by nature, are highly inquisitive beings who normally should become "high achievers" as a result of their curiosity, experimentation, discoveries, assimilation-organization-

use of information, perception of relationships, and memory. Gifted children are made into underachievers as a result of specific handicaps; a dull, meager curriculum that destroys motivation to achieve in school; inappropriate teaching strategies that are incompatible with their learning styles; or a lack of adult assistance to the child in need of learning how to handle socioemotional conflict, to gain self-control, and to set realistic self-expectations. (p. 132)

No nation can long tolerate the loss of these extraordinary human resources. This book is designed to help educators, parents, and other community leaders respond to the problems of gifted and talented children that so many responsible investigators have found in need of correction. There is solid research evidence that the specific human handicaps, the curricular limitations, the flagging motivation, the failure to capitalize on individual learning styles, the shallow and narrow instructional goals and objectives that stand in the way of high-quality education can be corrected in most cases. There is also competent proof that confidence-building adult-student relationships can replace those that are destructive to the mental health of gifted and talented children. A point made in the 1972 U.S. Office of Education report on the gifted and talented should be emphasized:

The boredom that results from discrepancies between the child's knowledge and the school's offerings leads to underachievement and behavior disorders affecting self and others. Early identification would enable schools to prevent rather than to attempt later on to cure underachievement. (p. 12)

Probably at no other time in history has there been such an effort to ensure that the most able young people of this nation have real opportunities to fulfill themselves and to contribute, in the process, to society. One vivid example of this effort is the toll-free hotline on gifted and talented education that has been launched under the sponsorship of the U.S. Department of Education. By calling (800)424-2861 one can obtain information and literature in Spanish or in English on research projects in gifted and talented education. The service also provides referrals to experts.

THE KNOWLEDGE BASE ABOUT GIFTEDNESS AND TALENT

A great deal of reliable information about giftedness and talent is available as a result of many serious and painstaking investigations. The first was in England more than a century ago (Galton, 1869). The number of psychosocial and psychoeducational studies is now estimated to be more than 1,000, and they provide an accumulation of research of major proportions and significant value. The sifting and winnowing of this mass of information by diligent and insightful analysts make it possible today to examine the nature and needs of gifted and talented individuals from a foundation of facts, well-documented generalizations, and principles.

A major point that emerges from a study of contemporary practices and thought is that giftedness and talent can be nurtured quite well while the separation of pupils into special groups is kept to a minimum. The great majority of gifted and talented children and youth can receive optimum education in their local schools, in classes with other children. This requires, first, that these exceptional pupils be recognized and, second, that regular teachers be furnished with sufficient in-service preparation, consultation from specialists, and the requisite time, materials, aides, and volunteers. There are differences of opinion on this matter, and the book acknowledges other approaches. We are satisfied, however, that the know-how is available and needs only to be carefully and thoughtfully applied.

THE CONTENT

To locate gifted and talented children and to deliver individualized education of high quality and of substance to them is an acknowledged objective in most nations today. There is now a sufficient knowledge base about the social and psychological qualities of highly able learners and about effective educational practices to reach that public objective. The thrust of this book is to provide educators and other interested groups with information regarding the nature and needs of able learners and the preferred ways to undertake their individualized education.

ORGANIZATION OF THE BOOK

The book is divided into five units. Units I and II identify the nature and origins of superior abilities. Units III through V reflect the needs of gifted and talented learners. The Unit Synopsis, Key Ideas, and Prototype establish a set for the subsequent chapters in each unit. Each unit concludes with a Summing Up and an Enrichment section, which suggests activities for the application of unit content. There are several competing approaches to the nurture of superior human abilities. Our preference is for individualized education programs, i.e., the orderly matching of aptitudes to curriculum content and resources. For us, high-quality education involves managing and maintaining that optimal match. Pupil attributes must be the foundation for program design. Their identification is the first step toward individualization.

A STARTING POINT

There are many definitions and descriptors of gifted and talented persons. One widely used definition was advanced by the U.S. Office of Education and became part of Pub.L. 91-250. This definition, with occasional minor variations, is used by a majority of state departments of education. It refers to gifted and talented children as:

> those identified by professionally qualified persons, who by virtue of outstanding abilities, are capable of high performance. These are children who require differentiated educational programs and/or services beyond those normally provided by the regular school program in order to realize their contribution to self and society.
>
> Children capable of high performance include those with demonstrated achievement and/or potential ability in any one of the following areas: 1) general intellectual ability, 2) specific academic ability, 3) creative or productive thinking, 4) leadership ability, 5) visual and performing arts, and 6) psychomotor ability.
>
> ... Evidence of gifted and talented abilities may be determined by a multiplicity of ways. These procedures should include objective measures and professional evaluation measures which are essential components of identification. (p. 10)

The adequacy of this definition is examined in Chapter 3. Our purpose in this Overview is to highlight significant points where there is broad agreement about what is meant by gifted and talented persons. We propose these points, in addition:

- *Gifted* and *talented* are terms applied to persons who may possess one, several, or all the attributes listed in the Office of Education definition. Consequently, persons should be viewed in the light of their particular profiles of abilities.

- Highly able learners tend to be positively and humanely motivated, stable, and well adjusted.

- A psychological assessment of intelligence, using individual standardized intelligence tests, is a very valuable means of determining a child's range and variety of abilities. Such an evaluation is one important index of potential or of performance. As seen in Units II and III, parent and teacher observations, as well as other data, can also be valid indicators of extraordinary ability.

• Most persons of high intelligence or talent show signs of their potential very early in life, long before starting to school. Attention to these budding abilities is highly important.

• Some children with great potential are limited by poor physical nourishment, by vision or hearing impairments, by emotional and social forces in their environments, and by neglect or abuse. Special efforts should be made to find and help these children.

• There are marked individual differences among gifted and talented persons in their backgrounds, their interests, their achievement motivation, and their attainments. The reasons for these differences are fertile fields for study.

THE CHALLENGE

The identification of superior human abilities, whether artistic, athletic, or academic, is a strong tradition in all the world's civilizations. The increasing complexity of life and the heightened awareness of human interdependency bring sharply into focus the imperative that the most valuable of all material resources, the potential of children and youth, must now command attention as never before.

Understanding and Describing Human Abilities

SYNOPSIS

Teachers, principals, parents, coaches, and recreation leaders who are responsible for instructing and counseling gifted and talented young people need an unusually thorough understanding of human abilities, including intelligence. The chief reason: the nurture of intelligence lies at the heart of every bona fide special education scheme for highly able young people.

An examination of the concept of intelligence as it is accounted for in major theories of developmental psychology can shed light on how psychoeducational scientists and practitioners arrive at definitions of gifted and talented persons that make sense in both theoretical and practical ways. Much of this unit is designed to supply the theory base of the concept of intelligence and to show the specific linkages between theory and the day-to-day work of those who guide and educate gifted and talented children and youth.

The temptation to look for common characteristics in all gifted and talented persons should be resisted. They vary in every direction, and so do their accomplishments. It should be noted that intelligence is not divorced from the rest of life; rather, it is a good indicator of a person's ability to make wise and personally profitable adaptations to the world's demands.

KEY IDEAS

Typically, intelligence is associated with terms such as mental ability, thought, wisdom, or cognition. Cognition is a troublesome word because it can be used in two different ways, both correct. It is frequently used as a synonym for intelligence. In psychoeducational terms, however, cognition is the manipulation, in thought, of objects, symbols, rules, sequences, and concepts. In order to perform mental manipulations (i.e., to try out notions, to achieve

1

understandings, or to construct plans) at least five psychoeducational processes need to be employed (Mussen, Conger, & Kagan, 1974): (1) perception, (2) memory, (3) generation of ideas, (4) evaluation, and (5) reasoning. Employing these five cognitive processes at progressively higher levels of complexity and accuracy is the substance of intellectual development in the years of childhood and youth. A rate of cognitive development that is consistently much faster than that of most age peers is one operational evidence of giftedness (Reynolds & Birch, 1977). The Bloom system uses some related terminology to develop essentially the same five components of cognition. A less common use of the term *cognition* is to signify a specific kind of behavior within the Guilford system.

Within the psychoeducational community, three theoretical systems for understanding intelligence arise from the writings and research of Bloom, Guilford, and Piaget. All the systems describe and explain how information and knowledge are processed in the human mind. They recognize, in common, practices called storage, retrieval, selection, application, and production, though their terminology may differ somewhat.

A knowledge of any of the systems can help educators, counselors, and parents of gifted and talented young people in at least three ways. First, the knowledge can add precision to everyday language, improving communication. Second, any system can assist in defining program goals and objectives, thus facilitating the assessment and evaluation necessary for program improvement. Third, an understanding of pupils in terms of a theoretical system can help to establish empathy in adults.

Human ability has its social-psychological context. Testimony from able persons and their parents reveals many situations that call for practical guidance. For parents, there is the constant need to manage socialization as it relates to accelerated development.

Attributes such as talent, aptitude, and creativity create persistent confusion, especially if they are not considered in relation to intelligence. It is not necessary to possess complete knowledge about the origins of talent, creativity, and aptitude in order to identify, encourage, and nurture them. There is now sufficient knowledge for appropriate home, school, and community program design and implementation.

One result of comparing human ability and human performance in their social-psychological contexts is the evolution of a definition. The best functional definitions summarize knowledge and guide practice. Definitions of gifted and talented persons are of three types. The federal definition describes outstanding attributes necessary for program operations. A view that is more associated with the individual's high degree of task commitment can be identified in other definitions. Finally, a view that emphasizes unusual skill in personal/social adaptive behavior can be observed. Each style of definition has values for those responsible for the optimum development of gifted and talented individuals.

With a sufficient background of knowledge, each counselor, parent, teacher, or principal can form a personally and scientifically defensible, responsible, and useful position on the meaning of intelligence and related concepts, a position that makes a firm base for both long-range planning and day-to-day guidance, instruction, evaluation, and problem resolution.

A PROTOTYPE

One major obstacle to understanding intellectual ability is sorting out the terminology. Michener (1978) made the point precisely in *Chesapeake* when he told of Edward Paxmore's efforts to build a sailboat without benefit of the shipwright's technical vocabulary:

> But always he lacked the essential tool without which the workman can never attain true mastery: He did not know the names of any of the parts he was building, and without the name he was artistically incomplete. It was not by accident that doctors and lawyers and butchers invented specific but secret names for the things they do; to possess the name was to know the secret. With correct names one entered into a new world of proficiency, became the member of an arcane brotherhood, a sharer of mysteries, and in the end a performer of merit. Without the names one remained a bumbler or, in the case of boat building, a mere house carpenter. (pp. 200–201)

Chapter 1

Understanding Human Abilities as Performance and Operations

Intelligence is the accepted name for the combined operations of attending, thinking, remembering, forecasting, and evaluating. In everyday terms, intelligence is what makes up the intellect, or the mind, and it includes inventive abilities. The brain is thought of as the seat of intelligence or of mental activity. In a colloquial sense, "brains" or "smarts" are synonyms for mind, intellect, and intelligence.

Intelligence is thought to be capable of growing, especially in the periods of childhood and adolescence. There is a pervasive, popular belief that, while there is a native wit that can show itself without benefit of formal schooling, the best opportunity for intelligence to blossom into its full strength is provided by years of consistently high quality education, complemented by thoughtful and warm-hearted stimulation at home and in the community. It is well-known, too, that two women or men with the same mental prowess can be totally different in what they know, what they like, how they relate to others, and in what they expect from life.

Within the domain of schooling, intelligence is viewed mainly in two ways. Initially, intelligence is thought of as a quantity; the more the pupil has, the more readily that pupil can grasp what is being taught. Thus, a student who has a great deal of intelligence is expected to do very well in school. Conversely, doing very well in school can be taken as an indication that a pupil is very intelligent. Equating little intelligence with low achievement is part of the same commonly held view.

A second way of thinking about intelligence in the school milieu suggests an additional and perhaps more useful way to think about it. This more recent view is that intelligence is developing during the preschool and school years and *that the growth of intelligence can be influenced significantly by how teaching is done.* True enough, individual children exhibit more or less intelligence at any one time, and the intelligence exhibited at any one time is a major determinant of how thoroughly and speedily things taught will be learned. But this new theory of intelligence proposes that the way things to be learned are presented, the way children are encouraged to study, the kinds of questions parents and teachers ask, the willingness with which adults and older children listen to children's ideas, the tone and attitude that accompanies correction and explanation, the rewarding of sincere effort, and the fostering of eagerness and ambition all can have powerful effects on how rapidly and richly intelligence grows. Adult behaviors can operate either to depress or accelerate the development and full use of children's intelligence. Formal education and other interactions with adults ought to increase individual differences both in present achievement and in the capacity for future achievement for all children, but especially for those who are gifted and talented.

Competing terms can interfere with communication. Synonyms for intellectual performance in common speech make an almost endless list: cognition, mental ability, evaluation, judgment, reasoning, logic, brillance, discernment, comprehension, conceptual agility, analytical aptitude, shrewdness, synthesis, problem solving, etc. Among contemporary scholars, cognitive, mental, and intellectual describe similar abilities. Of the three, cognition is often least clear as to its meaning. As used here, cognition describes the activities of a person in the processes of receiving, storing, and retrieving information. The manifestation of cognitive behavior is viewed as the ability to organize available information so as to achieve a purpose and to recognize when that purpose is achieved. Gifted and talented young people do these things much better than their age peers.

HUMAN ABILITIES AS PERFORMANCE: BLOOM

A Range of Behaviors

Bloom, Hastings, and Madeus (1971) offer a potentially useful way to consider what intelligence (as human abilities) is and how its development may best be encouraged under the guidance of teachers. They recognize that teachers are not content to teach only facts, but that they aim at increasing students' understanding and stimulating students' constructive use of what has been learned.

One of Bloom's reports (1956) has emerged as a very promising way of assisting teachers to describe their goals. This report has proved especially reassuring to teachers who want to determine if their aims are appropriately comprehensive in scope. Bloom and his associates described cognition as a universe of six behaviors: (1) knowledge, (2) comprehension, (3) application, (4) analysis, (5) synthesis, and (6) evaluation. These may be taken as building blocks in that each is a foundation for subsequent behaviors.

Knowledge objectives, according to Bloom (1956), may be tested by recall. The person neither transforms nor alters content. Knowing usually involves a relatively low level of abstraction, although abstractions themselves may be the subject matter for recall. Items of knowledge constitute a general fund of information, e.g., how to multiply a two-digit number.

Comprehension is the same as understanding. It is shown by a paraphrase of the material that transforms the original into a personalized interpretation without loss of meaning. Also, comprehension can be verified by interpretation, or extrapolation, beyond the original data. For example, knowledge of a definition of gifted and talented is an ability to recite it verbatim. Comprehension is shown by an accurate, deliberate expansion of the definition.

Application refers to the use of rules, principles, and general methods in concrete situations. The need for specific information must be recognized, and that information must be recalled. For example, word problems in arithmetic require (1) recognition that a given process applies and (2) recall of that process. Accuracy of application is required. Applications can be demonstrated by an understanding of implications, consequences, and effects.

Analysis calls for comparing and contrasting. It is exemplified in the procedures by which those in a given discipline examine its subject matter and their own methods of inquiry. Its essence is in the relationships that exist among pieces of information within a given information- and skill-based system. Analysis is the basis upon which original theories are constructed.

The remaining two dimensions of the Bloom (1956) report, synthesis and evaluation, have attracted especially strong interest from educators of the gifted and talented. Ability to perform these behaviors is frequently said to be characteristic of productive gifted and talented persons. Moreover, the emergence of these abilities is facilitated by instruction.

Synthesis means the creation of a whole out of its parts, usually involving information and ideas from a variety of sources. It includes behaviors such as anticipating and explaining consequences, deduction, appraisal, and classification. Students may be tested on their mastery of how professionals organize a plan of action. The gifted and talented learner evolves a personalized style of synthesis.

Evaluation requires an examination of the plan and the product developed by synthesis. It involves making the judgments necessary for implementation and continuing to make assessments as the plan is implemented. It also implies criteria of worth, accuracy, consistency, and logical validity. Evaluation culminates in defining the circumstances in which the goal will have been achieved. There are two main types of evaluation: (1) the formative type in which the internal consistency of the plan's elements and their logical fit is assessed and (2) the summative type in which the external consistency of the plan, i.e., its adequacy to achieve desired outcomes is examined. The latter is the ultimate test.

In teaching, or in measurement situations, these six dimensions present a sequence of increasing complexity. In performance terms, according to Bloom (1956), a person may be operating in several dimensions at once. Cognition defined by these six elements does fulfill a psychoeducational description of intelligent behavior.

Preparing Knowledge Outcomes

There are some things that children simply must learn to recall quickly and without help. Examples are their address; telephone number; directions like left, right, up, and down; the correct spelling of words; number facts; certain geographical place names; and the order of the alphabet. Items like these are more useful if they can be remembered quickly and through unaided recall. (Unaided recall or pure recall is producing information without assistance; writing a definition to a word is an example. Aided recall or recognition is remembering with the help of cues; a multiple choice item is an example.)

According to Bloom (1956) and Bloom et al. (1971), the ability to remember certain items is a prerequisite for subsequent attainments. Knowledge items (facts) are the foundation upon which subsequent skills are built. Hence, tests for these items can be useful in assisting the parent or educator to uncover gaps or errors in information among gifted and talented youngsters. Knowledge items usually center upon names, dates, definitions, terms, and the like.

There are two options for measuring factual knowledge. One is the recognition mode, in which answers are supplied and the pupil selects from alternatives. The multiple choice item, true-or-false statements, and matching items are examples. The other mode is unaided recall, which involves fill-in-the-blank, open-ended questions. In this instance, the child must supply the answer. Thus, it can be seen that "knowing" can be in two different modes. The recall mode is more difficult than the recognition mode for everyone, including gifted and talented individuals.

Knowledge test items should very closely parallel the original teaching. If a child has learned that $3 + 2 = 5$, it does not mean that the child immediately knows that $2 + 3 = 5$. That must either be learned separately as a new bit of knowledge or learned through the application of a higher order process, namely, transposition. Gifted and talented children tend to "catch on" quickly to transpositions.

Preparing Comprehension Outcomes

Comprehension, the step beyond the factual knowledge acquired by rote memorization, is important to any subject matter field. Bloom et al. (1971) suggest that the term *understanding* is an equivalent to comprehension. Key phrases can serve as indicators of comprehension. These include: (1) give an illustration; (2) interpret the meanings of maps, charts, and graphs; (3) write a summary; (4) interpret the context of a passage; (5) describe consequences from reading a report; (6) note and explain imagery in a painting; and (7) translate a French sentence into English.

Three distinct elements are involved in comprehension: translation, interpretation, and extrapolation. Translation is the act of changing a message into a different or altered form, for example, describing in words the exact, or literal, meaning of a graph. Interpretation is a skill that involves inferences, such as describing relationships among the dimensions of the graph. Extrapolation, in turn, calls for the ability to predict consequences from the graph.

Measurement of comprehension follows the same mode as knowledge items in that items can be supplied from which the student is to select a "best" choice, or an unaided recall response can be requested. As with knowledge items, comprehension assessment items should not go beyond what was taught, even with gifted and talented persons. Examples of comprehension assessment might include the following:

- A group of persons is engaged in the production of a differentiated curriculum. In lay language, what are these persons doing?

- In reading articles about giftedness and talent, one encounters terms such as basic scholar, intelligence test, the Terman studies, and the Bloom taxonomy of cognitive objectives. Describe in your own terms and in everyday experiences, what these words mean.

Bloom et al. (1971) observed that the traditional true-or-false test can be transformed into a multiple choice test of inference statements, such as (1) true, (2) probably true, (3) not sufficient information, (4) probably false, and (5) false. For example, given the federal definition of giftedness and talent mentioned in the overview, items could be constructed in which the following choices could be employed to obtain a measurement of comprehension:

1. The definition relies on intelligence quotients alone.
2. The definition is a national mandate.
3. The definition includes overt behavior.

Preparing Application Outcomes

Gifted and talented children may readily acquire knowledge, understanding, and even skill, that they may not be permitted to apply. Navigating ships or aircraft, driving automobiles, and operating complex industrial machinery may all be well within the competence of gifted and talented girls or boys who are much too young (by law or by custom) actually to do so. Yet, persons who grasp new material must be able to apply a great deal of what they learn if the learning is to be retained and if frustration is to be avoided. Meaningful application is desirable whether the subject be art, foreign language, mathematics, science, or sociology. This makes it necessary to move gifted and talented students beyond merely the recall and the understanding of what has been presented.

Material that can be applied immediately after learning is retained longer than material that is simply known or understood. Also, the ability to apply learning to new situations is a cognitive declaration of independence from the past. It is an example of transfer of training, the ability either to apply new learning to past events or to apply old learning to new events. The personal utility of application is plain. Instruction is not needed for every new situation; new situations can be encountered with confidence.

The measurement of ability to apply learning calls for special consideration. It cannot be measured by tests that call only for knowledge. Application requires the use of abstractions in real and concrete situations. Consequently, abstraction and situation are the key elements of the behavior called application (Bloom et al., 1971).

Abstractions may be either principles or generalizations. Principles are truths or laws accepted by scholars in a field. They are consistent results of observations and experiments, and they hold true for a wide range of conditions. Generalizations summarize inferences that hold true for a majority of instances, although there are acknowledged exceptions. Generalizations are less firm than principles. The gifted and talented person must be able to recognize the tentativeness of a generalization statement and the limited circumstances to which it can apply. The consensus of scholars in a field decides the extent to which any statement has the status of principle or generalization. For example, "a learned act is repeated if it is reinforced" is a principle, while "educational aspirations of schoolchildren are related to the fathers' occupations" is a generalization.

Abstractions, either as principles or as generalizations, can be ideas, procedures, teaching methods, educational theories, or they can take other forms. Some abstractions are accepted by wide agreement or by specific adoption, as in the case of a definition. Most frequently, principles and generalizations are established by observation of the frequency of the events with which they predict principles allowing firmer and more precise predictions.

The ability to apply, according to Bloom et al. (1971), may be demonstrated by any of eight possible behaviors (Table 1-1). Posing problems such as those in Table 1-1 for able youth is a genuine skill. Response is best to problems that may be encountered in real life. An adequate problem statement should (1) be solvable by use of principles and generalizations

Table 1-1 Example of Use of Abstraction Applied to New Situations*

(In order to determine whether a gifted and talented child is able to perform the kinds of behavior in the left column, the child can be asked to respond to questions that are like the ones in the right column. The content of the questions should, of course, be within the child's knowledge and comprehension.)

Behavior Type	*Example Item*
1. Determine which abstractions are appropriate or relevant. 2. Restate a problem as to which abstractions are necessary.	There is, according to some observers, a steady, long-term trend toward increased federal control of American life, including education. What information exists to support the eventuality of such control? What information suggests that the trend is temporary or transient? A misinterpretation?
3. Describe limits under which an abstraction applies. 4. Recognize exceptions to an abstraction and their reason.	The individual test of intelligence is considered by some authorities to be the best means of identification of gifted and talented children. What evidence supports this view? Are there other data that contradict that view?
5. Explain new results from known abstractions.	Creativity has been found to be associated with positive self-concept. How does this statement prove or disprove the stereotype of the thin line between genius and insanity?
6. Predict happenings in a new situation by application of abstractions.	Suppose all gifted and talented learners were required to attend specialized, residential schools. What would be the social and economic consequences of such a policy?
7. Justify a new course of action by use of abstractions.	People predict there will be an increase in programs for the gifted and talented when parents form a national association. If you were an advisor, what position about enrichment would you urge for national policy?
8. State reasons, or reasoning, to support use of abstractions.	Suppose the concept of individualized education programs were extended to all children in the public schools. What would be consequences of such an action?

*Adapted from Bloom et al. (1971).

already presented; (2) be new, or unfamiliar, but reasonably solvable; and (3) include at least one of the eight behaviors in Table 1-1.

Preparing Analysis Outcomes

Teaching pupils to be competent at analysis rarely appears as a general objective in the elementary school curriculum. It appears occasionally at the secondary school level and frequently at the college level, especially in courses for juniors and seniors. Yet it is clear that analysis training is appropriate and advisable for elementary age gifted and talented children.

Analysis is one means by which people cope with rapid social change and distinguish between facts and fancies. As a behavior, analysis is the use of knowledge, comprehension, and application to uncover the actual circumstances of events, their causes, and especially their interrelationships. It reveals both the explicit and the implicit data at the foundations of a problem. It involves the ideas, opinions, things, documents, models—whatever are the constituent parts of the problem. Analytic skills are learned through practice. Optimum teaching methods include (1) using problems that are real, (2) having vital documents or data available to students, and (3) judging the adequacy of pupil responses by reference to the opinions of competent persons, by use of factual evidence, or a combination of both.

In testing whether children can perform analysis it is best to use actual examples. The student should have documents and information readily at hand. The open-book examination, the take-home examination, and the term paper are preferred ways to provide data for the teacher to use to assess whether the pupil has mastered analytic skills. Of course, the questions put to gifted and talented pupils in such examinations must be searching ones, if they are to call upon the skills of analysis.

The characteristic language of questions that call for analysis includes such phrases as (1) distinguish between fact and opinion, (2) recognize an untested assumption, (3) identify motives, (4) verify the accuracy of an accepted hypothesis in light of data and information, (5) identify assumptions and information that are essential to a position, (6) identify underlying causal factors, (7) detect an author's view, and (8) identify the methods of inquiry used in solving a problem. Analysis involves at least six behaviors. Some are relatively passive; others require a more active engagement.

Table 1-2 displays the behaviors of analysis. The sample items show that the person must draw inferences beyond those explicitly stated by an author. This requires viewing a document as a whole, as well as in the societal context that surrounded its preparation. As a product, the gifted and talented person would be expected to produce an analysis that includes assumptions, motives, and purposes.

Bloom et al. (1971) observed that analytic skills correspond to Piaget's pronouncements about formal operations. It is the use of both the obvious and implicit that separates this ability from concrete operations.

Preparing Synthesis Outcomes

The ability to synthesize is one of the most frequently mentioned objectives for gifted and talented pupils. Attention to that outcome is almost universally viewed as an attribute of a high-quality program for these children.

Table 1-2 Examples of Measurement of Analytic Skills*

(Assume that each example item is based on or literally drawn from actual articles, papers, or books that are accessible to the person responding to the sample item.)

Behavior Type	*Example Item*
1. Recognize the use, function, and/or purpose of related elements in a document.	What would be an author's purpose and assumptions in advancing the following statement? "The scholarly concerns of psychologists include interest and support for programs for the gifted and talented."
2. Infer qualities, traits, or attributes not directly stated from available clues in a document.	How could Napoleon's concept of an aristocracy of merit influence public support for an environmental viewpoint regarding human ability?
3. Infer the conditions, assumptions, or criteria within a document that would define the validity of its conclusions.	It is true that, if a perfect correlation existed between measured IQ and creativity, then IQ could predict performance. Perfect correlation will not exist. Consequently, IQ should be discarded. Can this conclusion be defended?
4. Use criteria (cause, sequence, appropriateness) to discover an order, pattern, or arrangement in a document.	Suppose one has access to Terman's studies. How do his reports reflect the absence of modern statistical methods, his ability to gain recognition, the use of theory to guide his work, and the key attributes of the gifted and talented?
5. Recognize the patterns/principles of organization upon which a document is based.	
6. Infer the purpose or point of view on which a document is based.	

*Adapted from Bloom et al. (1971).

Bloom et al. (1971) described synthesis as a creative act and equated it to the Guilford concept of divergent thinking. They observed that knowledge, comprehension, and applications ordinarily represent convergent thinking, which is used in tasks that are fixed problems for which there are set answers. Analysis, depending upon teaching style, can be creative, but it is usually presented as a convergent task.

Education based upon synthesis frequently is a departure from the usual, often involving a highly individualized pursuit that departs from the content controlled by curriculum makers, teachers, and conventional test makers. The outcome of synthesis is a production that is uniquely the pupil's. There is pride of authorship, a sense of creativity, and an investment in communication. There is also the sense of accomplishment. Typically, a synthesis (a term paper, essay, thesis, project, composition) is the end product of a phase of education. The ability to synthesize well tranforms the person from a consumer of generalizations to a producer of generalizations. Early opportunities for learning the skills of synthesis for gifted and talented children increase the likelihood of early benefits to society.

The language of synthesis objectives suggests its attributes. It appears in phrases such as (1) organize to present ideas, (2) write creatively, (3) express ideas in clear and concise terms, (4) contribute to group discussions, (5) propose procedures for testing ideas, (6) devise methods for testing hypotheses, (7) design a unit of instruction for a specific teaching situation, (8) use space to fit a particular situation, (9) produce discoveries, and (10) deduce a hypothesis from logically related data.

Synthesis includes three behaviors: (1) production of communication, (2) design of a plan or proposed set of operations, and (3) derivation of a set of abstract relations. Communication can encompass any aspect of human ability and any medium, such as art, music, literature, the sciences, and mathematics. The gifted and talented child as a producer is expected to (1) convey meanings to others; (2) describe the effect to be achieved; (3) identify the nature of the audience to be influenced; (4) rationalize the selection of media, mode, or styles to be used; and (5) summarize the ideas, feelings, information, and experiences to be communicated. An example of an item to assess this behavior could be:

> Sometimes journals devoted to and designed for parents or teachers of the gifted and talented are criticized. Their articles are considered slanted to one view or irrelevant to day-to-day teacher concerns. You are to propose and explain what you think a journal for parents or teachers of the gifted and talented should be like. You may discuss a specific journal or journals in general. Present your ideas about the characteristics of a helpful journal. What should be its proper role? What should its responsibilities be? Who should formulate its policy? By what standards should it be judged? Do not merely write answers to these questions. They are intended to stimulate your thinking about the topic. Make sure that your points are clear and form some kind of progression. Take the time to critique, revise, polish, and proofread your answer before submitting it.

Plainly, to give a reasoned answer to this item, the learner must have access to a variety of source materials, plus ample time. To assess the quality of the response, the teacher should use criteria similar to those applicable to the analysis.

The ability to produce a plan, or proposal for operations, is assessed by means of a task or a problem. The topic selected should be of interest to the learner; the student should have either a free choice or full partnership role in topic selection. The task is only to propose a plan; there is no need to execute it. The gifted and talented individual is expected to (1) identify the requirements of the task, (2) gather the data to be taken into account, (3) satisfy the criteria and standards generally accepted in the field, and (4) conform to appropriate standards of expression. The following is an example of an item that, if assigned and completed, could be used to determine the learner's ability to produce a proposal:

> Educational policy regarding the gifted and talented is a reflection of social goals and respect for individual differences. Policies are also influenced by community attitudes and financial resources. The aspirations of educators are another significant source. In light of these comments, prepare an essay about education policy toward the gifted and talented. Describe the following: (1) principles that should guide practice, (2) the intentions/goals that policy should pursue, and (3) what policies should be instituted. Your response will be judged on the basis of your thoroughness and consistency, not by conformity to a particular point of view. Use citations, but do not allow them to substitute for your own point of view.

The third behavioral component of synthesis is the derivation of a set of abstract relations. The product might be a theory, a scheme, a design, or a model to account for relationships. Deriving abstract relationships involves making logical deductions. One approach to determining whether a person has this skill is to present three to five articles, essays, or experiments. The gifted and talented individual would be expected to derive their common features (abstract relations). Then the individual would be asked to identify others that would be similar. The following is another approach:

> Suppose you were able to travel into the future and study the culture of the United States 1,000 years from now. You find that all positions of status and honor are held by gifted persons between the ages of 15 to 21. You are told that this is because sensitivity, kindness, and competence are ideal attributes. Since it is believed that gifted persons of the 15 to 21 age group excel all others in these attributes, they automatically find themselves chosen. Write an essay to account for the influences that resulted in this situation. What significant social changes might be associated with such changes?

In order to provide a convincing rationale, the writer must seek reasonable relationships among age, high rate and level of cognitive development, and the qualities of sensitivity, kindness, and competence. Moreover, the essay's format must be historical, showing the interactions of those elements over time while specifying consequent changes of social significance.

Preparing Evaluation Outcomes

Evaluation, judgment about value, is not merely a reflexive act, a snap judgment of good-bad, or like-dislike. Rather, evaluation involves a choice from among alternatives through the exercise of knowledge, comprehension, application, analysis, and synthesis; it calls for a reasoned estimate of worth, merit, and usefulness. Standards must be used to determine accuracy, efficiency, effectiveness, satisfaction, and economical value. Judgments can be quantitative, qualitative, or both. Evaluation is essential to maintaining the quality and substance of citizenship. The exercise of evaluation by everyone, and especially by leaders, can be a protection against hazardous snap judgments. Evaluation almost always appears among objectives for secondary and college education. Analysis and synthesis abilities are essential prerequisites to sound evaluation.

The language of internal evaluation can be recognized by phrases such as (1) examine the accuracy, completeness, and relevance of data; (2) distinguish between valid and invalid inferences in a statement or a document; (3) determine if conclusions are supported by data, proper method of inquiry, and sound arguments; (4) reorganize bias and emotional motivation in a presentation; and (5) identify fallacies in assumptions underlying an argument or presentation.

The language of external evaluation is made up of phrases such as (1) describe standards of quality, (2) compare products with the highest known standards in a given field, (3) identify and judge the elements generally accepted as necessary for a plan of work, and (4) appraise the provisions of government services in relation to established criteria in recreation, protection, cultural stimulation, education, and other indicators of quality of life.

Evaluation is composed of six behaviors, three associated with internal procedures and three with external. Table 1-3 presents illustrations of the measurement of these behaviors.

Guidelines for Use

The outline, or taxonomy, of cognitive outcomes described by Bloom et al. (1971) has enjoyed increasing acceptance by educators. It is useful with all pupils, but especially with those who are gifted and talented. The document itself provides useful illustrations and examples in all subject matter and performance areas across all age levels, from preschool through college.

Table 1-3 Examples of Behavior Associated with Evaluation*

(Note that the last three behavior types on the left can be related to the last two sample items on the right.)

Behavior Type	Example Item
1. Judge a document or plan in terms of accuracy, precision, and the care with which it has been prepared.	Given two reports of investigations on the same topic, identify the areas that have been well controlled and the features that have not been well sampled.
2. Judge the relationships among assumptions, evidence, conclusions, and logic of a document or plan.	Same situation as above with the additional requirements of the elements of relationships. The student must make a choice between the two.
3. Identify the values and points of view used in any statement, document, or plan.	The statement is often made that psychology and sociology are basic sciences, while teaching and administration are derived sciences. What interpretations proceed from this view?
4. Judge a work or plan by comparison with other relevant works.	Suppose that a school district were serious about programming for its gifted and talented pupils. Its school board decides to require preparation in the education of the gifted and talented as a condition of teacher, principal, and counselor employment. Describe the circumstances by which the regulation would be proper or improper.
5. Judge a work or plan using a given set of criteria or standards.	The Terman studies are often praised for their enduring contribution to knowledge. This is remarkable, since they lacked a theoretical base. In a well-organized essay, state your degree of agreement with this statement. Your report should reflect your mastery of the content of the Terman project.
6. Judge a work or plan according to a personal set of criteria.	

*Adapted from Bloom et al. (1971).

Initial feelings of anxiety about using the procedures evaporate through practice, and the effort to attain mastery is usually rewarded by benefits for all learners.

Users find that the system lends precision and a degree of concreteness to outcomes that have heretofore been fuzzy and imprecise. At the same time, the system is not bound to any theory of learning or to any set of values. Also, it invites cooperative efforts; for example, teachers and parents can work together to decide which dimensions are to be pursued and which procedures are to be followed.

The system facilitates the development of assessment procedures tailored to the unique features of the immediate situation, although commercially available materials can be used. The care devoted to measurement encourages the matching of content and teaching tactics to individually selected learner outcomes. The diagnostic potential in the system's sequence facilitates the identification of foundation skills necessary for subsequent achievement. Responses to items can be the basis for designing and conducting further instruction. Not restricted to one kind of content or question, the ideas are appropriate for projects, seminars, laboratory work, independent study, and other types of school experiences.

Although the examples cited were essay questions, all levels of cognitive behavior can be assessed by objective short answer or multiple choice type items. Using such items together with essays provides both quantitative and qualitative results. Essay test methods can be used as a follow-up to more objective procedures. Although the system is neutral about teaching strategies, it emphasizes student participation in planning. Moreover, it places a value on student products and effort.

A formulation by Gage (1963) can help in summarizing. He spoke of teaching as:

> any interpersonal influence aimed at changing the way in which other persons will behave. . . . The influence has to impinge on the other person through. . .his ways of getting meaning out of the objects and events that his senses make him aware of. . . . These behaviors. . .may be classed. . .as the "cognitive," "affective," and "psychomotor" domain of the *Taxonomy of Educational Objectives.* (pp. 96–97)

What Bloom and his associates have accomplished is exceedingly important to the teaching of gifted and talented persons because their work is an orderly and useful classification of complex behavior encountered in the daily interactions of teachers and pupils. Moreover, they have contributed more than a static classification; they suggest ways to bring that classification to life in the teaching of gifted and talented students.

HUMAN ABILITIES AS OPERATIONS: GUILFORD

Guilford offers parents, teachers, and psychologists an instruction-oriented way to look at intelligence. He presents a neatly arranged model in which different intellectual abilities can be recognized and assessed. There are gaps in the model because, in Guilford's view, there are many yet undiscovered mental abilities awaiting the development of tests to name and measure them. However, and most important, many of those that have been identified await cultivation. This is both the challenge and the opportunity for anyone interested in gifted and talented children and youth. Guilford's conception of productive thinking and its function in problem solving and creativity suggests exciting approaches:

> A common use of the term 'creativity' means creative production. Production is output...output may be in the form of tangible products, such as a poem, a scientific theory, a machine, or a musical composition. To the psychologist, there can be productive thinking even when there is no tangible product (Guilford, 1965.)

Many teachers and principals feel that gifted and talented children currently must spend too much time on memory work and are not given enough time for evaluative thinking or exploring new or unusual ways to think about things. Practice in judgmental and divergent thinking, they believe, is an essential ingredient in teaching if bright young people are to acquire sound, responsible personal and social judgment. They must have opportunities to make judgments and to test them in a friendly atmosphere against the judgments of both peers and authority figures, such as parents, teachers, and other significant adults.

Outlandish, bizarre, and nonfunctional ideas are not to be valued just because they are divergent, however. Guilford emphasizes the key concept that productive thinking is much more than thinking quickly, originally, and in unusual ways. Productive and self-directed students are those who are able to harmonize the whole array of operations, from cognition and memory through convergent, divergent, and evaluative thinking.

From the standpoint of instruction, the educational goal for all pupils might be, in Guilford's view, to bring each individual's mental abilities into busy and organized engagement with the requirements of every task to be learned. This is hardly a new idea. Its significance in this context is that Guilford spells out what those mental abilities are in operational terms. Perhaps even more significant is Guilford's hypothesis that teachers and parents can intentionally shepherd those mental abilities along their developmental course, enhancing them by ensuring that they are exercised daily in class and individual activity.

What seems to be especially needed in order to realize that goal for gifted and talented pupils is attention from both teachers and parents to several activities. One is the lively involvement of each pupil's intellect over a wider curriculum content than ordinary. Another need is individually paced growth for each learner to grasp and master complex concepts. A third is daily exercise in employing knowledge for personal purposes, particularly in the storage, recall, and restructuring of information. The beauty of this theory is that these activities are already recognized as legitimate parts of schooling; the application of Guilford's concepts simply puts mental operations into clearly recognizable and usable form. The three processes mentioned are not only good for all pupils, but they are especially appropriate for gifted and talented pupils. The end product can be a strong and competent intellect, one that fosters imagination while keeping a firm evaluative hold on reality.

The practice of education requires the integration of three spheres of influence: administration, curriculum, and guidance. All are related to the sciences of sociology and psychology, and educational specialists have continually attempted to root instructional practices for gifted and talented pupils in proved social-psychological principles.

Meeker (1969) is one specialist who created an educationally oriented application of Guilford's (1966; 1967) work. Its main use is to help teachers, principals, and parents ascertain that gifted and talented pupils acquire experience in all forms of thinking, particularly in the higher order thinking processes that foster their creative potential. Meeker's motivation was to identify methods of assessment and instruction that would help teachers to individualize education and nurture human abilities. Meeker's application is based upon Guilford's structure-of-intellect conceptual model. It shows teachers how to make up questions to ask in class and how to construct test items that require students not only to recall facts and ideas, but also to manipulate those facts and ideas mentally so as to reveal new and more advanced concepts. Guilford (1969) acknowledged the contributions of Meeker in the systematic application of his model to educational practice. Recognizing the gap between his theory and its applications to educational theory and practice, he praised Meeker specifically for her derivation of education implications from his own psychologically oriented studies of human abilities.

Intelligence as Factors

Guilford's theories evolved from his studies of learning by human subjects. He concluded that human learning is the overt manifestation of what is called intelligence. He identified three dimensions associated with human learning: (1) content to be learned, (2) products that demonstrate mastery, and (3) the acts, or operations, by which content and products are linked. In practice, educators confront decisions on (1) content, (2) teaching methods, and (3) assessment of content acquisition. Educators and parents also realize that learning involves conscious effort. Consequently, Guilford's findings parallel real life situations.

Meeker (1969) reviews the three interrelated dimensions of Guilford's model. These are content (e.g., types of information to be processed), products (e.g., the forms information takes), and operations (e.g., the processes/behaviors of the person in responding to information). Typically, the model is presented as a three-dimensional grid to illustrate the interaction of these three dimensions.

Content

The information processed by the person, the content, is of four types. Figural, the first type, is the most concrete; data are expressed in shapes or presented themselves. The symbolic type involves a sign, or representation, such as numbers, letters, or musical notes. The content involves words. The critical dimension is the association of the word with the object, trait, or quality it represents. The final type is behavioral, i.e., the action that results from the interaction of a stimulus and response.

Products

Categories used by a person to organize and classify environmental stimuli are products. They range from the elementary to the complex, from simple units to classes, relations, systems, transformations, and implications. Units are viewed as a single idea, word, or fact. Classes are composed of like units. Relations involve the connections between classes. Analogy items require this type of product. Systems involve two related behaviors, for example, identifying methods of a procedure is one ability, and interpreting in one's own words is a related ability. Transformation is an abstract ability to produce a product of personal interpretation. Implications, the final and most abstract product, involve forecasting consequences. More than literal, narrow deduction and inference, they have the added dimension of planning.

Operations

The dimension of operations has attracted specialists in education of the gifted and talented because this is truly a behavioral description of human ability. The operations are descriptors of the able person. Five types of operations have been identified: (1) cognition, (2) memory, (3) evaluation, (4) convergent thinking, and (5) divergent thinking.

Cognition. As mentioned earlier, the term *cognition* is encountered as a synonym for intelligence or mental ability. In the Guilford sense, however, cognition denotes only the person's ability to discover, to recognize, and to comprehend. Cognition is the use of sensory and perceptual data. It includes processes such as (1) sorting a stack of objects into common groups, (2) completing a multiple choice test, and (3) selecting the best title for a story.

Memory. Recall, recognition, and remembering involve the memory. Accuracy (data can be retrieved in the same form as it was entered and stored) is a key attribute; data are not distorted or marred.

Meeker (1969) observed that memory is of two types—short-term and long-term. Short-term memory is defined as the remembering of information within one minute of presentation. Everyday examples are a telephone number, a person's name after an introduction, or directions to someone's house. Short-term memory is a topic of continuing investigation by psychologists, for it is much more complex than it seems. Gifted and talented persons are distinguished by their memory and their ability to convert and process short-term memory data into the long-term memory system.

Memory is usually assessed in two ways. Recall implies an open-ended restatement, while recognition involves choice from among options, such as the multiple choice test. As was noted earlier, recognition is sometimes dubbed aided recall.

Evaluation. Judgment and decision making make up evaluation, which includes the ability to recognize any discrepancies. Evaluation is often assessed by "how to" questions in which the appropriateness of the person's response is considered. The person can also be asked to identify relevant and irrelevant considerations as a measure of this activity.

Convergent Thinking. Although often grouped with divergent thinking in a single category, productive thinking, convergent thinking can just as easily be considered a separate category. This ability goes beyond mere rote retrieval of the correct answer. Rather, it is a complex form of thought, best characterized by descriptors such as systematic, determined, and orderly. The thinker examines given data from which a solution is deduced, much like the detective who assimilates clues to reach a conclusion that is a "best" solution. It characterizes the behavior of the historian who explains the common features of an event and the scientist who reaches a conclusion. For the problem solver, convergent thinking emerges as an essential. The highly practiced convergent thinker is recognized by the ability to produce extremely important results. Interpretation, for instance, of poetry as to mood, symbolism, and the like, is one example of this ability. Finding camouflaged items hidden in a drawing is another. Given a list of words, the person skilled at convergent thinking can group them into meaningful pairs. Predicting the missing number or letter from a sequence is another illustration (6 8 10 5 7 9   6), as is arranging random pictures in a sequence.

Skill and high quality in convergent thinking is a desired outcome in curriculum of the gifted and talented. Meeker (1969) did observe that this outcome is not necessarily restricted to the gifted and talented. She found certain convergently oriented outcomes in curriculum guides for normal children, Head Start programs, and for the mentally retarded. A continuing challenge for educators is to understand the extent to which convergent thinking is subject to training and which instructional tactics are most likely to facilitate such change. Environment appears to influence this operation, but it is not clear whether there is a genetic factor that predisposes humans to convergent or to any other form of thinking.

Tactics for teaching convergent thinking can be described as contrived versus natural and as direct versus indirect. The inquiry method of Suchman (1966) and other discovery methods are examples of tactics. In contrived methods, the educator arranges data from which the pupil, under guidance, excercises thinking abilities. Role play and simulation are also tactics of this type. A natural approach, on the other hand, involves student selection of data, which is then applied to problems chosen by the student. The indirect tactic uses specific convergent thinking "exercises" intended to produce skills that can be transferred to more formal school tasks and tasks of the professional. More direct approaches employ student-selected projects in which convergent thinking behaviors can be practiced. Research indicates that natural, direct tactics are most effective for teaching convergent thinking, especially for the gifted and talented. Gifted and talented learners who initially need the structure of contrived, indirect tactics will quickly grasp the idea and then proceed toward activities of the natural, direct type.

Divergent Thinking. The production of unique, varied, and high-quality responses from given stimuli or data is divergent thinking. The convergent thinker uses an array of data to produce a unified conclusion. By contrast, the divergent thinker generates a variety of responses from a given. This latter ability can be conceptualized figuratively as an hourglass. The upper half's inexorable flow of sand toward one point represents convergent thinking; the diffusion of sand in the lower half represents the thought process of divergent thinking. Meeker points out that the difference is between zeroing in (convergent) and expanding on (divergent).

Divergent thinking is the product of discipline and effort, just as convergent thinking is. Most inventions that are popularly thought to have been accidental have, in actual fact, been the result of controlled, sustained practice, observation, experiment, divergent and convergent thinking, and evaluation.

Guilford and his colleagues were very well aware that they were assigning a meaning to the term *originality* (and consequently to *creativity*) that was very different from many of its popular meanings. They said, "We wish to use it [originality] as the name for a psychological property, the ability to produce original ideas" (Wilson, Guilford, & Christensen, 1953). Then they went on to point out that:

> For measurement purposes, we have found it useful to regard originality as a continuum. We have further assumed that everyone is original to some degree and that the amount of ability to produce original ideas characteristic of the individual may be inferred from his performance on tests. (p. 563)

Certainly any mystique that may have tended to becloud individuality or originality ought to be dispelled by the frank and straightforward terms in which Wilson, Guilford, and Christensen presented their approach to the matter. They postulated that the divergent, or generated, product has three traits: (1) fluency is the numerical count of responses; (2) flexibility is the varied use of response categories; and (3) individuality, or originality, is a statistical infrequency of response. For example, a sample exercise might be to name things that carry things. Two children who produced 20 responses would be equal in fluency. However, one might produce 15 responses that center on cars and trucks plus "Mom carries baby brother" and "my sister carries a purse." This demonstrates two categories of fluency (e.g., vehicle and person). If the second child's responses include trucks, people, as well as "an ear carries earrings," "a cat carries a mouse," this youngster has produced more categories. Comparison shows that this child's latter two responses were the only ones of the kind that were produced; hence, these are original in the sense of statistical infrequency of appearance in the responses of similar children.

It is also common to identify another attribute, termed elaboration. As might be imagined, it refers to further expansions on any particular product.

Divergent thinking involves activities like the following. Given three sticks, make as many designs as you can. Given a cube, extend its lines into space; what would you find? Draw or write your expectations. Write as many words as you can that end in *er*, begin with *er*, end with *re*, and start with *re*. Can you describe the 49 ways to make 50 cents? How many other words can be made from the word exceptional? What are the uses of a brick? Interpret past and future events based on a single picture. The comments made earlier in regard to the origins and tactics of convergent thinking apply to divergent thinking as well. Teaching of divergent thinking should not be restricted to gifted and talented learners. Expected outcomes for Head Start pupils, mentally retarded and other handicapped persons, and normal learners ought to contain an emphasis upon this objective. However, instruction for pupils who are gifted and talented merits an especially high priority on this operation.

Divergent thinking is certainly *not* a synonym for creativity in the Guilford-Meeker lexicon. The qualities of flexibility and originality are also, in their scenario, essential characteristics of the creative person. Neither is creativity associated solely with the arts and humanities. In the structure-of-intellect context, divergent thinking, flexibility, and originality—in short, creativity—is indispensable to those in the professions and to technical, governmental, and commercial personnel, as well.

Applications of the Model

Meeker's (1969) summation remains a valid identification of applications of Guilford's model. In keeping with her intent to integrate psychology and education, she observed that assessment, learning style, and curriculum can be influenced by the model.

In assessment procedures, the intentions of test items should be clear. Items can be analyzed (in the Bloom sense) as to content, product, and operation, allowing informal or formal tests used in assessment to be linked to the curriculum goals they are supposed to measure. Meeker (1969) also shows how results from individual intelligence tests can be related to elements in the structure of intellect and thus to school behaviors. Another potential advantage is that the model encourages parent and teacher observation of the functional, day-to-day, social, and personal behavior of gifted and talented children and youth. Teacher and parent observation of movement, auditory modes, and the like can also be a source for assessment.

Instruction should follow and elaborate upon assessment. Learning, in the Guilford sense, is the exercise of operations upon content, resulting in products. For Meeker, content and product are incorporated into each operation. Learning can be viewed as a function of cognition and evaluation. The result of learning (e.g., change in behavior) is stored and retrieved through memory. The use of learned material (e.g., memory) can be further used in unchanged forms (convergent) or changed forms (divergent). Evaluation remains a continuing mediator to judge the adequacy of convergent or divergent production. Learning is rather like a cycle of cognition-evaluation, producing memory applied to productive products (convergent-divergent), with the whole process being monitored by continuing evaluation.

Operations can be descriptive, too, of a person's learning style. Gifted and talented individuals may become oriented toward either convergent or divergent pursuits. Persons whose intelligence quotients (IQs) are similar vary as to their mix of operations. The proportions contributed by the five operations of intelligence could generate a lengthy list of possible combinations. Since learning styles themselves are not inherent, but are acquired, they are amenable to change and improvement through teaching. Potentially, therefore, each gifted and talented child can be taught to use a variety of learning styles, matching them to the requirements of each particular situation.

The Guilford operations are not goals in themselves, but are means toward ends. If the operations are applied in the study of subject matter, the content will be learned and the student will attain skill and confidence in the conscious application of the operations to new content, be it in the form of new information or new problems.

Chapter 2

Understanding Human Abilities as Adaptation

A humble question, according to Spencer-Pulaski (1971), had a tremendous historical impact. The question according to these authors was:

> Some of my flowers are buttercups. Does my bouquet contain (1) all yellow flowers, (2) some yellow flowers, or (3) no yellow flowers?

The historical significance of the question was that it motivated Piaget to begin his studies of human development. As an associate of Binet and Simon in Paris, he interviewed children with similar questions. He observed that 11- and 12-year-olds could respond correctly, while younger ones could not. It was his curiosity about these observations that provided a continuing incentive for study. The problems of adapting to life's demands in personally satisfying ways as well as responding to reasonable sociocultural standards can be highlighted by the concepts of Piaget. With a knowledge about gifted and talented persons, it can be seen how adaptation is influenced by superior abilities.

INTELLIGENCE AS ADAPTATION: PIAGET

Guiding Concepts and Principles

Piaget has had a major impact upon American thought and practice regarding the nurture of children and youth at home, in school, and in the community. His theories, research results, and experimental designs continue to excite wide interest. Yet the literature of the gifted and talented reveals a much greater preoccupation with Guilford and Bloom than with Piaget.

Piaget's perspective regarding human abilities is a distinct contrast to those of Guilford and Bloom. For Piaget, intelligent behavior is adaptation. The central theme is that intelligent behavior requires a person to assimilate and to accommodate to the environment. Maturity is shown by the quality of that reaction. The term *accommodation* refers to the incorporation into one's self of environmental stimulation; the term *assimilation* describes how one responds to environmental stimuli. Adaptation, consequently, is the equilibrium between a person's control of environment and the environment's control of the person. Humans continually pursue the balance between previous mastery and new demands to be mastered.

Rowland and McGuire (1968) speak of adaptation as growing progressively and predictably more complex with increased age and experience. Accommodation is the taking in, or incorporation, of the external, whereas assimilation is the modification of the external into one's own frame of reference. In more behavioral terms, assimilation is what happens when a person generalizes or transfers a past experience to new circumstances.

Of special interest to parents, teachers, and other educators is the behavior that mediates between, or balances, accommodation and assimilation. Piaget (Rowland & McGuire, 1968) describes the mediation between accommodation and assimilation as operations, or actions. These operations can be internal or external. Each of the following could be an operation: reflex, habit, judgment, reasoning, inference, and logic. The operation a person uses shows how that person perceives the relationships (e.g., correlations, cause-and-effect consequences, inferences, habits) that regulate personal behavior. For many followers of Piaget, the use of particular operations can be equated with the presence of more or less intelligent behavior.

The Bloom perspective and the Guilford model view intelligence as the developmental expansion of common abilities, the essentials of which can be detected in infants. In their sense, intelligence may be likened to a computer that becomes increasingly complex over a lifetime. In the Piagetian sense, however, intellectual development is the successive exchanging of used computers of limited scope for new ones of greater scope. A central theme of Piaget's is that intelligence emerges through four successive stages: (1) sensory-motor, (2) preoperational, (3) concrete, and (4) formal. Each is characterized by essentially different and higher level operations. They appear in gifted and talented children at earlier ages, though their essential characteristics are the same for all children.

Prevailing conceptions of how intelligence develops have it growing in fairly smooth sequence between birth and about 17 or 18 years. The growth curve is highly accelerated in the early preschool years; then the rate is reduced until a near level plane is reached in the late teens. The growth continues, but at a very modest rate, until the 40s. In this view of intellectual development, it is the ability to employ what was there from the outset, namely, attention, perception, association, judgment, reasoning, and the like, that increases with age. Piaget's viewpoint, though, is substantially different. He believed that qualitative changes in intelligence take place as the child matures because of the emergence of new stages of development that bring with them new capabilities. True enough, the older capabilities remain and can be built upon, but the new capabilities are not simply extensions of use of the old ones.

Piaget's four stages of operations should be approached with care. For instance, impatient investigators are inclined to confine operations to specific age periods. Piagetians typically employ the term *invariant sequence,* but they do not mean that the stages always appear at the same age—only that the sequence is always the same. The sensory-motor stage is the foundation for the preoperational stage, as the preoperational stage is for the concrete stage, and so forth. Persons differ as to the amount of time (e.g., rate) with which they complete the sequence, but no behaviors of any stage of operation can be skipped, eliminated, or ignored. Progress through operational stages cannot be rushed, although environmental stimulation can enhance maturity.

The readiness principle, in Piagetian terms, says that the next level of operational behavior appears when all the conditions are right. Readiness involves the person's maturity of resources: sufficient physical dexterities, available information, differentiation of information, and coordination of available information. The Piagetian view of readiness is that each person possesses an internal time clock. Consequently, while it may seem convenient administratively, not *all* children can be expected to be ready to read at a given time and after a specified period of training. The Piagetian principle requires individualization of assessment. The implication is obvious that teaching methods should be timed to the individual's particular growth rate. Moreover, calling a child a failure because he or she does not read by age six or deferring a precocious child's reading instruction until age six are both inappropriate practices of applying group norms without taking into account an individual's own profile. The importance of individualization is reinforced by the Piagetian insistence on matching instruction to the child's stage of development. The concepts of Piaget have attracted interest among such widely disparate groups as educators of preschool children, science educators, and those interested in ungraded primary programs.

In addition to the constructs of adaptation, operations, invariant sequence, and the readiness principle, there is another very significant principle for gifted and talented child development derived from Piaget's work. It is the principle of imperfect understanding. Early in his studies of children (in association with Binet), Piaget noticed that, by adult standards, children frequently gave incorrect answers to standard questions. The answers often possessed a logic rooted in concrete childhood experience, however, and the children demonstrated a great deal of consistency in that "incorrect" response. In one classic example, two lumps of clay of equal size were shown to a child. One was rolled into a thin cylinder, the other, into a round ball. Younger children said the cylinder contained more clay, but older children recognized the two pieces to be the same. Similar responses were noted when a thin, tall glass was compared with a wide, squat glass. The former was said to hold more water, even if water were poured from one glass to another. Also, a stick was labeled as bent when placed in water and straight after being withdrawn. Similar responses are observed in language behavior. In English, for example, children may talk about "wolfs" and use an expression such as "I sleeped." Technically, the responses are incorrect. To the thoughtful observer, however, these responses possess a certain logic and approximation toward more complex behavior. In the Piagetian sense, such responses reflect an imperfect understanding, *not* a lack of understanding.

The principle of imperfect understanding justifies the emphasis upon the quality of response as well as the quantity, or accuracy, of response in the literature of the gifted and talented. The outcome is respect for how a person responds to a task rather than a preoccupation with response itself.

Finally, the work of Piaget confirms an intimate association between affect (e.g., feelings, attitudes) and cognitive operations.

Piaget's work on cognitive development can be summarized as centered on three concepts. Adaptation describes human development as a balance between accommodation and assimilation of the new with old experience and demands. Secondly, operations are the mediators of assimilation and accommodation. A third concept is the developmental and evolutionary sequence of operations.

At least four principles drawn from Piaget's work have gained wide acceptance. *Invariant sequence* describes a fixed sequence but acknowledges an individualized rate of progress. The *readiness* principle endorses the practice of timing of educational tasks to the person's as opposed to group, maturity. The principle of *imperfect understanding* respects the logic of children. It does impose adult standards, but prizes an empathetic view of a child's view of events. Piaget's works also generates a principle of the *integration* of cognition and affective behavior. The concepts and principles of Piaget, when joined with those of others, reinforce the press for individualization of instruction. A rationale for individualization is, perhaps, the summative theme of Piaget's contribution.

Up to recent times, Guilford's and Bloom's very valuable models have dominated the thinking about preparation of teachers and other educators for work with the gifted and talented. During the same period, Piaget has become a major influence in the preparation of teachers in other educational areas, such as preschool, mathematics, science, and general elementary education. Those practitioners who are prepared in Piagetian principles are now beginning to employ them in the practice of individualized education for the gifted and talented.

The Four Stages

Wolf and Wolf (1977) observe that a Piagetian orientation views the learner as the architect of intellectual growth. The role of educators is to create opportunities for language, social interchange, and shared experience. Such opportunities are essential if giftedness and talent are to flower.

The four operations can be summarized according to their focal attributes. For example, the sensory-motor period is characterized by reflexive responses to objects made without much internal mediation beyond pleasure-pain. In the preoperational period, the person responds with internal perception, but it is highly personalized and ego-centered; the individual is bound by personal experience. The ability to order and to recognize consequences of actions is only emerging. *Concrete* operations pertain to the child who is able to relate consequences to actions clearly, but in limited ways. The child can order and classify with systematic criteria within his or her personal experience. The period of *formal* operations approximates that of adult intelligence. The central ability is prediction of the possible without reference to actual events. This stage allows for theory development, explanations, and deduction.

Stephens and Simpkins (1974) described the four operations as stages through which a person changes from a reflexive organism (sensory-motor operations) to an inventive producer (formal operations). The continuing task of the developing person is to accommodate new ideas and skills, and to manage new structures of cognitive or affective responses. The increasingly complex structures arise from the person's own schemata.

The sensory-motor period, which is characterized by a transition from simple reflexive action to an organized stimulus response system, is composed of five substages. The *reflexive* stage is a simple response to external stimulation, such as kicking and blinking. The *primary circular reaction* describes behavior that is coordinated to produce an effect, such as in kicking a crib to shake a mobile. By 9 months, *coordination of secondary schema* (e.g., secondary circulatory reactions) emerges. Acts are observed to be clearly intentional; for example, a child can reach behind a cushion to retrieve a ball. By 12 months, the *tertiary circular response* appears. This is exemplified by the child who reaches a music box resting on a pillow by pulling the pillow. Between 18 months and 24 months, the *invention of mental operations,* e.g., using a stick to reach an object, can be observed. The theme of the sensory-motor period is circulatory, the connection between stimulus and response. These seemingly humble associations are the origins of human intelligence, and it is essential to stimulate them in very young children if an existing potential for giftedness and talents is to be realized.

The preoperational period includes actions based upon a single trait. This period ordinarily ranges from age four to seven years, with speech and language as the principal growth areas. Thought, per se, is complex, and the preconceptual stage is characterized by imitation and verbalism. There is repetition of language; judgment is egocentric. Thought has an egocentric inflexibility; for example, "to the right" means to *my* right.

Concrete operations extend generally, for typical children, from age 7 to 11 years. Judgment remains tied to acts and evidence, although the ability to reason is increasing. Rather elaborate forms of classification, reversals, and associations are manifest. By age 12, formal operations emerge in that the person can form hunches, derive explanations, and check solutions. Thought directs actions and observations.

Examples of Applications

Proponents of Piagetian viewpoints have identified a number of applications. As adults become sensitive to their own mastery of the system, they gain an empathetic understanding of ways to approach a new and unfamiliar system. Ideally, adults can transfer this understanding to children. Piagetian techniques of assessment can also be translated into teachers' and parents' practices with their young charges. The central theme is the conscious application of formal operations to instructional situations.

Serious pursuit of Piagetian concepts, with applications to very able youth, requires direct review of his experiments and his interpretations of them. These interpretations reflect the deductive nature of formal operations and indicate how a knowledge of formal operations can become a valuable tool in the nurture of gifted and talented children. The work of investigations of Piagetians are characterized by formal operations such as hypothesis building, hypothesis testing, verification, and elaboration of conclusions in order to begin the cycle again. It is the use of questioning in everyday situations that most closely approximates the practice of education.

Brearly and Hitchfield (1972) described Piaget's use of questioning as a "clinical" method. The questioner considers both obvious and implied responses. Questioning is increasingly specific to the child's level of understanding, and all questioning is conducted in psychological safety. It is made clear that there are no necessarily "right" answers, and neither amazement nor disdain is shown for a lack of comprehension or error by adult standards. This psychological safety is especially important for gifted and talented children, because it encourages them to make logical leaps, employ rational and accurate shortcuts to problem solutions, and to reveal themselves in other ways with impunity. It guarantees freedom from reprisal if the child engages an adult in a no-holds-barred intellectual confrontation. Even more, it ensures that the adult will encourage such encounters and will allow the child to share in rule making.

This original method also takes into account the fact that appearance is significant. For example, gifted and talented children may respond as they think adults want them to respond. A related consideration is identifying the assumptions of the child's answers. For example, suppose there are two sheets of paper of standard size. One has 12 buttons concentrated in the center, and the other has 12 buttons equally spaced over the sheet. Children are asked to identify which sheet has more buttons. According to Spencer-Pulaski (1971), the child in the preoperational period will identify the sheet with the concentrated buttons has having fewer buttons; the child is attending to the white space. The child with concrete operations will count the buttons and conclude they are identical in number. The child in the formal operations stage will be puzzled by the question because the correct response requires only a glance. Questioning by teachers can be used as an ongoing assessment as well as an instructional tool. Psychological safety of response contributes to this.

Spencer-Pulaski observed that Piaget acquired his techniques of questioning through studies of psychotherapy. To counselors, psychologists, and school social workers, the resemblance is immediately plain.

Another example of the application of Piagetian concepts can be seen in the life of Piaget, who was himself a gifted and talented person. His life reflected the influence of nurture on ability, since his family provided early access to information and supported his curiosity. By age 10, he had published original papers in biology. A museum director furthered his abilities; Simon and Binet provided individualized encouragement. Employers were willing to encourage and sponsor the ongoing activities of his institutes. One is struck by the significance of what Pressey (1955) called "furtherance" in the life of this remarkable scientist. Also striking is the Spencer-Pulaski (1971) account of Piaget's willingness to nurture and encourage others. His career integrated biology, philosophy, and psychology into a comprehensive plan for investigation. Piaget recognized psychology as the mediation between the biological structures of the nervous system and the philosophic structure of knowledge.

A VIEW FROM THE TOP

A perspective of superior ability shared by a leader of the Mensa Society might be called a view from the top. Fixx (1972), a member, gives details about this society in which membership is restricted to persons of verified high intelligence quotients (IQ's). His views are based upon interviews and observations of Mensa members who are found in varied economic levels and occupational groups. The Fixx account is rewarding reading for several reasons. It offers an insight into the adult world of gifted and talented individuals, and it highlights the ways in which the Mensa mind attacks problems. It suggests methods for the identification and instruction of young gifted and talented individuals, shows there can be an almost impish quality about the Mensa mind, and makes it plain that superintelligent persons (Fixx's term) view this label as but one personal attribute, not their *sole* source of identity.

Life's Problems and Rewards

Fixx believes that there is little sympathy for bright persons; perhaps this is because problems encountered by bright persons may be of a nature undreamed of by others. They must cope with earlier and sharper awareness of tragedy, greater sensitivity to life's complexities, and heightened vulnerability to injustice. Fixx noted the precocious sensitivity and consequent early emergence of problems that combine cognitive and affective tones. For example, an adult may ask children which of the following numbers can be divided by 2, given the following series: 1, 2, 3, 4, 5, 6, and 7. A gifted and talented child may say all of them. The teacher may retort with "Try again and, this time, think!" The child may defend the first response by pointing out that 5 divided by 2 is $2\frac{1}{2} + 2\frac{1}{2}$. The teacher may reply with a chilling remark about smart-alecky kids!

Another true example involves a class of high-school students who were asked to find the height of a building by using a barometer. The most obvious and typical solution was to drop the barometer from the top of the building and observe how long it took to hit the ground. Another common solution was to climb the building, noting the change in air pressure. Either way, the solution is a mathematical calculation of two known elements to predict a third. One student, however, suggested that one could offer the owner of the building a really nice barometer in exchange for being told the height of the building. Fixx reported that the student was in deep trouble for the lack of a *serious* approach to problem solving.

Another such incident took place in a college engineering class. The question was: Given a three-pound beef roast and a 325-degree oven, how long will it take for the center of the roast to reach 150 degrees? One student was reported to disclaim an exact solution, but produced an elaborate research proposal that would take six months to complete. A more practical student obtained an oven, a three-pound beef roast, a watch, and a meat thermometer; this student solved the problem while eating roast beef sandwiches. Reasoning that beef tissue is like water, a logical student applied heat transfer principles to obtain an answer that was very similar to that of the second and fourth student. The fourth student, a resourceful type, provided the quickest response; his solution was to ask his mother!

The most resourceful students in these examples reflected an inventiveness beyond the obvious, but their originality is not always prized by the conventional mind. Perhaps it is because their solutions appear to be too easy, advanced without seeming effort, that they are not valued. Rejection of original solutions can cause persons to conceal abilities, or even to repress them. Being expected to function in a conventional way can produce boredom and feelings of insufficiency in gifted and talented persons.

Life for gifted and talented individuals has its beguiling features, however. The good part of life at the top is the enjoyment of ideas and the delight in solving problems. Agile and accurate use of abilities in numbers, logic, words, and reasoning holds out the same kind of fun. Persons who are rich in gifts and talents have many opportunities to enjoy themselves (Fixx, 1972).

Attributes of the Mensa Person

Some of the attributes of the superintelligent can be detected in their approach to solving problems. For example, given this series of letters, OTTFFSS, what is the next single letter? The obvious solutions are triad patterns of double letters, or intervals between letters. Perhaps the shapes of letters offer a clue. Perhaps it is the sounds of letters. Then, perhaps the clue is that the letters stand for something. After this discovery, sheer persistence will solve the problem. That is, the order of letters stands for *one*, *two*, *three*, *four*, *five*, *six*, *seven*, and the answer is *eight*. Having enough confidence to give thorough consideration to each alternative before moving onto another is helpful. So is willingness not to linger over apparently lost causes and the readiness to move to other alternatives.

Consider this nine-dot puzzle:

The task is to connect all nine dots with only four straight lines, although it is permissible to cross lines. The solution may seem to be impossible. However, the Mensa mind realizes that the result does not have to be four equal lines, nor do the lines have to conform to the boundaries of the dots. Hence, the following completed puzzle:

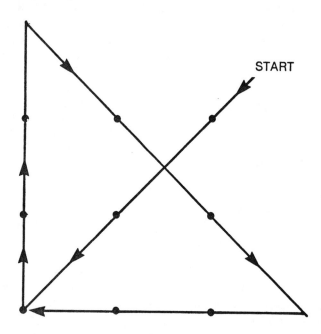

The Mensa person does not impose or accept restrictions on the mind. In a sense, the individual has broken free of restrictive assumptions.

Fixx (1972) shared another example. How many times can the number 9 be found in the series 1 to 100? Instantly, the answer of 10 is rejected, but the answer of 11 has a certain appeal as *9, 19, 29, 39, 49, 59, 69, 79, 89, 99*. After examination for a loophole or an overlooked dimension, it is realized that the answer is 20 as in *9, 19, 29, 39, 49, 59, 69, 79, 89, 90, 91, 92, 93, 94, 95, 96, 97, 98, 99*.

A final example is the puzzle of the three boxes. One box is labeled oranges, one box is labeled apples, and the third box is labeled apples and oranges. The problem is that none of the boxes is labeled correctly. The task is to examine only one box to know the contents of the other two. It is frequently assumed that selecting a fruit from one box will reveal nothing about what is in the other boxes. For example, if an apple is selected from a box labeled oranges, then oranges can be in *either* of the remaining boxes. The Mensa mind grasps an alternative principle, however. It recognizes the opposite of the assumption and proceeds. That is, if an orange is selected from the apple and orange box, then the other two boxes cannot contain oranges. Given that all boxes are mislabeled, it is simple to switch the labels to obtain the answer.

An analysis of how Mensa minds attack and solve such riddles shows that a restless mental agility is part of their character. Furthermore, there is the willingness to abandon a fruitless approach in order to select another, no matter how improbable it may at first seem. The Mensa mind is interested in pursuit of a solution; if no solution exists, it pursues why there is no solution. Persistence is evident.

Nurture

Intelligence can be confused with IQ, a score from an intelligence test. A single test score, or even two or three scores, may fail to indicate valuable types of intelligence. Sometimes, too, gifts and talents can be very specific. For example, a man whose IQ was 60 could defeat people of average or above ability at checkers, and a man whose IQ was 29 could calculate the day of the week for any date between 1959 through 1979. IQ is but an inference about a person. The point at issue, for Fixx, is the use a person makes of his or her abilities. A responsive environment nurtures intelligence by enabling the person to *do* more with available abilities. Varied forms of interaction with the environment increase the person's armamentarium of responses and heightens flexibility and self-confidence.

The informal observations by Fixx (1972) are confirmed in research summaries by Torrance (1971, 1980). The Torrance reviews create a composite image of the productive gifted and talented individual as one who has developed a personalized wisdom about life. This individual believes that existence is filled with opportunity of varied kinds. Such a person recognizes that departing from tradition may invite distress but is willing to accept a certain amount of stress in the belief that a new order will be created.

Thoughtful adults, especially parents and teachers, understand that these attributes of personality are indeed susceptible to influence by the social and physical environment. In short, they are to a great extent learned. Therein lies one of the great opportunities and challenges for educators.

Chapter 3

Describing Gifted and Talented Persons

IDENTIFYING DIMENSIONS

The very term, gifted and talented, can be read with an emphasis on either separation or combination. It is possible to view giftedness and talent as distinct, separable behaviors and even to distinguish between giftedness and talent in the same person. A confounding condition is that giftedness and talent operate in a social and cultural context of values. For example, Edgar Allan Poe existed in Baltimore on little more than dandelion greens. Yet, decades after his death, a note he had written to a neighbor sold for $10,000. Recognition of talents or gifts and material rewards for performance are received only if there is a corresponding societal judgment that they are deserved.

There are three areas or dimensions of human performance that have both cultural-social sanction and educational relevance: talent, creativity, and aptitude. They are overlapping clusters rather than distinct, separable dimensions. Figure 3-1 summarizes the everyday language that describes these attributes.

A review of superior human performance under the headings of talent, creativity, and aptitude has been advanced by Arieti (1976). His work is grounded in research investigations and in the life histories of eminent persons. From these data, Arieti postulated generalizations about the nature of superior human performance.

According to Arieti, talent, creativity, and aptitude are related, though separable, human attributes. Talent is most often identified with a product or a demonstrated performance, generally restricted to the arts. Creativity is more likely to be described in connection with a process. Operationally, the process can be described as synthesis in the Bloom sense or as divergent thinking in the Guilford sense. Aptitude is the capacity to benefit from instruction. It is assumed that aptitude refers to intelligent behaviors applied

Figure 3-1 Everyday Language to Describe Performance

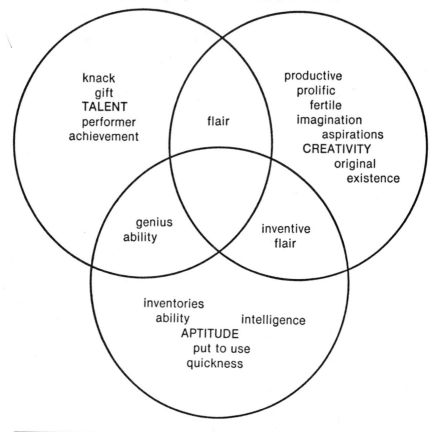

and directed toward process and product, e.g., the ability to perceive data (cognition in the Guilford sense), memory, judgment, and persistence.

Within the American educational and psychological communities, the process of creativity (defined as divergent thinking) has received the most attention. Measurement of aptitude, as an inference, has also received attention. Talent is cultivated, although this remains a relatively neglected area. In the everyday language of professionals, creativity is used in an interchangeable manner to denote process and product. Talent is usually restricted to the performing arts.

Talent and creativity can exist in the same person. The talented person is usually judged by products and accomplishments. To the extent that the talented person has intended and can explain the procedures used to develop the product, this person is also labeled creative. The phrase "teaching is an art, not a science" can serve as an example. Teaching as an art can be translated as meaning that others have judged the teacher's performance to be superior; however, the teacher may not be able to explain the sources of the performance. Teaching as science means that the teacher can personally explain the processes used and is consciously following a lawful pattern. In this sense, creativity serves as mediator between aptitude and talent.

Talent and creativity result from effort and practice to refine aptitude. Genetic endowments *and* a high intelligence quotient (IQ) are not sufficient explanations. Personality and the social context play important parts, too. Personality factors most significant here are persistence, self-confidence, and a personal commitment to success. This commitment has been noted by researchers for years. It has been variously called zeal by Galton (1896), ambition by Terman, and most recently task commitment by Renzulli (1978). Social influence can include early attention, recognition, and guidance from a competent person. Some gifted and talented persons seem to have persisted even without social nurture, but that is more the exception than the rule.

A person's status can change, and a person may possess several attributes simultaneously. A child, for example, who is believed to have a high aptitude, can attain the status of talented by comparison of performance. Piaget was recognized prior to his teens for both the product of his biological research and for his innovative process for classification. While most often the status of talent and creativity can be reached only by adults, superior performance (e.g., product and process) is not restricted by chronological age.

Performance is an enduring pursuit of the persistent person. There is also an element of humility about lifelong learning. The person seems to recognize and operate on the principle that the more questions answered, the more questions to be asked. The so-called burn-out is more a function of developmental tasks than of exhaustion of capabilities. For example, F. Scott Fitzgerald and Sinclair Lewis achieved status, but their inability to manage success thwarted their continuation. Ernest Hemingway and Margaret Mead are more typical examples of continuing achievement.

Research and theory can describe products and processes as they exist, but the sources of products and processes are still not well understood. There is, however, sufficient information regarding motivation and development for the design of nurturing environments. Motivation, as a task commitment, can be a rallying point for organization of resources. For example, adequate prenatal care, adequate nutrition, preschool intervention, enlightened parenting skills, individualized educational programs and instruction, and personalized guidance do *not* await further breakthroughs in research findings. These are essentials that can be applied immediately.

Humor (e.g., wit, puns, jokes, and proverbs) has emerged as a promising area for the scientific investigation of talent and creativity. Humor has the creative element of combining varied and diverse ideas into new unexpected forms. As process, it has the attribute of quickness to summarize and even to inform. As talent, it has performance dimensions in its delivery and creation of context. As aptitude, humor obviously requires the use of memory and appropriate application. Humor can be used as a means to gain social approval and as a defense mechanism. Moreover, humor can be applied to the qualities and attributes of the listener, since anticipation, comprehension, and applications are involved. Arieti's (1976) study certainly validates humor, in either its active or passive sense, as a functional means for identification of gifted and talented pupils.

Table 3–1 is a summary of both the Arieti (1976) discussion and this section.

Table 3-1 Dimensions of Human Performance in Talent, Creativity, and Aptitude

	Talent	Creativity	Aptitude
Inferred by	Historical and cultural sanction; demonstrated performance	Attribution and descriptive of a role or person; demonstrated performance	Statistical frequency, estimate of potential to benefit from further instruction
Role models	Artist, writer, musician, conductor, performer	Used as a modifier to an occupation in the professions, administration, and education	Used as a modifier to describe a student as having aptitude for ____
Evaluative criteria	Awards bestowed by recognized peers; judgments of competent critical reviews of performance; public approval or acceptance	Awards bestowed by competent peers; position of influence by promotion or public acclaim	Recognition by teachers, peers, or a mentor; significant above average test performance designed to predict skill acquisition rate
Demonstrated by	Performance in the arts—visual, music, dramatic, dance, and literature; coordination of physical dexterity and mastery of norms; performance above the norm	Performance in the professions as in politics, law, medicine, education, science, theology, commerce, labor, management, etc.; performance usually in decisions, ability to inspire and persuade	Test scores or observation of *current* performance; expectation that a nurturing environment will encourage future talent and/or creativity

DEFINING GIFTED AND TALENTED

Values and Utility of Definition

Gifted and talented is an expression applied to a person or a group; it is not always a badge of honor with automatic status and benefits. A label, according to Hallahan and Kauffman (1978), should maximize advantages and minimize adverse consequences in order to serve the interests of the person or group so stamped. Hallahan and Kauffman recognize that labels alter the perceptions of nonlabeled persons. They note, for example, that the label gifted and talented can set the labeled person apart from his or her peers. That set-apart status may have positive or negative connotations, or a mixture of both.

Definitions of the gifted and talented have significance chiefly for identifying persons who have already demonstrated superior attainments or those who are capable of future superior attainments. In either instance, there is no guarantee that present or potential abilities will automatically flourish. It should not be assumed that young gifted and talented persons can fend for themselves, they need helpful intervention from informed adults. To be sure, some do. Even in these unusual instances, however, strong foundations for self-esteem and the will to persevere must be laid early in life by exceptional parents or other significant adults.

Negative effects of labeling may include alterations in adult expectations of the learner; loss of identity as an individual person; and exclusion from facilities, social interaction, and experiences normally available to others. For gifted and talented children, for example, attending special schools or participating in "pull-out" programs has often limited their socializing experiences with typical children. Positive advantages of labeling can be pragmatic ones. Labeling may result in increased funding, facilitate communication among professionals, and create public support for programs. Since labels will probably persist, scientific and professional employment of them may, in the long run, minimize offensive usage.

A label can be justified only to the extent that the person or group so labeled receives a benefit and to the extent, also, that all others not so labeled are not limited or deprived of opportunities. If there is no such tangible result, the process of labeling is meaningless. Well-made definitions can direct effort toward appropriate home, school, and community services and away from restrictive practices.

Attributes of a Definition

Renzulli's (1978) rationale for defining gifted and talented learners offers guidance to persons who must devise their own local specifications. He offers three criteria by which to evaluate a definition. A definition should:

1. be derived from the best available research studies investigating the attributes/characteristics of gifted and talented learners
2. generate criteria for the design of identification systems, including the selection of procedures and instrumentation
3. provide direction for programming practices that deal with the gifted and talented as a learner with special needs.

Adequacy of the Federal Definition

Definitions can be borrowed from legislation, policy documents of agencies, the research literature, and the literature of advocates. Renzulli analyzed definitions from these sources by applying his criteria of research base, guidance for identification, and directions for programming.

A difficult, yet central, task in constructing a widely useful definition, has been to balance objective criteria (e.g., data such as test scores) and subjective criteria (e.g., value judgments rendered by parents, teachers, and other experts). Objective criteria may exclude potentially eligible pupils, but subjective approaches can be so inclusive that they create confusion as to what areas of performance should be incorporated into the judges' opinions.

Renzulli (1978) and others (Kirk & Gallagher, 1979; Reynolds & Birch, 1977) have noted the limitations of the federal definition (see Overview):

- Motivation sources as attributes of superior ability are neglected, although research identifies motivational sources as significant influences.

- There is an indiscriminate mix of aptitude and process. Creative or productive thinking, leadership ability, psychomotor ability, and the like are processes that are the applications of general aptitude. It is doubtful that creativity and leadership exist apart from specific performance areas to which they are applied.

- Interpretation of elements of giftedness and talent as outlined in the definition have been misinterpreted and misapplied, at least partly because the structure of the definition encourages the common but inaccurate assumption that the categories are separate entities rather than overlapping attributes.

In spite of these limitations, the federal definition does call attention to the need for programs. Moreover, this definition attempts to include a wide range of abilities, many not covered by strict measurement criteria. There has been a tendency, however, to seize upon this definition without considering its applicability to local circumstances. It can be hoped that the relationship between definition of an intended population and resulting practices will be increasingly recognized.

Defining Human Ability as Task Commitment

Renzulli (1978) has advanced an operational definition of gifted and talented learners that he feels can be scientifically verified, indicates identification criteria, and is a trustworthy guide to program practices:

> Giftedness consists of an interaction among three basic clusters of human traits—those clusters are above average general abilities, high levels of task commitment, and high levels of creativity. Gifted and talented children are those possessing or capable of developing this composite set of traits and applying them to any potentially valuable area of human performance. Children who manifest or are capable of developing an interaction among the three clusters require a wide variety of educational opportunities and services that are not ordinarily provided through regular instructional programs. (p. 261)

Like the federal definition, Renzulli's definition identifies creativity and general intellectual ability as descriptors and relates abilities to areas of performance of merit and worth. It emphasizes demonstrated performance and prediction of capability, and it advocates modification of standard school practice.

The Renzulli (1978) definition has several advantages over the federal definition. It adds task commitment as a dimension; moreover, it proposes that general intellectual ability, task commitment, and creativity are equal partners in describing performance. In addition, Renzulli's definition is based on published documentation. The evidence discounts measured intelligence and achievement test scores as the *sole* basis for either definition or identification procedures and also casts doubt upon grade point average as the criterion for identification. In fact, participation in extracurricular activities can be a more valid predicator of performance than grades per se. Renzulli does not reject objective criteria, but rather he rejects exclusive reliance on these variables as either identifiers or descriptors of gifted and talented learners.

Task commitment refers to the energy brought to bear upon a specific problem over an extended period of time. Productive persons are distinguished from less productive persons by showing more of this quality. Task commitment is shown by persistence in accomplishment of goals, integration of diverse goals, self-confidence, freedom from inferiority feelings, drive to achieve, and eagerness. Persons with these qualities are not necessarily proficient acquirers of test information, though they may have that quality, also.

Creativity poses enormous problems for measurement and assessment. A creative person possesses or demonstrates (1) an originality in solving problems; (2) a willingness to set aside established, conventional procedures when appropriate; and (3) an ability to fulfill the major unusual demands of a career. While these traits may sound vague and imprecise, panels of judges are able to reach agreement in their evaluation. Renzulli noted that actual performance and measures of self-concept of ability could be as useful as "tests" of creativity for identification of gifted and talented learners; although he did not advocate rejection of contemporary "creativity test" results. He did, however, recommend that persons in particular fields of endeavor develop specific criteria for identification of creativity and performance. For example, teachers could identify and describe attributes of an educator who is original and effective in performance.

The three clusters do not function in a vacuum, but are best recognized as they are brought to bear upon performance areas. Work remains to be done on the sources, causes, or etiology of these three attributes.

DEFINING HUMAN ABILITY AS ADAPTIVE BEHAVIOR

Educators of the gifted and talented are not the only practitioners for whom defining a service population is an ongoing task. The definition of learning disabilities, for instance, is continually under revision. The same could be said for the definitions of all educational problems at the edges of current knowledge. It has been recommended by Lucito (1963) that a definition of the gifted and talented could be adapted from definitions proposed for other aspects of intellectual development.

The study of mental retardation is an example of an attempt to assemble relevant information into a concise statement. A group chaired by Grossman (1973) identified the essential components necessary for definition as (1) condition, (2) developmental period of life, (3) intellectual functioning, (4) functioning in adaptive behavior, and (5) comparative, relative status. Condition implies biological correlates associated with an efficient nervous system. Developmental period of life denotes the period between birth and age 18 as a formative period for personal growth and development. Intellectual functioning essentially refers to the results of an assessment of cognitive development by a competent psychologist. Adaptive behavior refers to maturation, learning, and social adjustment. Maturation denotes the skills associated with physiological maturation, particularly psychomotor and communication skills. Learning means the rate at which skills are acquired, as well as mastery of school tasks. School adjustment signifies conformity to reasonable community standards as well as vocational productivity. Relative status describes an individual's position in relation to a population distribution. In usual practice, the upper and lower three percent of a population are those who are likely to be noticed, because the usual community environment and processes do not fit them comfortably. For example, attention is drawn to a very tall person because doors, beds, and ready-made clothing are not adjusted to scale. Similarly, scouting, public libraries, recreation activities, and schooling might well be out of synchronization for gifted and talented children and youth, defined as the most able three, two, or one percent of all children and youth.

An application of the same concepts could define giftedness and talent as:

> A condition resulting from a responsive biological and social environment that is manifest during the developmental period of life and describes significantly above average performance inferred by current performance and estimates of future performance contingent upon the person's task commitment to attainments in adaptive behavior.

This proposal possesses no additional disadvantages over current definitions and might have certain advantages. For example:

- It recognizes that environmental influences are significant correlates to ability, which creates a sense of urgency about the nurture of human ability.

- The concept of manifest implies the need for sensitivity to a variety of attributes that constitute evidence of potential and present capacity.

- The emphasis on the developmental period reinforces the importance of the preschool period and the impact of family life and parenting.

- The use of the term "significantly above average" allows for a range of abilities to be included, instead of restricting the population to a narrow upper one percent range. The percentages can be moved up or down, depending upon local circumstances.

- Estimates of performance allow the use of both objective criteria and actual performance. Additionally, identification could be based upon inferences of future performances that would rely on validated predictive procedures.

- Incorporation of task commitment acknowledges the influence of motivation. In turn, inclusion of motivation also acknowledges the influence and need for responsive environments.

- The inclusion of adaptive behavior suggests both program direction and program content. The three elements of adaptive behavior (e.g., maturation, learning, and social adjustment) imply direction at all age levels, especially preschool levels. It also suggests that identification procedures vary as to age levels. Finally, adaptive behavior implies continuity of programming from preschool through adulthood and suggests dimensions of curriculum outcomes as well as a variety of assessment procedures.

Some professionals might have certain reservations regarding the acceptance of this definition, including:

- Since this proposed definition parallels one in existence to define mental retardation, there could be credibility resistance.

- The proposal does not require demonstrated superior intellectual measurement for labeling as gifted and talented. It allows for either performance *or* achievement as sufficient criteria.

- Inclusion of task commitment may seem to be imprecise.

- Reference to adaptive behavior may create resistance because it requires acceptance of responsibility for preschool programming. In some localities, preschool programming may not be viewed as a public (e.g., tax-supported and free) sphere of activity.

- Reliance on measured IQ may seem to be a rejection of alternative descriptions of intellectual behavior.

- The emphasis upon responsive environments may disrupt existing genetic explanations.

- The concept of significantly above average can create confusion because the numbers to be served could range from one percent to five percent of a population.

Any given program requires a definition of an eligible population to serve. Educators can choose definitions from a variety of sources, including legislation, the literature, and expert opinion. Educators, of necessity, develop their own local definitions to guide identification and programming decisions; such decisions are required to assign relative weights to dimensions of human ability. Available evidence suggests that ignoring the range of dimensions results in programming for a narrow spectrum of learners.

Summing Up

UNDERSTANDING HUMAN ABILITIES AS PERFORMANCE AND OPERATIONS

In everyday language, terms such as *intelligence, cognition,* and *mental abilities* are synonyms. In more precise situations (e.g., curriculum goals, assessment, parent guidance), cognition is used in two diverse ways. In one sense, it is one attribute of intelligent behavior.

Bloom and his associates have identified six performance dimensions: (1) knowledge, (2) comprehension, (3) applications, (4) analysis, (5) synthesis, and (6) evaluation. These dimensions describe how information is stored, retrieved, and put to use. Bloom's description, or taxonomy, of performance has been endorsed by those in general education, as well as by specialists in the education of the gifted and talented. Bloom's dimensions of analysis, synthesis, and evaluation can be employed to describe higher order abilities. The concepts of content, instruction, and assessment can be defined by reference to Bloom.

Bloom and his associates have been specific in the application of their system to the gifted and talented. They noted a relationship between their description of synthesis and creativity as process.

Guilford and his associates have produced a model of intelligence that integrates intelligent behavior with its products and forms. The description of behavior as operations, which have been labeled cognition, memory, evaluation, convergent thinking, and divergent thinking, has attracted interest among educators of the gifted and talented. The operation of divergent thinking has attracted the most attention among these educators. There is an unjustified belief that divergent thinking is an operational definition of creativity as process. Guilford's model and his operations have served as sources for curriculum goals, instructional materials, and assessment.

The educational literature of the gifted and talented has reflected a significant indebtedness to both Bloom and Guilford, especially for assessment and precision of educational outcomes.

UNDERSTANDING HUMAN ABILITIES AS ADAPTATION

The work of Piaget has attracted wide attention among American psychologists and educators. His view of intelligence can be expressed as the adaptation to internal and external influences, i.e., the equilibrium between accommodation and assimilation. Piaget's enduring contribution has been the view of intelligence as different accommodations and assimilations.

Implications and contributions of Piaget can be listed as operations (e.g., sensory-motor, preoperational, concrete, and formal), invariant sequence, readiness principle, and imperfect understanding. Educators can also model Piagetian skills of questioning and probing.

The views of gifted persons themselves could be termed "Mensa views." In these views, there is a continuing theme of persistence, confidence, and gratification for mastery of problems; a humility about intelligent behavior; and an emphasis on the importance of social encouragement and opportunity that can be termed nurture.

DESCRIBING GIFTED AND TALENTED PERSONS

Superior human performance is described as talent, creativity, and/or aptitude. These attributes do not operate independently from intelligence, but a superior IQ (e.g., 130+) is not sufficient for superior performance. A favorable social context is also important.

Talent has the dimension of performance or production of a product that is culturally and socially valued. Creativity has the dimension of a process or a series of behaviors. Aptitude is an inferred ability to profit from subsequent training.

The study of humor shows promise as an area for controlled studies of talent and creativity. Humor possesses the sociological and psychological qualities necessary for understanding quickness, relationships, and reactions.

Definitions serve useful purposes for program direction and allocation of resources. Labeling benefits the person if an individualized education program results; otherwise, labeling is meaningless. Definitions should be evaluated as to (1) their grounding in the scientific literature, (2) their potential for guidance in the design of programs, and (3) their direction for program goals and activities. The federal definition has been widely adopted. It can be expanded to include task commitment as an attribute of the gifted and talented person. Another expansion could be to include the concept of adaptive behavior.

Enrichment

UNDERSTANDING HUMAN ABILITIES AS PERFORMANCE AND OPERATIONS

1. Review the course descriptions in a college catalog. What elements of Bloom appear most frequently? Review descriptions for high school courses. What differences exist? Are there loadings on any one dimension to the exclusion of others?

2. Obtain copies of final examinations, either objective or essay. Review these copies in light of the Bloom procedures. What loadings do you notice?

3. Examine a workbook in spelling according to the Guilford model. Select three pages for comparison. How would you describe each page as to its operations, content, and products? What loadings do you observe?

4. Try the "how many uses for a brick" exercise on various age groups of children and adolescents. What categories of originality do you find? Are your perceptions about children altered? How?

UNDERSTANDING HUMAN ABILITIES AS ADAPTATION

5. If you were unfamiliar with either Piaget, Guilford, or Bloom, you probably needed to resolve accommodation and assimilation. How did you manage these complex and somewhat diverse systems? How would you advise others? Do you find yourself drawn to one more than others? Do you find equal merit in all parts of all the systems? What might this tell you about yourself?

6. Review the section entitled "A View from the Top". Try a few examples on others, such as the nine-dot puzzle, the OTTFFSS_____puzzle, and/or the how many nines used in the sequence of 1 to 100. What qualities of the Mensa mind do you observe? Try the barometer and beef problem on others. In how many instances is the Mensa solution found? Are there any attributes of the persons who suggest Mensa solutions that distinguish them from those who did not give Mensa type answers?

DESCRIBING GIFTED AND TALENTED PERSONS

7. Consult the Arieti (1976) discussion. Do his distinctions among talent, creativity, and aptitude make sense? How could his distinctions be helpful in initiating programs?

8. Observe a TV talk show. Record examples of wit, use of puns, and/or stories told. How do they reflect the creative process as unique uses, the use of the unexpected, etc.? What categories do you notice? Why did some examples seem funny and others "bomb?" What clues about context, performance, and expectation do you observe? What dimensions of language are readily evident?

9. Consider the three definitions at the conclusion of this chapter. Suppose these were the only ones available. Imagine that Piaget, Guilford, and Bloom were brought together to endorse *one* of the definitions. Which one would Piaget endorse? Guilford? Bloom? Might there be total agreement, two out of three, etc.? Cite your reasoning for your perceptions.

10. Write the three definitions on one sheet of paper, and share them with others. Which one emerges as the most favored? What reasons are given? What improvements are suggested?

11. Write your own definition of gifted and talented persons. What dimensions do you emphasize? What would be the consequences if your definition were adopted within your school district?

Understanding the Social Context of Human Abilities

SYNOPSIS

This chapter begins with a review of the major landmarks of human development, particularly as they relate to gifted and talented children and youth. Then the social context of human behavior is considered, with special emphasis upon the family and allied social institutions. The importance of widening the social context on behalf of highly able persons is stressed.

KEY IDEAS

Human development continues throughout a lifetime. Research has uncovered significant periods or cycles that are characterized by age-specific tasks for mastery. Life cycles research can offer guidance on projected curricular outcomes that may assist in effective and satisfying adaptation.

Human ability has a social context. Testimony from able persons and their parents reveal a number of situations that call for practical guidance. For parents, there is the recurring need to manage and monitor the child's socialization and accelerated development.

Highly constructive human performance, described as talent, creativity, or giftedness, also has a social context. One feature is the interaction between personality and performance, which depends on environmental influences. A second is the subjective nature of judgment about what constitutes unique and valuable performance.

Underachievement is a serious hazard for many gifted and talented boys and girls. The hidden form is probably the most widespread, although reliable figures are lacking. Most important, underachievement can be detected and corrected.

The social context of educational opportunity is widening, as illustrated by developments for gifted learners who are handicapped either by emotional,

53

learning, or sensory impairments; physical impairments; and/or unexplained underachievement. Parallel thrusts promise aid for minority groups and for persons limited by the circumstances of poverty. These interests originate from research that has confirmed the diversity within the population called gifted and talented.

A PROTOTYPE

This true story illustrates the nurturing influence of family. The Hunter family proved adaptable (Associated Press, 1977).

He's a Froshboy

East Lansing, Mich. (AP)—While most sixth-graders are struggling with geography tests, 11-year-old Kam Hunter is gearing up for advanced mathematics and chemistry at Michigan State University.

Hunter was among 43,000 students who began classes Thursday at MSU. He's taking honors courses, since he scored in the top 5 per cent of freshmen taking entrance examinations.

While Hunter isn't the youngest student ever to enroll at MSU, he's not far from it.

Michael Grost, now a mathematics professor at the University of Wisconsin in Milwaukee, was 10 when he entered MSU in 1946. At the time he was the youngest ever to enroll at any university in the country.

Richard and Sally Hunter said there were early indications that Kam was an exceptionally bright child. He was speaking in complete sentences at six months and reading children's books by three. He entered the first grade when he was six years old, taking two high school courses on a trial basis.

One year later, he entered high school after teaching himself to write.

The Hunters have two younger children at home in Lansing. Kam's father, a pharmacist in nearby Ionia, moved the family to Lansing to be close to MSU. He and Mrs. Hunter, an elementary school teacher, commute to Ionia each day.

Hunter, a "sports nut," retrieves balls during MSU football games.

"I love sports. I'll play anything—football, basketball, tennis, swimming, golf," he said. Hunter also plays the guitar and piano and says his musical tastes run more toward rock 'n' roll.

Hunter reads a lot and enjoys it. He likes mysteries and sports stories.

"He has never required much sleep," his father said. "He's up reading until midnight and sometimes, perhaps once a week, until 3 a.m. We used to worry about his not getting enough sleep, but have since been reassured that he apparently just doesn't need as much sleep as the rest of us."

Being in the MSU honors program means Hunter's education is flexible and he can progress as rapidly as he wants.

Chapter 4

Understanding Life's Sequence of Tasks

Human development consists of acquiring and mastering increasingly complex physical, cognitive, and personal-social behaviors. Life cycles research, which emerged in the mid-1970s, has extended previous views of human development. Just as there are significant periods in the lives of children and youth, life cycles research has identified epochs of significance in adulthood.

Reseachers in human development agree on several common concepts. First is the notion of developmental tasks (Havinghurst, 1953). The essence of Havinghurst's research was to identify critical periods, which are characterized by (1) a time period; (2) the acts, expectations, and behaviors encountered in that period; and (3) their consequences for subsequent development. Havinghurst's work should *not* be considered simply an inventory of what happens. Rather, his emphasis is on the process, the movement through each period and from period to period, the interactions between the person and the environment (Muller, 1969; McMahon, 1974). Persons become more complex as the result of physical maturity, encouragement, opportunity, and reinforcement for effort. Gifted and talented individuals are capable, potentially, of reaching very high levels of complexity relatively early in life. The work of Levinson, Darrow, Klein, Levinson, and McKee (1974), as well as that of Sheehy (1976), complements and extends into adulthood what is known about development in childhood and adolescence. This can be used as a base for examining the development of gifted and talented persons in more detail.

The developmental task system has some important uses. Curriculum design and content can be timed to the readiness of learners; needs of learners can be more precisely described and assessed; and methods and materials can be constructed for age and maturity levels. A full range view of development can provide a "map" for the future. Additionally, life cycles research can help teachers, principals, and parents arrange home and school environments that will help pupils to manage their tasks.

The developmental task approach is valid for gifted and talented persons. For these persons, both mental age (MA) and chronological age (CA) are reference points. Gifted and talented individuals move more rapidly through development periods, although the periods follow the same sequence (Havinghurst, 1953). In order to adjust the gifted and talented child's expected age and rate of speed in the passage through the developmental periods, the following procedures are useful:

1. Note the child's actual age (CA) to the nearest month. For instance, Robert's might be ten years and five months. Mary's might be nine years and six months.
2. Convert the CA to months: Robert, $(10 \times 12) + 5 = 125$ months; Mary, $(9 \times 12) + 6 = 114$ months.
3. Obtain individual intelligence test results for each child, preferably either the Stanford-Binet or the Wechsler tests. (These must be administered by licensed or certified public school psychologists or clinical psychologists. If you have access to test results obtained by such specialists within the previous three years, and if there have been no marked changes in the child's school performance or health in the meantime, those results may be used.) Assume that Robert's full scale intelligence quotient (IQ) proves to be 135 and that Mary's is 150.
4. To find the MA of each child, mark off two decimal places in the IQs (1.35 and 1.50) and multiply the child's CA by the appropriate decimal fraction. For instance, for Robert: $1.35 \times 125 = 168.75$; for Mary: $1.50 \times 114 = 171$.
5. Round the answers to the nearest whole number, divide each by 12, convert the decimals to months, and the result is the MA, in years and months, for each child, as of the date of the calculations. For Robert: $169 \div 12 = 14$ years and 1 month; for Mary: $171 \div 12 = 14$ years and 3 months.

These results can be important to both teachers and parents. Although Robert is almost a year older than Mary, they are at almost the same level of current mental potential, as estimated from MA. Robert's mental potential at this time is 3-⅔ years beyond his CA. Mary's is 4-⅔ years above her CA. Finally, the rate of Mary's mental growth is more rapid than Robert's (1.50 mental years per life year, as against 1.35 mental years per life year). Thus, a year from the time of this calculation, Mary's mental potential will probably have drawn appreciably ahead of Robert's, as it will continue to do each year until potential mental development peaks at near 17 or 18 years CA.

These pieces of information derived by teachers and principals from individual intelligence test results provide the best single available basis for predicting the ages and the speed with which gifted and talented children will move through developmental stages. They are far from perfect predictors, but they are much better than CA alone. (For discussion in depth about the uncertainties and values associated with these procedures see Sattler, 1974.)

Used with reasonable care, MA and IQ allow teachers, principals, and parents to be more effective as they plan for gifted and talented pupils and evaluate the results of their plans. Obviously, other factors influence a pupil's rate of development and can serve as aids in prediction. For example, inadequate nutrition, repressive or abusive parental treatment, or lack of educational opportunity will ordinarily slow intellectual growth. So when MA and IQ are employed in planning, it should be in the context of what is known about the life of the pupil.

One more word of caution in the use of this prediction procedure. A child of age 10 with a mental age of 15 is obviously not the same as a child of age 15 with a mental age of 15. Many physiological changes take place in the years from 10 to 15, just as they do over any other five-year period in the first two decades of life. Also, five more years of living means five more years in which to learn from experience. It is true that gifted and talented children learn faster and with unusual richness of understanding for their years. Even so, it is sensible to be satisfied with goals that are set a little short of what MA might suggest. Objectives that lie between CA and MA are appropriate. For instance, for the 5-year-old with a MA of 8, an adjusted expectancy of accomplishment equivalent to 6 to 7 years would be reasonable, as would an adjusted accomplishment expectancy of 10 to 11 for a youngster of 9 whose mental age is 12. These expectancies should not be considered ceilings, however; gifted and talented children should not be held back to fit these calculations. Rather, these procedures should be thought of as ways to set up reasonable anticipations of progress, to be corrected if necessary.

The use of MA and IQ in the way just described once enjoyed a widespread vogue. It was practically abandoned in the 1960s and 1970s, largely because serious errors in application were rife. With proper precautions, they can be valuable professional tools for teachers, principals, and other educators.

Six broad developmental periods can be identified. Such age divisions are arbitrary, since persons vary in rates of progress, but they are useful to show what usually occurs and to highlight the ways in which gifted and talented persons may differ. These six divisions parallel epochs of educational preparation and continuing learning throughout life.

EARLY CHILDHOOD

The period from birth to approximately age five is referred to as early childhood. Piaget and Freud had an early influence on thinking about this period. More recently, the impact of contemporary investigators like Bruner,

Connolly, Bronfenbrenner, Kagen, and White has been felt through an increased understanding of how very young children grow in competence. Sensory-motor and preoperational behavior characterized this period according to Piaget. Freud's contributions, apart from his opinions on sexuality, have been to (1) dignify the study of early childhood and (2) confirm that the early years and experiences are very significant for subsequent development.

By age three, typical children have mastered major elements of self-care skills, motor coordination, and language. The coping behaviors necessary for later periods are well developed and represent major moves toward independent action. Language proficiency jumps ahead, especially the use of sentences. Some gifted children move ahead cognitively even more swiftly in this exciting period. For example, the prototype for this unit illustrates this point.

By age five, typical children have a mastery of perceptual consistency, emergence of conscience, and awareness of skills. Perceptual skills are sufficient for beginning reading, there is an elementary view of right and wrong, and a sense of confidence about performance has developed. These characteristics tend to emerge earlier among gifted and talented children.

Beyond question, planned, deliberate education in the period from birth to age three is desirable for all children. Very early childhood education involves parents, is conducted in the home, and begins with the very earliest parent-child interactions. Demonstrations of the benefits of such prompt beginnings, when supervised and coordinated by professional educators, abound in contemporary early childhood literature (see Chapter 10). What may not be so well-known is that there were excellent examples of the benefits of early education for gifted and talented infants and toddlers in the psychological and educational literature of America even when Piaget was a young man. Several of the case illustrations resemble contemporary single case experiments in applied behavioral analysis.

For disadvantaged populations, early preschool education can prevent subsequent school failure. Similar outcomes are obtained with children with mental, physical, or sensory impairments. Kindergarten is certainly not early enough to begin the education of these children. Affective outcomes of positive self-concept and self-control are equally important with cognitive and psychomotor outcomes, and all of these have their roots in what is learned in the earliest months and years of life.

CHILDHOOD

Usually bounded by ages 5 through 11, the period of childhood overlaps Piaget's stages of preoperational and concrete operations. During this time, for typical children, practical intelligence grows with common sense and approximations of reasoning. Physical skills associated with group games and activities become evident. Peer relationships are important for the child in and of themselves as well as for the establishment of sexual role and identity. A major emphasis for most children during this period is the acquisition of academic skills. There is a transformation from self-centeredness to an increasing awareness of the needs and expectations of others, as well as an ability and willingness to conform to them. Reasoning becomes useful in peer relationships and activities. Self-confidence grows. Normally, this is a strategic time to begin a consideration of careers. These years, too, mark the physical transition to adolescence.

For gifted and talented children, physiological changes tend to come somewhat earlier, but it is in the cognitive domain and the affective domain that they leap ahead even more noticeably. In a stimulating atmosphere, they are capable of very rapid development in these domains. Even in the period called childhood, many of their achievements are far from childish. Their development can be precocious in many directions at the same time.

A stimulating atmosphere does not have to resemble a pressure cooker. Curiosity and zest for learning go hand in hand. The entire world is the gifted and talented child's curriculum. Good teaching at home or in school consists in large part of setting the stage and then giving encouragement while the gifted and talented child takes the initiative.

ADOLESCENCE

The period of adolescence spans age 12 to 18. Formal operations, or adultlike intelligence is refined. Adolescents become more and more comfortable with abstractions and with the consideration of ideas that have no concrete, tangible, sensory reference points. There is a steady increase in the power to cope with the consequences of puberty and to form a philosophy of and about life.

Adolescence is a transitional period between the dependence of childhood and the independence of adulthood. Conflict arises in several ways. First, the adolescent seeks freedom, but does not wish to abandon the security of limits. Second, adolescents and parents differ as to their readiness to accept decreasing dependence. Conflict is natural, however, and can be constructively managed.

The adolescent is in transition between the new and the old, the familiar and the unfamiliar. The period piles choice upon choice regarding careers, marriage, and ethical dilemmas. Career preparation often requires separation from family so that each of these significant tasks is complicated by the other.

YOUNG ADULTHOOD

Most agree that young adulthood extends through the late 20s. Sheehy (1976) says it has two parts, pulling up of roots and getting a running start into life. The shift from dependence to self-sufficiency is made economically and psychologically. Separation from the family, in a geographical and physical sense, is often a natural consequence. If parents are overreluctant, separation can have enduring adverse effects.

Starting a career means acquiring the skills, competencies, and interpersonal relationships necessary for vocational success. Young adults must combine the pursuit of material success with a sense of personal purpose in life that involves identifying their own values, as opposed to the values of their family. The period is filled with both personal excitement and vulnerability. There is a sense of career accomplishment paired with an awareness that others have control over one's progress.

A mentor is a mature person who is selected by the young adult to serve as a role model, a consultant, and source of practical guidance. Research on this life period shows that mentors are indeed selected and that these mentors have an extremely potent influence on the developing young adults.

MIDDLE AND FULL ADULTHOOD

The notable contribution of life cycles research, pioneered by Levinson et al. (1974), has concerned the age group of the 30s and 40s. Evidence on the dynamics and tasks of the 30s validates life cycles research and its view of later human development as more than an extension of young adulthood and childhood experience. There are unique forces at work during this time. The period is one of establishing a personal identity.

The 30s can be the best and worst of times. These years are as turbulent, in their way, as adolescence. Material goals lose their appeal; control by things is rejected. There is persistent restlessness and questioning about career, vocation, and commitment to goals. Marriage and career are vulnerable to change. There is almost total self-centeredness, but it is difficult to be one's own person. It is disquieting to try continually to live up to idealized images or to fulfill the demands of others.

The 40s, the deadline decade, bring the first conscious recognition of one's own mortality and a sense of a last chance. It can be a positive period, however. Marriage and its values are rediscovered, and the personal power to control one's own life and future events is recognized. Many men and women in the 40s find themselves taking on and being rewarded by the mentor role with younger adults.

Full adulthood can combine a graceful retreat with a period of renewal. The person who has resolved the highs and lows that come with the 30s and dealt with the realities of mortality that come with the 40s, finds that contentment and fulfillment come with full adulthood. Gaps between dreams and reality diminish in importance. Coping with physical infirmity takes on increased significance, and caring for aged parents may become a major responsibility.

The sharp edges of value differences cleave friendships less often. The older adult concentrates on the simple pleasures and cherishes family and a few companions. Retirement can be a highly productive and creative period of life; it may be considered going *to* another phase of life, not leaving a career.

Those who possess gifts and talents have the potential to enter adulthood earlier, in a personal-social and career sense; to do so with fewer destructive disruptions; and to enjoy individually and socially significant productivity longer. Follow-up studies make it clear that the form and quality of home life and education during childhood and youth influence profoundly whether adulthood will fulfill the promise of the early years (Barbe, 1956; Reynolds & Birch, 1977; Sellin & Birch, 1980; Whitmore, 1980). The old adage that begins, "As the twig is bent . . ." applies with special force to gifted and talented children and youth.

Chapter 5

Understanding Family and Social Influences

FAMILY INFLUENCES

A Parent's View

Families are a definite source of nurture, although some are more effective than others. Parents, if willing, can be full partners with educators in the planning and implementation of education programs for gifted and talented learners. Many parents of gifted and talented children, however, have an uncertain or mixed image of their role.

A life experience shared by Grost (1970) provides insight into the social context of the family and the educational system. This account is useful in helping parents and others anticipate experiences that may be encountered. In telling the story of her son, Grost illuminates the consequences of certain attitudes toward the gifted and talented.

By age three, her son was reading fluently, doing some writing, and had a vocabulary of 500 words. As an infant and toddler, the boy was a master of complex puzzles, building blocks, and Tinkertoys. As the child approached kindergarten age, difficulties began to emerge. A local child guidance center dismissed the family as pushy, prideful, and conceited when they tried to have the boy tested in order to confirm their suspicions of giftedness.

The kindergarten and first grade experience with the public school was a continuing crisis. The teachers and the principal viewed the boy's academic accomplishments as calling words and memorization of pages. A classmate using a blue crayon told the boy, Mike, that it was her favorite color. Mike observed that it was the color used by an eminent artist in one of his periods of exploration. Mike's teachers dismissed this and similar incidents as the effects of a "pushy" family who were attempting to fulfill their own personal ambitions through their child.

Mike soon noticed that his own reading style was different from that of his classmates. He began to imitate the halting, word by word, finger pointing of

65

other pupils. This pattern was noticed with relief by the school establishment, since it confirmed their belief in the family's overzealousness.

Friends and relatives urged treating Mike as a "normal" child. Their advice was to leave the schools alone and let Mike progress in the standard manner. It was distressing to the family to observe Mike as a third grader pursue original reports using encyclopedias at home in the evening while studying from a single text by day. Furthermore, while the school administered a psychological text that indicated Mike's intelligence quotient (IQ), its results were closed to the parents. The family felt helpless and isolated. It was time for help.

Grost paid tribute to Dr. Elizabeth Drews, a faculty member of a university in the immediate area. She was able to arrange enrollment in college level courses and served as advocate and mentor for Mike, as well as advisor, to reassure the family. The university was able to manage and thwart the interest of the sensationalistic media.

By age 12, Mike had a college degree, a full list of Cub Scout achievements, and a distinguished record at third base for his Little League team. He completed a Ph.D. by age 16 and found employment as a member of a department of mathematics at an urban university. His academic skills had not outstripped his interpersonal skills. Consequently, he was accepted by his first year undergraduate students, although he was barely older than they. (This advanced social ability has been confirmed in other instances.)

Mike's sponsoring institution has been able to attract similar students because of its demonstrated competence to manage an individualized program. It is little wonder that the Grost family remained so positive about both Drews and the university. They have a sense of escape from a possible disaster because of the human and humane resources that they located.

Outcomes of Family Influences

The family has a direct influence upon self-concept, aspirations, and school achievement of the gifted and talented child (Thiel & Thill, 1977). When parental perceptions of children's abilities were compared with children's self-reports, it was found that significant discrepancies between father and son were associated with school achievement below the child's measured capacity.

Aldens (1973), however, could not isolate any specific family behaviors that discriminated between the creative and noncreative children per se for a sample of 620 third grade gifted and talented children. Siegelman (1973) drew very cautious conclusions about parent behaviors and creativity. His sample consisted of 418 college students in the sophomore and junior years of college; they were divided into two groups—creative and less creative. Their task was to recall the practices of their parents.

Overprotection was found to curb creativity, especially between fathers and daughters. In this sample, fathers emerged as more protective of their daughters than of their sons. Demanding, domineering, and conformity-oriented parents were more frequently found among the less creative group. The parent who was viewed as a causal agent, an encourager, a facilitator of the child's aspirations was most frequently found among the creative group.

The most perplexing finding, according to Siegelman, was the parental dimension of rejecting versus loving. Detached, seemingly remote parents were found among the creative group. Parents who were recalled as loving were viewed as less likely to encourage the autonomy of their child. Siegelman speculated that creativity originates in an atmosphere of freedom to explore interests without undue parent pressure. The perplexing variable is the balance between encouragement and control that smothers. The utility of intervention is illustrated by the Myers (1971) study. His report reflected significant academic gains for children whose parents learned techniques of accepting, nurturing behaviors.

Family Backgrounds

The backgrounds of families with children enrolled in education programs for the gifted and talented are remarkable in the lack of specific traits that distinguish them from other families. There is no typical, or average, family of the gifted and talented. A 1956 report by Barbe indicated that gifted and talented children are to be found in all ethnic, economic, educational, and social class levels of American society. The families in this study were found to have lower divorce rates, greater family integration, and slightly above average economic security. A 1977 study by Cox produced similar results. His report, like that of Groth (1974), found that multisibling families are more frequently encountered, although not all siblings are necessarily equally able.

Recent work reported by the U.S. National Institute of Mental Health supplies persuasive evidence, at least for boys, that the firstborn in families of two or more has a dual advantage. First is the early stimulating interaction with adults only. Second is the intellectually enriching opportunity to be, from every early childhood, a teacher and mentor for a younger sibling. These conditions account for the higher achievement of firstborns.

CONCERNS OF THE FAMILY

Good educational management for gifted and talented learners necessitates collaboration between the home and school. Bruch (1975) culled from research those conditions that increase the likelihood of effective contact between parents and educators. For example, the need for early identification, especially at preschool and primary grades, has created an urgency about parent involvement. According to Bruch, educators can expect to be asked to advise parents regarding questions and choices about educational tactics to manage and monitor their child's accelerated development as well as to nurture the child's abilities. Moreover, accelerated development and nurture are both topics for individualized planning. Moreover, the family and the educator must be concerned with effective development in addition to cognitive and psychomotor attainments.

Socialization

Family members are the child's first teachers. Parents continue to exercise influence over a lifetime; a "retired" parent is exceedingly rare. Parental influence affects mainly the socialization of the child, i.e., the process of learning to mesh one's own needs with those of others, especially those in authority. Socialization involves learning skills as well as acquiring the values and beliefs that regulate family and neighborhood group behavior. The families of gifted and talented children have particular influence upon (1) language development, (2) sex role identification, (3) task orientation, and (4) self-actualization.

Language development is a major index of the amount and the rate of cognitive development. Although early motor development is not particularly related to subsequent academic achievement, early language mastery is a highly accurate predictor. More than a large vocabulary is involved; complexity of vocabulary and use of sentence structure are key variables. For example, some children may be familiar with the word *Mars* as a town in Pennsylvania, as a candy bar, or as a planet. It is the preschooler who realizes that it also means defaces who demonstrates truly unusual language development.

Not only do parents provide language models for imitation, they also are sources of stimulation and encouragement for language development. Acquisition of language is the foundation for intellectual skills such as comparisons, classification, and directions to complete tasks. Parents are almost always receptive to practical suggestions to assist their child in this significant area of development.

Sex role identification has major implications for career guidance. In the past, certain characteristics, careers, and even courses of study have been viewed as either a masculine or feminine domain. For example, sensitivity has been viewed as feminine, while independence has been viewed as masculine. Studies of creativity suggest that neither of these is tied exclusively to one sex, although both are attributes of the creative person. There is a noticeable move toward the elimination of career stereotypes, also. Mathematics is no longer a male domain. Preschool education is attracting larger numbers of males.

Teachers should ensure that parents of gifted and talented children are aware of these changes in career opportunities.

Parents can be valuable allies in the development of task orientation. Parents will not support school goals, however, unless they are meaningfully included in the process of establishing those goals. Such inclusion enables parents to transmit their own internalized endorsement to their child.

Self-actualization, a term from the literature of counseling and guidance, connotes a sense of self-confidence in managing personal goals. It is a companion to self-realization. Positive self-concept and internalized locus of control are similar concepts. Parents are in a crucial position to influence their child's feelings about self-actualization, and educators can help them.

Accelerated Development

Today an overriding consideration that binds the educator and parent together is how to achieve individualization of instruction. Gifted and talented children are not a homogeneous group; both parents and teachers recognize the wide diversity of these children, and the Individualized Education Program (IEP) has been a response to this mutual concern (see Chapter 6). For example, tactics of acceleration and enrichment should be selected with consideration of the person. Their selection must meet the same professional standards of precision as would the selection of a reading method.

Given that individualization must be based on data from assessment and evaluation, these procedures require interpretation. Assessment usually involves both quantitative and qualitative procedures to test or estimate present achievements and potential for the future. Parents have an obvious interest in understanding how the procedures are used, why they are selected, and what options result.

Program goals require interpretation so that parents comprehend how guidance, instruction, and other services facilitate their child's accelerated development. If there is unevenness in attainments, parents want to know how these differences can be accommodated or corrected. Moreover, the gifted and talented child who is handicapped by physical, sensory, learning, or emotional disabilities benefits from special forms of parent involvement. Parents are concerned that goals are well rounded and comprehensive. For example, they often probe into the development of physical skills and request guidance in the best use of leisure time.

Social Relationships

The child's need for social relationships with persons of equal ability and motivation must be satisfied. It is also necessary for the child to maintain contact with all of his or her chronological peers. Social and emotional development does not necessarily occur at the same rate as mental/ intellectual development. Certainly, the gifted and talented as a group are socially and emotionally well adjusted. However, experience and individual differences must be taken into account. Each child's socialization calls for a great deal of contact with both psychological and chronological peers to avoid the consequences of isolation. It is widely believed that a gifted and talented child's emotional needs more closely approximate what is normal for chronological age than what is normal for mental age. Actually, there is too little information on this matter to be certain, but it is clear that social relationships are essential and that their development and growth vary from one gifted and talented child to another.

Parents require basic information concerning the nature of accelerated human abilities. A gifted and talented child may be the first in a family clan. Parents are not necessarily free of stereotyped ideas about the gifted and talented merely because their child is gifted and talented. Moreover, according to surveys, expectant parents hope for a "bright" child rather than for a genius. Parents may feel incompetent or overwhelmed by the financial resources needed to nurture their child. Their lack of financial resources may cause them to deny the youngster's ability. Some parents may be confused by technical terminology used by educators and psychologists. Just as some teachers may feel ill prepared to teach the gifted and talented, some parents may feel ill prepared to nurture a gifted and talented child. Parents require reassurance that their skills do indeed apply and that their child's teacher is available for consultation.

Values Conflict

Serious disagreements can surface among the home, the school, and the gifted and talented learner. The future for a gifted and talented boy or girl can be filled with ambiguity. At the same time, parental, teacher, or pupil tolerance for uncertainty can be very low. The resulting differences can become the source of immense frustration. For example, a child's preference for a creative career can cause deep concern as to the practicalities of earning a living or can foster religious conflicts.

Certain youngsters may resist being pushed faster than their own internal sense of timing, others may rebel at too slow a pace. Some family values may not be reinforced by the wider culture, such as tolerance for the ideas of certain leaders, which can place the gifted and talented learner in an awkward position. Parents may feel frustration over the lack of provisions for the gifted and talented in their school district. They may feel excluded from influence (not control) on educational policy. Educators and parents must build mutual advocacy arrangements in the best interests of the gifted and talented.

THE SOCIAL CONTEXT OF PERFORMANCE

Talented or creative human performance has motor, cognitive, and affective components. Consider a room in a "Y" on a Saturday morning. An artist turned educator is working with a dozen elementary school children. The adult dominates the room, but her sense of art as serious, no nonsense work has not entirely subdued the "school's out" attitude of the children. She reminds the children that Art is Work, Art is Labor, and that the time for play is *after* the product is done. All eyes are now in focus. There is expectation.

The teacher holds up a lump of clay about the size of a lemon. She observes that this humble lump is three dimensional (3-D). People can walk around it and view all sides. She elaborates on the degree of relief and detail in 3-D sculpture. She challenges the pupils to devise hollow, 3-D objects out of clay. With a smile, with sincerity, she encourages. She expects mistakes and false starts. With a twinkle in her eye, she urges the pupils to err boldly.

Some pupils consider what could be hollow and 3-D. Some think of an object and how to make it 3-D and hollow. By the end of the period there are models of cars, cans, snakes, birds, baseballs; everyone has produced a hollow, 3-D representation. There has been joy in creation; there has been accomplishment in responding to the challenge. The teacher also feels a sense of accomplishment. There has been meshing of cognition, affect, and motor activity in relating a medium to a purpose. It has been a good session.

Composites of Performance

Every personality is a composite that reflects not only external behaviors but also the internalized impressions of personal adequacy. Three clusters about the personality of the gifted and talented are especially significant for parents, educators, and others who guide the development of these children (Jacobs, 1971). One cluster centers on the need to allay misconceptions about the personalities of gifted and talented persons. A second cluster focuses on personality as a means of identifying gifted and talented learners. A third spells out the educator's role in the design of environments to nurture the emerging personality.

Jacobs compared gifted and average pupils of kindergarten age. His general conclusion that the developmental sequence was the same for both, but that the gifted and talented moved through the stages more rapidly, conforms to many other findings. Jacobs was interested, too, in the stage of moving from dependence upon adult direction and approval to reliance upon a personal sense of direction and approval. This movement from the external to the internal is usually termed by psychologists as a change in locus of control.

Educational equivalents would be becoming mature, developing self-confidence, and acquiring independent work habits. Jacobs' gifted and talented learners made significant gains over other children in (1) motivation to succeed, (2) practical common sense, (3) emotional sensitivity to the needs of others, (4) productivity of assignments completed, (5) flexibility in response to situations calling for the discovery of solutions, (6) self-reliance for initiation of work and confidence in their own solutions, and (7) independence from the need for adult approval.

Teacher reactions to the rapid development of their gifted and talented learners was often mixed. For example, the self-reliant child was frequently perceived as stubborn. The reflective child was perceived as lazy, inattentive, or immature in study habits. The child of high initiative was perceived as bossy or domineering. The highly motivated child was perceived as a showoff. The very traits of ability were considered disturbing behavior. The Jacobs report is instructive in that it illustrates how misunderstanding and misinterpretations of the gifted and talented can arise from the personal experience of teachers, principals, and other educators. Whitmore (1980) observed the same phenomena in the primary grades.

In an early study, Kurtzman (1967) investigated the acceptance of adolescents in relation to IQ, measured creativity, school attitude, and peer acceptance. Sex differences regarding attitudes toward the school experience were found within the sample. In general, the males were more positive (for

Table 5-1 Attributes of Personality Associated with Performance*

Facilitative Attributes	Mean Scores**		Nonhelpful Attributes
	Males	Females	
Outgoing	6	6	Reserved
Bright	5	5	Dull
Mature	7	6	Emotional
Dominant	5	4	Submissive
Enthusiastic	6	6	Glum
Conscientious	5	6	Expedient
Venturesome	5	5	Shy
Tender-minded	6	7	Tough-minded
Trusting	5	5	Suspicious
Imaginative	7	7	Provincial
Forthright	5	5	Shrewd
Placid	4	4	Apprehensive
Experimenting	7	6	Conservative
Self-sufficient	7	7	Dependent
Casual	6	6	Controlled
Relaxed	5	6	Tense

*Adapted from Halpin et al. (1974).
**7 is most positive, indicating possession of the facilitating attribute to a high degree.

reasons unspecified) than the females. Both groups were found to be extroverted, sociable, and accepted by others. Those who scored high on creativity measures were self-confident and open to new experiences and activities. The results of this early study are confirmed by Halpin, Payne, and Ellett (1974). Their sample consisted of 360 high school students who had been selected to participate in a Governor's Honor Program. The investigators identified selected attributes that were associated with demonstrated performances. Table 5-1 presents a resumé of self-reports by the participants. Slight sex differences were reported; however, curriculum interest was the significant predictor. Social science, science, and art students were found to have facilitative attributes most often: English, mathematics, and drama majors were next, while the music and foreign language majors had these attributes least often. It is not known if the measure of creativity really assesses creativity in general or is sensitive only to certain curricular dimensions. At any rate, the Halpin et al. report illustrates the diversity of gifted and talented students and the attractive and appealing typography of their personality attributes.

Sources of Motivation

Recognition was identified by Thistlewhite (1959) as an important factor in personality, especially in motivation for subsequent studies in college. The sample consisted of students who had all received certificates of merit for participation in a state program, but the amount of newspaper coverage their achievements had been given was not the same. Verbal aptitude, sex, geographical region, and socioeconomic status were controlled. Recognition increased the person's (1) favorable attitude toward intellectual pursuits, (2) interest in careers in research and/or college teaching, and (3) requests for scholarship aid. Pupils of nonprofessional parents became motivated to seek professional careers. Furthermore, recognition had similar motivational effects upon pupils of low verbal ability. Recognition seemed to act as an incentive.

Roweton (1975) found that students can motivate each other. Student recognition was more potent than that of teachers or other external judges as a stimulus to continued pursuit of excellence among fourth grade gifted and talented pupils.

Correlates of Performance

Self-confidence tends to be positively correlated with quality of production. Production can be of at least two main types. The known, or a given, can be used to produce or generate a unique and valuable creative product. The second type involves observations, analysis of data, and a fresh conceptualization that culminates in a product of merit. In certain instances, both types are involved in a single production as when information is used to arrive at new possibilities.

Continuing research has attempted to (1) clarify the difference between creativity and mere novelty, (2) understand the personality traits that give rise to creativity, and (3) identify those environmental sources that nurture creativity. None of the problems is yet fully solved.

An early study by Getzels and Jackson (1960) compared the upper 20 percent of a group of high school pupils on measured IQ with the upper 20 percent of the same group on measured creativity. Creativity was measured by response to items featuring word associations, use for things, hidden shapes, interpretation of fables, and completing open-ended stories. The combined mean IQ for both groups was 132; the mean IQ of the higher creative group was 127, and that of the higher intellectual group was 150. No differences were found in standardized achievement scores, although teachers expressed a preference for the higher IQ pupils. In terms of career orientation, the higher creative group expressed preferences for more unconventional occupations, such as inventor, adventurer, and writer. The higher IQ group was more oriented toward occupations of lawyer, physician, or professor. The higher creative group was more likely to find humor and make a playful response to open-ended exercises. A number of attempts have been made to replicate the Getzels and Jackson study, but the results have been far less clear-cut. It may be that the findings of Getzels and Jackson are peculiar to the pupils with whom they were working.

Some studies of curriculum organization as a source of performance have shown promise in isolating guidelines for the design of helpful educational environments. For example, Torrance (1969) observed that imposing time limits on an exercise can keep pupils from expressing curiosity. His elementary gifted and talented children were judged by teachers as high versus low curious. Each group was asked to develop questions regarding unusual uses of ice. Under timed conditions, both groups produced equal numbers of similar questions. Under take-home conditions, the high and low curious produced equal numbers of questions.

Curriculum structure, as a condition of environment, was investigated by Ogilvie (1974). He compared the creativity scores of 140 elementary children under various conditions of teacher control of activities. One condition was complete teacher direction (structure); another was absence of control (anomie). Other conditions varied in the proportions of teacher-pupil planning. The two extreme conditions produced the least gains in creativity. Taylor (1970) reported similar results, except that his report identified a potentially helpful sequence that merges teacher and pupil participation. This sequence included phases of (1) exposure to new ideas, materials, and possibilities introduced by the teacher; (2) implosion of new information into the pupil's existing framework of knowledge—an assimilation and accommodation process; (3) exposure to new possibilities usually manifested by the pupil as insights for planning new projects; (4) an explosion phase characterized by activities necessary for completion of a project; and (5) the culminating production phase. The Clark (1965) report confirms the influence of curriculum and personality aspects of the producer and consumer orientation of persons. Creativity seems to be associated with flexible thinking, pursuit of wide and varied interests, and selection of varied careers. Teacher overcontrol produces pupils who are confined, prefer safe careers, have a placid attitude toward the school curriculum, and respond to novel situations in standard ways.

Self-Concept

Self-concept, defined as one's opinion about one's own ability, was investigated by Milgrim and Norman (1976). They studied 159 elementary school gifted and talented children who were enrolled in an after-school program and compared the relationships among measures of self-concept, creativity, and intelligence. They found no significance between self-concept and measured IQ, but they reported a significant relationship between high measured creativity and high positive self-concept. Their report confirms an earlier investigation by Sisk (1972). Her sample consisted of 45 mentally advanced learners (e.g., a Binet IQ greater than 130) who were identified by trained teachers as noncreative. These learners were withdrawn and shy, terminated assignments, required prompting for assignments, and preferred external direction. Sisk described a ten-week Saturday morning enrichment program in which classes were organized into three separate groups of 15 pupils each. These classes were conducted by trained graduate students preparing to be teachers of the gifted and talented. Interests were pursued on an individualized basis, and opportunities were provided for group discussions, role playing, and project sharing. Sessions were designed to promote freedom to experiment with novel ideas and to experience success for effort. The content centered upon art, poetry, social institutions, and literature. All pupils showed a decrease in those behaviors by which they had been identified in the original sample selection. Seventy-five percent of the pupils were noted by their classroom teachers to be significantly improved in school performance. Sisk appears to have brought about marked changes in the learning styles of these pupils. Krippner and Blickenstaff (1970) noted similar performance gains as a result of an arts workshop.

These studies are representative of the literature of the gifted and talented in two respects. First, performance and self-concept are associated positively, although which "causes" the other is not known. However, it is reasonable to assume that confidence is an attribute for persisting in a given endeavor. Second, self-concept is susceptible to responsive environment; individualized attention creates the self-confidence needed to pursue complex tasks and to produce unique, personalized results.

THE CONCEPT OF UNDERACHIEVEMENT

Performing consistently below one's capability or potential is considered underachievement. In school, it is scoring lower on achievement tests than expected when the expectation is based on sound evidence of higher ability. Until recently, underachievement was blamed on the underachievers (lacking in drive or ambition, unwilling to try, a "get-by" attitude, personal maladjustment) or on the home and family situation (parental neglect, parental overindulgence, nonstimulating home environment, conflict in the home). Currently, attention has turned to the school as a major cause of underachievement, particularly for gifted and talented girls and boys. The substantial amount of underachievement among gifted and talented children and youth all too frequently results from a combination of inappropriate curriculum and instruction, but there are effective ways to prevent and correct most underachievement.

Sound education for gifted and talented children can be established only if there is a real effort on the school's part to optimize intellectual, social-emotional, and motor development and to prevent underachievement in any of the three categories. That is the school's problem, not the child's. If underachievement is to be corrected, the school must accept responsibility. To blame the child or the child's background accomplishes nothing. Strong empirical support for this view comes from Whitmore (1980), whose ten years of close attention to this matter lead her to conclude that:

> chronic underachievement by gifted students can be prevented by the provision of appropriate educational programs and early patterns of underachievement can be reversed through special education in the elementary school. Educational programs for achieving or underachieving gifted students are one and the same: the only difference ... is the amount of teacher time and effort directed toward such objectives as enhancing self-esteem, developing social skills, and remediating academic deficiencies. (p. 197)

There is no "best" set of instructional and curricular options, even for most cases. Instead, each teacher must study the individual child and the known instructional and curricular resources while considering these questions:

- What changes in behavior (mine and the child's) are desirable?

- What can be used to modify self-perceptions and build self-esteem?

- What materials and procedures will help most in developing citizenship and leadership skills?

- Which approaches should I choose to remediate the child's underachievement and close the gap between capability and attainment?

More than one possible prescription may emerge. Consultation with the child, with parents, and with colleagues often helps in determining the initial approach. In any event, a thorough trial, with good records, can be expected either to correct the problem or to indicate the next steps to be taken.

LEVELS AND FORMS OF UNDERACHIEVEMENT

There are three levels of educational underachievement among highly able individuals: (1) natural, (2) covert, and (3) overt. A knowledge of all three is helpful in understanding giftedness and talent, and all three of the levels are of practical significance, each in its own way.

Natural Underachievement

The difference between the rapid rate of cognitive development and the slower acquisition of life experiences in a gifted and talented child may produce natural underachievement. For instance, a 10-year-old with an intelligence quotient of 140 has a mental age (level of cognitive development) of 14 years. However, it is not reasonable to expect a 10-year-old to behave cognitively (think) like an average 14-year-old. There are physiological differences, differences in both quantity and quality of experience, differences in personal and social expectations by and of others, and differences in self-perception and self-concept. Thus, some shortfall in achievement if the criterion is mental age seems "natural." Moreover, gifted and talented children grasp and verbalize that concept. Given rapport and opportunity, they can freely discuss their perceptions of being "different" in this regard and their understanding that it is "normal" for them. (At this point, too, teachers and parents can reinforce behaviors and feelings that contribute to sound mental health in the face of being "different.")

If some degree of underachievement is to be accepted as "natural," the question is, How much? We opt for the rule of three-fourths in matters that are chiefly academic/cognitive skill learning, such as reading, arithmetic, oral language, spelling, and hard sciences. In matters that are more social or affective, we prefer the rule of two-thirds. These areas include history, the social sciences, world cultures, philosophy, and interpersonal and group skills. In the motor domain, and still with mental age as the criterion, a rule of one-fourth seems defensible. This area involves the typical physical education curriculum, individual and team sports, and physically active recreation pursuits. These fraction rules apply to girls and boys alike. The rule of three-fourths is computed as follows:

> Take three-fourths of the difference between chronological age (CA) and mental age (MA). Add the result to the chronological age. Use that result as an indicator of the child's achievement expectancy. For example, given that MA = 14 years, CA = 10 years, IQ = 140,

$$MA\ (14) - CA\ (10) = \text{Difference}\ (4)$$
$$\tfrac{3}{4} \times 4 = 3$$
$$CA\ (10) + 3 = 13\ (\text{Achievement expectancy age})$$

> Using the common procedure of subtracting 5 years from CA to obtain grade equivalent (13 − 5 = 8), the child's achievement expectancy is 8th grade level.

The rule of two-thirds and the rule of one-fourth can be used in the same way to obtain achievement expectancy grade level estimates. For example, grade level expectancy for this child in the motor domain, using the rule of one-fourth (barring such things as physical handicaps or health problems) would be (11 − 5 = 6) or 6th grade. The application of formulas like these has a long history. They are quite valuable if accepted as rough approximations. Efforts to refine such formulas to make them specifically diagnostic have failed, however. The main reason is that, while the original measures of intelligence or achievement have ample reliability for general estimates, they do not have the precision necessary to pinpoint diagnosis. That remains for professional judgment by well-informed specialists. Although the natural amount of underachievement can be readily calculated for any gifted and talented child, it must be remembered that the result is an approximation and should be bounded by ± one year. Thus, if the child in the example has actual reading skills achievement of grade 7.1 or more, achievement would be considered on target. Achievement less than grade 7.0 would be cause for concern, for there might be either covert or overt underachievement that needs corrective attention.

Covert Underachievement

Often disguised by better than average progress in school, covert under-achievement accounts for the great bulk of what studies like those of Marland (1972) have called the educational neglect, misunderstanding, and lack of fulfillment of gifted and talented young people. Covert underachievement is exemplified by the fourth grade child who is earning As and Bs, whose standardized and teacher-made achievement tests show attainments at about fifth grade level, but whose actual grade level expectancy is about seventh or eighth grade or higher. Because parents, teachers and such children them-selves are unaware of their higher capabilities and because they are all sufficiently rewarded by consistently reaching their own too low objectives, the child's significant underachievement remains undiscovered.

The consequences are predictable. One is the shock of confrontation with peers whose education has been more appropriately matched to their capabili-ties and who have learned to use their cognitive powers optimally, not minimally. This shock most frequently coincides with school transfers or shifts to more advanced levels, (e.g., middle to high school). Since the needs for social success and achievement remain dominant, the covert under-achiever either scrambles for positive responses from a suddenly demanding environment or drops out because of the emotional stress and social conflict. If remediation and counseling are available, the prognosis is good. More often than not, however, neither corrective instruction nor counseling is available.

Underachievement can also lead to serious personal and societal loss as a result of the failure *ever* to recognize the potential for higher level perfor-mance. The outcome commonly is a life of underemployment, few close friends, a series of attachments to esoteric causes and pursuits, and mild but chronic social maladjustment, chiefly manifested by detachment from neigh-bors and associates at the work place. "Bad luck" is blamed for any and all disappointments, and the locus of control is always believed to be external and beyond personal influence.

The covert type of underachievement can be detected by the same proce-dures used to detect the natural form. In general, it is necessary to look carefully at all pupils' actual achievement and compare it with levels of achievement expectancy, as determined by the fractional rules. More than a year's discrepancy at any grade level is cause for concern.

Overt Underachievement

For different reasons, overt underachievement may go unnoticed, too. It appears in children who do not seem to be gifted and talented to themselves, their teachers, or their parents. Their underachievement is quite apparent to everyone, however, because they do poorly in comparison to their age peers with the tasks of their regular grade classes. It is no wonder, then, that teachers, parents, and the children themselves are surprised and sometimes unbelieving when informed that psychological assessment results show very high rates of cognitive development.

After a most intensive study of gifted and talented underachievers, Whitmore (1980) concluded that the great majority of such youngsters fell into one of these four groups: (1) children who are learning disabled, (2) those who are behaviorally disordered or emotionally disturbed, (3) those who are neurologically handicapped or minimally brain damaged, and (4) those whose idea of perfection is so rigid that no efforts could be made for fear of unsatisfactory results. Happily, the special educational needs of these children are sufficiently common across categories that it is not essential to classify each child for educational purposes. Also, it is possible to correct the children's behavior so that the categorical distinctions disappear, along with the underachievement. This is done by instruction that focuses on matching, i.e., teaching the child specifically what personal and academic assessment show to be missing. Most often, it involves adapting to the child's learning style and providing many opportunities for self-direction and independent thinking, challenging curriculum adaptations keyed to the child's interests, a teacher-guided social climate that is open and not teacher-dominated, and conscious but nonthreatening cultivation of the child's self-esteem in mentally healthy ways.

Forms of Underachievement

Within each of the two problem levels, covert and overt, attention should be called to the forms, or types, of underachievement, general and specific. This is an educationally useful distinction because the two forms call for somewhat different approaches to remediation.

General underachievement covers those instances in which the problem is very broad and underachievement is essentially a way of life. Children who show general underachievement are not reaching reasonable expectancy in academic, social-emotional, or motor areas. It may be difficult to take corrective action, especially if the underachievement is overt.

Specific underachievement indicates an uneven profile. A child may be at expectancy in motor skills, but be covertly underachieving in the social-emotional sphere and overtly underachieving in the academic area. Some children may also show marked differences within the academic area, for instance, high in mathematics and low in social studies. Where there is some achievement that is consonant with giftedness and talent potential, it is often easier to arrange instruction that remedies deficits in other areas.

In summary, underachievement among the gifted and talented takes on a variety of appearances, some not easily detected at first. There are no firm data on its incidence or prevalence, but both are thought to be high, especially at the covert level. Enough is known, now, to keep the occurrence of underachievement to a minimum and to remedy it whenever it is identified.

Chapter 6

Widening the Social Context of Opportunity

HUMAN ABILITY, CULTURE, LANGUAGE, AND POVERTY

Educators are motivated to "do something" for pupils whose backgrounds do not match those of the majority. Common labels attached to such children are culturally different, economically disadvantaged, children of poverty, bilingual, culturally deprived, low socioeconomic, underachieving, failure-prone, ethnically different, high failure risk, inner city children, minority group, low social class, failure to thrive, and similar distinguishing (and usually perjorative) terms. The indiscriminate use of such expressions to categorize children and their families is a matter of concern.

> Traditionally educators have attached labels to children in an attempt to identify their educational needs—labels such as culturally disadvantaged, mentally retarded, learning disabled, hyperactive, gifted, emotionally disturbed, and high risk. There is reason (both logical and empirical) to question the usefulness of such labels for educational planning. Furthermore, the use of labels is debilitating for the persons to whom they are attached. Children so called typically develop ... [problems of] ... self esteem, are not well accepted by normal peers, and are treated differentially [in a negative sense] by their teachers. (Neisworth, Willoughby-Herb, Bagnato, Cartwright, & Laub, 1980, p. 114)

Labeling language should be used with utmost professional discretion, if it is used at all, for it tends to promote and maintain prejudice.

It is true that the expressions listed and similar ones can be accurate descriptions of certain pupils and their families. It is not true, however, that these conditions are synonymous with parental or societal neglect and ignorance. Seldom do these conditions, singly or in combination, actually cause educational problems. Educational problems are more often caused by the failure of counselors, psychologists and other educators to accommodate the varied backgrounds of these "different" pupils.

The practice most likely to lead teachers and others into mistakes is the tendency to lump cultural, language, economic, ethnic, and racial differences together. It has a certain arbitrary convenience, but it is like putting trees, tomatoes, and tanks together because they all begin with *t*. The following observations should make that even more relevant:

- Cultures that differ are neither better nor worse. Everyday life patterns in suburban Boston are quite different from those of an Amish or Mennonite community in Pennsylvania.

- Being economically disadvantaged (financially poor) is neither a disgrace nor evidence of sloth. Many hard-working and highly intelligent people have little or no material wealth. Sometimes it is because of the nation's economic conditions, and sometimes it is because they have not had opportunities for education and vocational advancement. Sometimes it is by choice, as in religious orders.

- Immigration often introduces non-English-speaking children into American schools. Some children born in the United States grow up in homes where Spanish, French, German, Chinese, or another foreign language is the primary tongue. These children are frequently from families that place a high value both on education in general and upon the ideals of American democracy. Yet, when such children come to school, the fact that they have at least rudimentary conversational competence in two languages is too often treated as a problem rather than the asset that it really is.

- From the standpoint of ability to learn, there are no important differences among children of different national origins. The similarities in learning potential among national and ethnic groups hold also for racial groups. A range of gifted and talented, average, and retarded pupils can be expected in all ethnic and racial groups. None has a monopoly on exceptionality or on ordinariness.

- In the midcity life of metropolitan areas there are a great many clean and well-kept homes, loving parents, active and concerned citizens, young and old, and enterprising business people. Civic-minded groups work hard to maintain and elevate the recreational and cultural tone of the inner city.

It is necessary to look in different ways to pick up the early signs of giftedness and talent in children whose backgrounds differ from that of the majority of children. For the same reasons that stereotypes about racial minorities, ethnic groups, and others must be combated, so must stereotypes about evidence of giftedness and talent.

In the Yourtowne Public Schools, a task force of educators has the responsibility of ensuring that the school system adapts to the needs of children whose backgrounds are unusual. This fall, for instance, an American Indian family, a Russian family, and a Vietnamese family moved to Yourtowne. All had children, and they ranged from preschoolers through high school age. The American Indian, skilled in structural steel work, took a position that let him settle down as foreman-instructor for a company that specializes in putting up the girders and other structural metal for buildings and bridges, and supplies the crew leaders for such work. He brought his family, a wife and four children, ages 4, 6, 9, and 11, from the reservation where they had lived and gone to school to live in Yourtowne. The mother and father in the Russian family had both been employed in New York City at the United Nations headquarters, she as manager of finances for the Russian delegation and he as a translator. There they met, married, began a family, and decided to defect to the United States. They elected to settle in Yourtowne, away from their previous associates. Their first child was old enough to start kindergarten. The Vietnamese group was an extended family: an elderly aunt, a middle-aged uncle, a husband and wife with three children, ages 10, 12, and 15, and two cousins, ages 3 and 5. The latter's parents died at sea as the group sought sanctuary outside their homeland. A church organization sponsored the settlement of the Vietnamese family in Yourtowne. In Vietnam, the father had been a high school mathematics teacher, and the mother had worked part-time as a salesperson in a bicycle shop.

When the children of these families appeared at various Yourtowne schools for enrollment, the task force was alerted. At each school, the parents received immediately a small, clearly phrased booklet that described enrollment procedures. They were told that, in a few days, with their permission and cooperation, some assessments would be made of the educational status and learning styles of their youngsters to help arrange the most appropriate school programs for them. The parents were invited to witness the assessments and help provide information.

The task force, chaired by a school psychologist, consists of another school psychologist, a school social worker, and the principal or a designated representative from the school in which enrollment is sought. Usually, only one school psychologist serves in a given instance, but two are kept up-to-date on assessment procedures particularly designed to circumvent unusual background or developmental differences. To accomplish this, the two psychologists are sent annually to workshops conducted on the topic by professional associations. Also, the newest assessment materials are purchased, and the two psychologists conduct in-service training for their associates in Yourtowne on the application of these procedures. The psychologists and the social worker, among them, have good command of black speech and of Spanish; a roster of community members fluent in other languages is kept by a local service club, and these can be called on for assistance as needed. As the task force nears completion of the assessment of a given child, the teacher most likely to have chief responsibility for that child is brought in as a partner to give educational substance to the plan being developed. The school social worker and the teacher decide together how best to bring the parents (and perhaps the pupil) into final decision making.

Naturally, the task force's workload varies. Most of the time, the members pursue their ordinary work in the schools. The task force is always ready, however, to come together and do what is necessary to design and initiate plans for children who need unusual attention.

Options and Choices

Torrance (1977, 1980) and Frasier (1979), on the basis of available research, identified issues related to identification and programming. Three of these can be summarized as follows:

1. Instrumentation and content of programming. So-called intelligence and creativity tests can be more accurately described as achievement tests than as measures of capacity for future performance. Present instruments can be faulted for their lack of adaptation to the children of poverty who have acquired low self-esteem and motivation for schooling. Furthermore, intervention efforts have proceeded on the basis of a deficit model, which implies a disability or defect nonresponsive to nurture, rather than a difference model, which assumes alternative methods to achieve common ends.
2. Neglect of knowledge, abilities, and values prized by specific and known groups. The content of instrumentation can be so centered upon culture-specific reference points that it excludes appropriate alternative responses. Responses may be culturally "right" but mainstream "wrong." For example, in certain regions of the United States, a "right" definition of the word *tonic* would be soft drink, but it would be typically considered wrong, unless the evaluator recognized its logic.
3. Negative effects of testing procedures. There is a persisting belief, a mistaken one, that all children are equally motivated to respond to test

procedures and settings. Users of tests sometimes have too little regard for the child's emotional reactions to tests and for their responsibility to develop rapport.

Emerging Trends in Identification

Trends are now emerging that can benefit all children and will reduce the risk that gifted and talented children will be overlooked because they are not in all respects members of the majority. These trends include:

1. translation of standard texts such as the Stanford-Binet and the Wechsler tests. Both are now available in Spanish. Problems that persist within this promising approach are: (a) translations do not always eliminate items of cultural bias, (b) item translations do not always allow for dialect variations, (c) an easy item in English may turn out to be a difficult item in Spanish, and (d) prediction of future performance is relatively weak.
2. modified administration of standard procedures which include extending time limits and use of nonverbal directions by the examiner have also been refined.
3. emergence of psychometer procedures that are not culture-bound, e.g., autobiographical inventories and tests that accommodate background differences. The system of multicultural pluralistic assessment (SOM-PA) developed by Mercer and Lewis (1976) is an example.
4. emergence of nonpsychometric assessment. This trend is growing and appears to have merit.

If settings are to be designed to foster learning by children whose gifts and talents do not surface immediately in typical school situations, deliberate efforts must first be made to locate those children. Second, these children must be invited to take part in the learning environment. Third, the individualized education programs (IEPs) for these children must be drafted with their particular characteristics in mind.

To find gifted and talented children who are not always detected by well-established psychometric tools like the Wechsler, a number of adaptations of available methods and several specialized devices have been proposed (Table 6-1). These are not unduly complicated. In each case, they try to bypass interference caused by language differences, lack of experience, or sensory deprivation and to probe for indications of high cognitive power or creative potential as shown in situations familiar to the particular child.

Reynolds and Birch (1977) supply anecdotal material and additional suggestions regarding ways to locate gifted and talented pupils who evade

Table 6-1 Psychological Tests of Intelligence and Creativity Applicable to Special Groups

Group	Test
Urban children whose only life experience has been confined to the region close to their community	Stallings Environmentally Based Screen (SEBS) (Stallings, 1972)
	Alpha Biographical Inventory (Taylor et al., 1966–68)
	Relevant Aspects of Potential (RAP) (Grant, 1974)
Culturally different groups in general	Torrance Tests of Creative Thinking (Torrance, 1971)
Disadvantaged black children	Abbreviated Binet for Disadvantaged (ABDA) (Bruch, 1971)
Disadvantaged black, Chicano, and Anglo children	System of Multicultural Pluralistic Assessment (SOMPA) (Mercer & Lewis, 1976)
Mexican-American children	Prototype Identification Instrument (Bernal & Reyna, 1974)
Blind children	Blind Learning Aptitude Test (BLAT) (Newland, 1969)
	Hayes-Binet and WISC Verbal Scale (Hecht, 1905)
Deaf children	Leiter International Performance Scale (Birch, Stuckless, & Birch, 1956)
	Hiskey-Nebraska Test of Learning Aptitude (Hiskey, 1966)
	Performance Wechsler Scales
Physically handicapped and speech handicapped children	Leiter International Performance Scale (Matthews & Birch, 1949)
	Raven Progressive Matrices (Taibl, 1951)

detection because of socioeconomic, racial, language, geographical, and cultural or ethnic differences.

The gifted and talented qualities of these children are sometimes disguised behind excessively withdrawn behavior or, conversely, obstreperousness. If a child or youth is a leader in mischief, the teacher must, of course, deal effectively with that overt behavior. At the same time, however, the teacher should realize that the troublesome pupil is also showing leadership, initiative, and independence, all features associated with giftedness and talent (Whitmore, 1980). The timidity or shyness of the withdrawn child may be more difficult for the teacher to penetrate. One way is to initiate a one-to-one relationship by asking the pupil to help in an easy and unobtrusive task, such as sorting papers, when few other pupils are on hand. Joint teacher-pupil activities create climate for incidental conversation. The teacher than can listen for the way the withdrawn child uses language, as well as for clues to the child's interests, hobbies, and general likes and dislikes.

Teachers who believe that disadvantaged children may also be gifted and talented often find their optimism justified. It pays to keep in mind that disadvantaged pupils are not automatically and irrevocably weak in the areas of cognitive, motor, and social-emotional skills. Rather, their indications of high potential may be simply different from those of the majority of students. A deliberate search for the gifted and talented among the disadvantaged can prove to be a rewarding professional treasure hunt.

Finding the gifted and talented among the disadvantaged is not the only problem. The factors that make them hard to locate may also make their needs different from those of most gifted and talented pupils. Two needs tend to stand out. One is for growth in self-direction and self-control. The other is for upgrading academic skills (Frazier, 1979). Meeting these two needs calls for both counseling and specific teaching. Growth in self-direction and self-control can be fostered in a variety of ways, including the use of mentors and models. In-school activities that easily can be linked to social studies and to career and vocational development are Decision Making Skills for Life Planning (DLP), authored by Frasier (1974), and Future Problem Solving Bowl (Torrance, 1976). Some upgrading of academic skills, particularly communication skills, can be readily tied into DLP. It is crucial, however, to avoid dampening enthusiasm and participation by being overcritical of technical writing and speaking errors. In general, the improvement of academic skills ought to be approached in straightforward style, as recommended in journals such as *The Directive Teacher* and *Teaching Exceptional Children.*

The seriousness with which efforts are being made to provide opportunities for gifted and talented pupils from disadvantaged backgrounds is shown by the work of Whitmore (1980) and others who have maintained that focus for years. It is certainly pròper that disadvantaged groups and individuals should have this attention. It is the right of every child to have a high-quality education that matches individual abilities and needs. It is also in the enlightened self-interest of all of society to ensure that no gifts or talents are wasted.

> To give a fair chance to creativity is a matter of life and death for any society. This is all-important, because the outstanding creative ability of a fairly small percentage of the population is mankind's ultimate asset, and the only one with which only man has been endowed. (Toynbee, 1964, p. 4)

THE GIFTED HANDICAPPED

Maker (1977) analyzed available information regarding gifted and talented persons who are visually impaired, hearing impaired, physically disabled, learning disabled, and emotionally impaired. The Maker report is remarkable for its insights into the range of human potential.

Attributes of Handicapped Gifted and Talented Persons

Maker's report is summarized in Table 6-2. It should be noted that the table's statements apply to groups; there are individual variations. The material has a number of possible uses. First, it can be seen that handicapped gifted persons on the whole do not differ substantially from other gifted persons in intelligence, divergent thinking, and self-concept. Second, the material suggests that individualization of instruction must take into account both the giftedness and the precise nature of the individual's handicap. Third, it offers a number of hints as to topics that need to be investigated more thoroughly. Finally, the suggestion is made that closer cooperation with professionals who specialize in other forms of special education might prove fruitful.

Educational Considerations for Physical Disabilities

The physically impaired (e.g., crippled and health impaired), although the reasons for their impairments are diverse, are usually considered together for special education. Key procedures and concepts are to (1) emphasize self-direction as a goal, (2) stress mobility skills, and (3) develop a "buddy system" among a number of nonimpaired persons to assist as needed. It has been found that physically impaired persons are sometimes the victims of embarrassing and distressing misunderstandings. For instance, their non-handicapped peers may laud them for heroism beyond reasonableness for their achievements or may treat them as totally incompetent. Nonimpaired gifted and talented persons are sufficiently mature to include the handicapped persons in both curricular and extracurricular experiences. This is consistent with both parental and pupil wishes and with the mainstream concept. Modification of physical space is now required in all public buildings to accommodate those who require it, whether they be pupils, teachers, or parents.

The visually impaired as a group preferred to be included in programs for the gifted and talented rather than in special programs for visually impaired persons. While those interviewed recognized the limitations of nonspecialists in mobility and Braille, the emphasis upon intellectual stimulation was considered sufficient compensation. Their suggestions for educational adap-

Table 6-2 Summary of Attributes of Gifted Handicapped Persons*

Attribute Clusters

Handicap Attribute	Intelligence and Ability Structure	Creativity and Divergent Thinking	Self-Concept
Visually impaired	Comparable to normal Memory and general information are strengths Certain superiority in auditory perception	Verbal fluency Curiosity related to mobility skills Adaptation to disability related to flexibility	Wide gap between "ideal" self and "true" self Concern with identity as person
Hearing impaired	Comparable to normal	Comparable to normal persons in general Slower emergence of specific abilities, dependent upon increasing age	Self-concept as a learner not a significant concern Concern about ability to succeed as a person in social situation
Physically impaired	Not given	Not given	Not given
Emotionally impaired	Limited evidence as to IQ after intervention for disturbed; preadmission measures of IQ emphasized in studies Comparable except perhaps in evaluation as defined by Guilford	Limited data complicated by limitations in the ability of adults to comprehend unique products/processes Slight evidence to suggest divergent thinking is different	Concerns about peers, acceptance by parents, academic achievement Services for the gifted and talented provided by school a significant source
Learning disabled	Higher level abilities such as reasoning and problem solving less likely to be impaired Less efficiency in perception and short-term memory	Creativity masked by underachievement	General problems in self-esteem Tends to be unable to resist loss of self-esteem without adult support

*Adapted from Maker (1977).

tations favored an arrangement that would both stimulate abilities and accommodate impairment. There have been a number of demonstrations of the feasibility of this approach. A specific priority was to discourage the use of abstract expressions by sighted persons, which could encourage verbalism, i.e., the use of words without comprehension, unless the visually impaired person also had opportunities to develop tactile, auditory, or olfactory reference points and descriptors. Additional priorities are to (1) stress vigorous physical exercise, (2) initiate mobility training early, (3) provide assistance in coping with fatigue, (4) teach the repair of clothing and appliances, and (5) encourage self-directed learning. Instruction in sexuality and sex education also surfaced as a relevant matter.

Educational considerations for the hearing impaired reflected a different pattern. Students had quite positive feelings toward their special classes for the hearing impaired. At the same time, they reported that it is entirely possible and often desirable to cope with hearing persons in a regular class, if enough support is available. Helpful considerations include: (1) sharing lecture notes, (2) using clear visual aids, (3) rephrasing questions, (4) using term papers as well as formal examinations to evaluate class performance, (5) facing the person when explaining items, and (6) asking fellow students to take notes. A prime suggestion involved self-concept development among the hearing impaired. Maker found a range of feelings regarding inclusion in programs for the gifted and talented. The ease of participation in a nonhearing world was attractive, but the gifted and talented hearing impaired recognized a common bond with nonimpaired persons committed to academic excellence.

There is definitely an increase in local school educational opportunity for pupils with physical and sensory impairments. Maker also leaves the distinct impression that a gifted and talented person with a handicap recalls with respect and appreciation those persons who responded to needs for challenge, stimulation, and achievement.

Educational Considerations for Emotional and Learning Handicaps

Gifted and talented learners with individualized programs designed to foster and nurture their superior abilities are not likely to manifest emotional or social disorders. This generalization links school practice to the mental health of gifted and talented learners. The learner who is asked to perform appropriate tasks and who has the companionship of equally motivated persons is at low risk for emotional difficulty. In the absence of an adequate adaptation, however, the gifted and talented are at high risk. Maker's message was explicit in its assumption that appropriate education for the gifted and talented can help to prevent emotional problems in these children.

The educational priority for education of the gifted and talented person who is emotionally impaired is treatment. The opportunity to express inner feelings could help to relieve the person's inner tension. Drama, writing, and artistic expression can be used for this purpose, in addition to their primary curricular purposes. Techniques akin to values clarification, which has a proved applicability to a wide range of teacher-pupil interactions, can be used to open and maintain the lines of communication.

The incidence of emotional disturbance within gifted and talented populations is less than that in the general population. The scientific investigation of the attributes of the gifted and talented has exploded the belief that there is a thin line between genius and insanity. Where emotional problems are found, they tend to be among the gifted and talented whose needs are not being met. Such persons experience unusual stress when they recognize the discrepancy between their potential and their performance; they feel frustration over their lack of opportunity and guilt over wasting their ability. Maker reinforces the generalization that emotional disturbance is environmentally induced by failure to render services rather than by constitutionally originated etiology.

One educational characteristic universally connected with learning disability is underachievement, i.e., attaining less than might reasonably be expected based on the other evidence of potential for achievement. The reasons for underachievement among gifted and talented students (Goldberg & Passow, 1958; Whitmore, 1980) are often elusive. Typically, school underachievement is described as a discrepancy between (1) actual performance of the person expressed in achievement test scores or grades and (2) an estimate of the person's potential performance as inferred by intelligence test scores, teacher judgment, or both. While this kind of discrepancy analysis approach appears straightforward, it is open to significant error. One can with confidence describe underachievement as a discrepancy between actual performance and an estimate of performance only when: (1) the estimate is free of error of measurement, (2) the estimate is a valid indicator of performance, (3) performance is related to measurement, (4) performance is not masked by environmental factors, (5) measurement of potential is not masked by environmental factors, and (6) chronological age is not the only discrepancy focus.

Error can arise when any of the preceding descriptors is ignored. Error, according to Maker (1977), increases in proportion to frequency of neglect of these descriptors. For example, a *sixth* grader who is achieving at seventh to eighth grade levels may not be thought by the teacher or principal to be an underachiever. However, if the student's potential (as determined by mental age criteria) were for ninth to tenth grade achievement, the picture changes and underachievement is evident. Before that, the pupil's superior performance in the sixth grade environment had effectively masked the serious gap between what the pupil's achievement was and what it should have been. (An example of what we call covert underachievement.) But this demonstrated underachievement does not necessarily mean that a learning disability is present. Diagnostic teaching may eradicate the discrepancy between potential and actual performance, leaving no reason to believe a learning disability was ever involved. On the other hand, if diagnostic teaching does not close the gap, there is reason to begin the search for a learning disability.

According to Maker, observation of class behavior is more promising than objective measurement per se. This approach is not always easily executed, even though research has identified prerequisite behaviors for school achievement. If a trait is considered a continuum, the learning disabled person will be more extreme in the possession or lack of this trait. Table 6-3 provides a contrast of behaviors of successful gifted and talented persons, underachieving gifted and talented persons, and gifted and talented persons labeled as learning disabled along such a continuum. This table identifies traits that exist at the time of identification. Intervention can minimize these negative consequences, since they are learned traits that are susceptible to modification.

The sign of learning disability among gifted and talented pupils is a significant discrepancy with an uneven pattern of achievement that is not associated with neglect, lack of opportunity, inappropriate teaching, environmental deprivation, or socioeconomic disadvantages and that does not yield to straightforward, individualized, diagnostic teaching aimed at removing the discrepancy. The educational significance of learning disability is seen in affective development, task persistence, and processing of information. Iden-

Table 6-3 Comparisons of Behaviors of Educational Significance for Three Groups of Learners*

Significant Attribute for Intervention	Achievers	Underachievers	Learning Disability
Attending	Attentive; able to persevere	Work consistently incomplete	Distractible; inattentive
Self-control	Able to regulate emotions	Self-control occasionally lost	Impulsive
Locus of control	Successful as a result of one's own efforts	Success as a matter of luck	Explicit structure required
Activity levels	Able to manage physical energy	Restless, moves from task to task	Hyperactive
Perception	Stimuli consistently perceived and labeled accurately	Inaccurate in association of stimuli and labels	Stimuli consistently distorted
Socialization	Socially motivated; popular	Aggressive; withdrawn	Inappropriate in attempts to interact
Self-concept	Positive view of self; anticipates success	Negative view of success	Self-defeating attitude; low self-esteem

*Adapted from Maker (1977).

tification is a significant first step, and intervention should be initiated immediately. It should focus upon affective development as well as academic performance, and higher level cognitive skills should not be ignored. Collaboration with a consultant in learning disabilities is essential to devise appropriate compensatory techniques. Whitmore's (1980) work confirms that corrective procedures can be very effective.

Eliminating Handicapism

Constructs such as racism, sexism, agism, and intellectualism are familiar reminders of the need for sensitivity. An *ism* alerts a nonaffected person of the ways in which language conditions, opinions, values, and behavior may influence others.

Mullins (1979) studied the stereotyping of handicapped persons within the educational community. This stereotyping can be viewed as a form of handicapism. Consider examples such as *lame* brain, turning a *deaf* ear, *crippled* by a strike, short-*sighted, blind* as a bat, threw a *fit, brittle* personality, *sick* job, *twisted* logic, *deaf* to reason, and *myopic* point of view. Consider examples such as *standing* tall, a fair *hearing,* a man of *vision,* source of *strength,* and rapid *movement.* The Mullins exposition documented the ways in which handicapism in language and educational media isolate handicapped persons from certain aspects of everyday life and limit them in career preparation and employment opportunities. She also documented that increased sensitivity to language and presentation in educational media is an improvement for everyone.

Mullins (1979) lauded the work of the National Center on Educational Media and Materials for the Handicapped, which represents an alliance of advocates, handicapped persons, and educators to eliminate handicapism from educational media. She summarized guidelines by which to judge the adequacy of educational materials. The proposed guidelines have sufficient validity to serve as criteria for elimination of other *isms* as well. These guidelines can be summarized as follows:

1. Representations of exceptional persons should be included in materials at all levels (early childhood through adulthood) and in curriculum areas such as career education, health, language arts, mathematics, physical education, science, and social studies.
2. Representations should be accurate and free of stereotypes.
3. Representations should show handicapped persons participating in everyday activities with nonhandicapped persons.
4. Representations should use language that is nondiscriminatory and free of value judgments.

5. Interaction between handicapped and nonhandicapped persons should be shown as mutually beneficial.
6. Representations should provide a variety of appropriate role models for handicapped persons, especially vocational models.
7. Emphasis should be upon the uniqueness and worth of every person rather than upon differences between the handicapped and nonhandicapped.
8. Tokenism should be avoided and comprehensiveness should be encouraged. For example, represented persons should not be limited to the physically disabled. Furthermore, severe as well as milder forms of handicaps should be displayed.

Representation of about ten percent of content would be evidence of commitment to elimination of handicapism. Mullins noted that omission is much more frequent than unfavorable representation.

Promising Trends

Opportunities for gifted and talented handicapped persons were expanded during the 1970s on three broad fronts: (1) legislation, (2) self-advocacy, and (3) enlightened recognition.

Legislative enactments such as Pub.L. 94-142 and Section 504 of the 1973 Rehabilitation Act have been called significant protection for handicapped persons by Flygare (1979). In general terms, Pub.L. 94-142 provides a federal mandate that each handicapped person of school age shall have a free and appropriate education based upon an Individualized Education Program (IEP). This legislation also states that education should take place in the least restrictive and most normalized setting, usually the child's local school. The intent and content of individualized planning have attracted the interest of educators in both general education and education of the gifted and talented.

Pub.L. 94-142 is called the Education for All Handicapped Children Act. Gifted children as such are not included in it, nor are they ordinarily thought of as handicapped in the most common usage of that term. For good reasons, however, Pub.L. 94-142 has turned out to be landmark legislation for gifted and talented children. The fact that gifts and talents appear among handicapped children has drawn attention to the need for IEPs that take giftedness and talent into account. Also, a number of states have elected to make Pub.L. 94-142's provisions applicable to their gifted and talented school-age populations. A third reason is that the IEP, so central to the law's thrust, is an excellent example of what ought to be employed in personalized program planning for gifted and talented pupils.

Self-advocacy describes the activism of handicapped persons themselves to inform public and private sectors about the legal rights, educational opportunities, and career/employment opportunities of the handicapped. For example, with the cooperation of the American Association for the Advancement of Science, handicapped scientists have organized a Foundation for Science and the Handicapped. According to Sharpless (1979), handicapped scientists can be found in every career/professional category, e.g., mathematics, physics, chemistry, astronomy, geology, biology, anthropology, economics, engineering, medical sciences, agriculture, zymurgy, industrial technology, education, dentistry, pharmaceutical science, computer science, statistics, as well as atmospheric and hydrospheric sciences. The Council for Exceptional Children, as cited by Mullins (1979), has also provided opportunities for self-advocacy by handicapped persons in the arts as well as sciences.

Enlightenment parallels self-advocacy. This dimension, however, describes the efforts of nonhandicapped persons and the gifted and talented who are handicapped to eliminate handicapism. The United States Office for Handicapped Persons (USOHP) monitors progress for both groups by advocate organizations. The very existence of USOHP is an indication of progress as well as a resource for technical assistance. The USOHP issues a publication, *Programs for the Handicapped,* that educators and parents can use for help and guidance.

RESPECTING VARIATIONS

In addition to minority groups and handicapped persons, other very able persons who are not readily identified should have greater educational opportunities. Such individuals reflect variations within the gifted and talented group. Drews (1963) discovered that, while adolescents appear similar in their scores on group IQ test and achievement tests, their talents and learning styles actually vary a great deal. She uncovered a minimum of four distinct patterns: (1) high achieving studious, (2) creative intellectual, (3) social leader, and (4) rebel. The attributes associated with these patterns are summarized in Table 6-4. In reality, no one person can be described by one pattern entirely; however, a given pattern can be used to express the general orientation a person has developed toward school tasks, motivation, and values. Exceptions are found, of course. For example, in school subjects in which a person has experienced success and demonstrated early competence, the creative intellectual pattern is usually dominant. In subject matter areas in which the person has had minimal success but is motivated to succeed, the high achieving studious pattern emerges. From time to time, the social leader pattern might emerge as a function of applied interest. The rebel pattern is also a possibility in the event of alienation toward teachers, parents, and/or curriculum structure.

The Drews report and the Torrance (1971) resumé document diversity in the descriptors of the gifted and talented. One implication of the diversity of attributes is that identification procedures must be equally diverse.

Table 6-4 Examples of Diversity among Able Adolescents*

High Achieving Studious	Social Leaders	Creative Intellectual	Rebel
Hard-working	Popular	Achievement test scores higher than grades	Individualistic
Attuned to adults	Well-liked		Creative nonintellectual
Conforming	Conforming to peers	Original and fluent on creativity tests	
Work before pleasure	Less adaptation to teachers		Nonconformity to serve their ends
Not school leader	"Good" student	Provocative questions on below the surface detail	Rejection of regimentation without intellectual or social purpose
Not creative or original	"Good" grades		
Productive in numbers or items attempted	Preference for social activities rather than reading about social philosophy or taking an exam on the topic	Desire for free choice	Low achievers
Structure preferred		Structure rejected	Leader in a subculture
Ambiguity rejected		No desire for rewards, approval	Rejected by teachers
Favored by teachers		Readers on topics outside the usual avoided	Low measure on social responsibility
Service to others		Scientist but not engineer	High score on nonverbal tests
Living by the rules		Oriented toward performing arts	Low score on fluency in creativity but highly oriented
			Possible responses to appeal directed toward their gain rather than a "social" purpose

*Adapted from Torrance's (1971) discussion of Drew (1963).

The styles of behavior presented by Drews appear to have been learned over the childhood and early youth periods. If this assumption is correct, these behavior styles and others are amenable to direction and to alteration by parents, counselors, psychologists, and educators.

Behaviors of Interest

Torrance (1977) speaks of a nonpsychometric approach to identification of gifted and talented learners. He singles out clusters of behaviors in school-age learners that have validity for identifying gifted and talented learners. These behavioral indicators are seen in the child who (1) is mature for age, (2) imitates and elaborates adult behavior, (3) is regarded as a leader with influence, (4) makes suggestions that are valued by peers, (5) mediates disputes and plans strategy, (6) tries new ideas, (7) persists in pursuit of tasks and ideas, and (8) initiates and maintains contact with adults.

A 30-item checklist can guide the observer's perceptions of classroom incidents (Torrance, 1977, pp. 89–90). An advantage of the checklist is that it takes in both teacher–pupil interactions and pupil–pupil interactions. They cover behavioral themes of (1) improvisation, (2) humor, (3) enjoyment, (4) responsiveness, (5) originality, (6) fluency, (7) speed of response, and (8) problem centeredness. Situations in class that allow for observation include (1) play/recess, (2) arts and crafts, (3) movement activities, (4) formal and informal language, (5) role playing and dramatics, and (6) problem solving/ unit teaching.

Torrance also proposed a teaching/instructional process for the observation of these traits. His elements of process included:

- discovery. Observations of the child at play can be a method of identification. Indicators are inferred by use of common materials for toys, games, and use in creative dramatics. Use involves the unexpected and unintended.

- importance. Autobiographies of gifted and talented persons reveal childhood preoccupation with improvisation from common materials. This attribute is found in both majority and minority group children. It allows for appropriate comparison.

- implications. Improvisation can be used to facilitate problem solving in group-oriented instruction. Career implications could be applied to occupations in (1) crafts/trades, (2) product development, (3) designing, (4) creative endeavors, and (5) science.

While the number of traits may eventually be reduced, expanded, or modified, Torrance's (1977) process of translating observed behaviors into practical applications will probably endure.

Emerging Alternatives for Programming

There is, at present, no single approach that is applicable to the diversity of gifted and talented learners, although common goals can be identified. It is the means that vary. A common goal is to translate the positive aspects of cultural diversity into fulfillment of mainstream requirements. For example, language systems can become more varied in imagery and affective content than standard English. The goal is to retain the richness while orienting the learner to the conventions of standard English. The mainstream language system must be taught without either attacking the child's system or causing the child to feel deflated or devalued. Torrance (1977) identifies three alternative ways to this central goal: (1) the talent development center, (2) the future studies center, and (3) the creative studies center. These centers would each have a different focus. The center approach requires a qualified director, criteria for admission, varied scheduling of classes, varied curriculum content, and rewards for performance. These concepts are most useful if they are applied in regular schools and classes, not in physically separate locations for gifted and talented pupils. Also, they need not be mutually exclusive.

Excellence in Education

A parallel alternative, EXCEL, has been organized by Jackson (1978). It is an expansion of his movement labeled PUSH (People United to Save Humanity). Organized in 1975, project EXCEL is not restricted to gifted and talented minority group learners per se. Its chief merit lies in its emphasis upon quality in education, which can benefit all children and youth. A further merit is its inclusion of pupils, parents, educators, and community to achieve equity, ethics, and excellence. EXCEL is a movement for quality and substance, to which parents, counselors, recreation leaders, and educators can look as a model for goals, organizational inclusiveness, and adherence to sound educational policy. The central themes of EXCEL are upward mobility and an agenda of action.

The goal of equity pursues the theme that everyone should have an opportunity for excellence. Employment and education are linked together as opportunities, since persisting unemployment and underemployment among adults creates negative influences for pursuit of educational goals. Jackson (1978) noted that IQ tests should be redemptive procedures, used to detect and diagnose problems, not punitive procedures, used to defeat or eliminate persons.

The goal of ethics involves the discipline necessary to defer immediate appetites for the later attainment of worthy personal and social development. EXCEL emphasizes the pursuit of truth, the educator's role in its pursuit, and a genuine respect for the learner's potential for self-discipline. EXCEL should not be thought of as anti-intellectual, according to Jackson. EXCEL does, indeed, stress attributes of the mind; however, it also stresses values. It seeks a balance among intelligence, integrity, drive, commitment, and concern beyond one's own immediate needs; a balance among "academics," career education, and moral education. This latter cluster includes belief in (1) oneself, (2) children's ability to learn, (3) parental capacity, and (4) life as having purpose.

Strategies to achieve equity and ethics are varied. Areas of emphasis include the school, the family, and policy makers. An example of the school's response would include the principal who delivers an annual State of the School address that contains a definition of goals, establishes rules, clarifies expectations, and describes a plan for the academic year. Graduation would include the student who receives a diploma as a symbol of knowledge and a voter's registration card as a symbol of responsibility.

The family's response could involve pledging. The student would sign written pledges to study for two hours with no outside interruptions, such as social visits, TV, or telephone. Parents would sign pledges to monitor their child's study hours, pick up report cards, and visit the school to review the child's progress.

The community's response would be a willingness to strive for equity and ethics. Examples of involved groups would include the school board, superintendent, administrative staff, principals, teachers, parents, pupils, religious institutions, the mass media, and the nonminority community as well. The intent of involvement is to establish an educational system that is a balance of liberal arts education and career education. This type of balance exposes learners to knowledge and the repetition of information, gives them the opportunity to internalize knowledge. From these steps develop convictions and values, as well as the ability to apply knowledge.

Summing Up

UNDERSTANDING LIFE'S SEQUENCE OF TASKS

Human development is not merely a recitation of what happens; it is an unfolding of increasing maturity and complexity. Development can be usefully described as tasks that are pertinent to specific periods of life and will meet both immediate and future needs. Development is a continuing dialogue between the person and his or her environment.

The pioneering work of Havinghurst has been updated. Life cycles research has evolved as the study of adult tasks that complements what is known and understood about childhood and adolescence.

Developmental tasks involve physical maturity, cognitive (e.g., intellectual) abilities, and interpersonal relationships. An understanding of developmental tasks can assist persons of varying ages to be empathetic toward one another.

The role of mentor has many implications for gifted and talented persons. Such persons may have mentors or may be mentors.

UNDERSTANDING FAMILY AND SOCIAL INFLUENCES

The families of gifted and talented persons exert a positive influence. The family's need for guidance is evident. Socialization and management of accelerated development are likely points of contact between the family and the school. Parents can also be competent partners in the educational process.

Self-concept, locus of control, and motivation are outcomes of one's social context. These outcomes can be attributed to practices within the home and school. Early recognition for efforts surfaces as a significant factor.

WIDENING THE SOCIAL CONTEXT OF OPPORTUNITY

The social context of opportunity for nurture has been extended to the children of poverty. Project EXCEL is an example of involvement of the home, the school, and the community. Functional observation of behavior in school and community can be a valid way to identify gifted and talented children and youth.

Another dimension of opportunity has been extended to handicapped persons. Legislation, self-advocacy, and enlightenment have been helpful sources. Scientific and technical careers are increasingly available to such persons.

There is diversity of abilities among the gifted and talented. Recognition of the four possible patterns encourages comprehensiveness of programming.

Enrichment

UNDERSTANDING LIFE'S SEQUENCE OF TASKS

1. Reflect upon the review of the resumé of developmental tasks. Consulting the original sources may be helpful. Does the listing make sense in terms of your own life, the lives of your parents? In what ways are there similarities or significant differences?

2. Do you believe that developmental tasks could be adapted as curriculum goals for your school district? Why or why not?

3. Explore the concept of mentor. How does a review of the life histories of notable people illustrate the existence of a mentor(s)? How have such persons been mentors? What appear to be key attributes?

4. Can you think of a person in your life that reminds you of a mentor? Have you been a mentor? How would you summarize the relationships as to quality and outcomes?

UNDERSTANDING FAMILY AND SOCIAL INFLUENCES

5. Prepare an outline for a parent education unit for families of the gifted and talented. What points would you stress with respect to definition, socialization, and managing accelerated development? What resources would be available within your community and your school district?

6. Free associate the ways in which the home, the school, and the community can recognize the abilities of the gifted and talented. Do you find evidence of public recognition within your community? What types of performances are rewarded?

WIDENING THE SOCIAL CONTEXT OF OPPORTUNITY

7. Inventory your community and your school district. What provisions are made for minority group members who are gifted and talented? Are there modifications of community and school practices?

8. Review the observational checklists within this section. Observe in schools and community agencies. Does any specific list prove more helpful in altering your perceptions?

9. Does your community have project EXCEL? Interview its coordinator. What provisions are made for the gifted and talented? Also, determine if your school district has a Teacher Corps project. What provisions does the project make for gifted and talented pupils?

10. How does your school district provide for handicapped persons? What provisions are made for gifted and talented pupils with handicaps? What evidence is there of interaction with the nonhandicapped?

11. Review the Mullins (1979) criteria on representation of the handicapped. Consult a sample of textbooks used in your school district and reference books in your public library. How do these books conform to the guidelines identified by Mullins? What improvement could be made? What positive examples do you note?

Understanding Needs and Priorities of Gifted and Talented Learners

SYNOPSIS

Four needs and priorities are associated with adapting informal and formal educational practices to accelerated and superior human abilities. One need involves the process and procedures of identifying gifted and talented children. Using the curriculum of one's expertise is a second need in the individualization of education. The third need is to match the learner's current educational level and needs with the content and processes to be learned in and out of school. The fourth need is to maintain and manage this optimal match.

KEY IDEAS

Four priorities for informal (home and community) and formal (school) educational programming for gifted and talented learners can be derived from an understanding of the nature of superior human ability and its social context. These four priorities are addressed to the matching of the curriculum of the school with the attributes of the gifted and talented person. They include (1) the recognition and location (identification) of gifted and talented persons; (2) the adaptation and appraisal of the existing home, neighborhood, community, and school curriculum; (3) the match between the learner and appropriate instruction; and (4) the maintenance and management of the optimal match.

The process to fulfill these priorities begins with assessment. The activities of assessment involve appraisal of the context of each person's formal and informal educational situation. It is a summation of pertinent information from which a deliberate instructional program is generated. Needs assessment describes the assembly and appraisal of both identification data and program data necessary for decision making for individual children, both in and out of school. Consumer opinion (parents and student) is an important source of assessment and evaluation. An inventory of the learner's interests and hobbies is another important source of information on which to base decisions for program improvement.

For a teacher, the immediate outcome of understanding learning conditions is a format for a lesson plan. For a parent or mentor it is also a plan, but probably a less formal one. These plans might well be linked to one another, however.

A PROTOTYPE

Thinnes (1978) has provided an account of one consumer's life experience. His theme was that having a high intelligence quotient (IQ) is not a guarantee that life will be beautiful. This account creates a sense of urgency about educational intervention.

Life at the Top of the IQ Scale Can Be Difficult

Forty-one-year-old Diane Simon (not her real name) is living proof that having a high IQ (intelligence quotient) is no guarantee that life will be a bed of roses full of nothing but golden moments.

Twice divorced and the mother of two children, she is trying to carve out a new career for herself, armed with a high school diploma freshly earned last week and renewed optimism bolstered by the fact that she is a member of a rather exclusive club of intellectuals.

She belongs to American Mensa Limited, which draws its membership from the people who score in the top two percent when they take various certified IQ tests. Wags have labeled Mensa members as "eggheads" and their groups have been referred to as "think tanks."

But as far as Diane Simon is concerned, it has sometimes been mighty lonely at the top in that two percent and it's only been recently, since her association in area Mensa circles with other "high IQ-ed" people, that her outlook on life has fully blossomed.

A dropout . . . as a sophomore, Diane stayed at home to take care of her younger sister until she turned 18. She joined the Marine Corps in 1955, but only after she "smoked" a high school equivalency exam and dropped 40 pounds.

On the Binet scale (the most popular IQ measurement), Mensans score at 135 and upwards. So why should a student, who had the smarts to qualify as a "Whiz Kid," quit school?

"I really don't know, " she said. "I got straight A's, but I didn't like school. I wasn't challenged enough."

Mensa draws its name from the Latin word for "table" because the organization is supposed to be a "roundtable of equals." Diane, who is an officer and the coordinator for the Western Michigan Mensa Chapter, says it is basically a "social organization."

"We have no set creed," she said. "The only thing we want to do is arrange to have people with high IQs get together and communicate. We have different senses of humor and look at things differently. Let me tell you! It is sometimes brutal to be a high IQ child."

If Mensa has one political aim, she said, it is to promote and stimulate special classrooms and educational activities for youngsters with academic talents and gifts. "I think that would have kept me in school," she said.

Diane, who is cashier at a grocery in a small community, is testimony to the fact that Mensa membership is not just limited to college professors and nuclear physicists. Her chapter contains 101 members. There are about 25,000 Mensans across the nation in all kinds of occupations and jobs, from doctors to factory workers, from farmers to police officers, from lawyers to housewives. There are children in Mensa. There are prisoners who are active members.

"One in 50 Americans could be eligible," she said. "They aren't because they have either never heard of us or they are scared to try. Taking the test is a private matter. The local chapter is never notified until a person passes. You have two chances at it." There is a fee to take the test and annual membership dues.

Why get involved?

In Diane's case, "It changed my life," she said. "I have a whole new group of friends. I have more confidence. What's really great about a Mensa meeting is that you can always find somebody interesting to talk to and something interesting to talk about. We bring in speakers to focus on certain topics, unidentified flying objects, for example."

The Mensa society was formed in England in the mid-1940's as a "think tank" to solve the world's problems, but that lofty ideal never really materialized. Now, it's more of a social organization dedicated to personal enlightenment.

A high divorce rate is common among Mensan women, said Diane. Her two marriages were to a Navy medical corpsman and to a career Army officer. She has two children: John Simon, a college junior majoring in advertising, and Laura, a junior in high school.

As a Marine and as a military wife, she traveled all over the United States and lived in many different installations.

Returning to her hometown in 1972, Diane's second marriage started to disintegrate and she went to work, on assembly lines and in grocery stores, sometimes working 70 hours a week on two jobs.

"I remember when I was working on the line at Kal-Equip," she said, "and the word spread about my high IQ. One day, a guy came over and said, 'If you are so darn smart, what are you doing here?'"

Comments like that made her think, so she enrolled in Plainwell's adult high school program to polish up her secretarial skills. And, with her Marine background, her job experience, and her score on the GED (Graduate Equivalency Degree) test, she discovered that only a half-credit class in government was keeping her from a high school diploma. She polished that off quickly and now she's ready to go to work as a secretary.

"You know," Diane said, "just having a high IQ doesn't guarantee success. And having an average or low IQ doesn't mean that a person is doomed to failure. Success is a matter of education. It's a function of personal drive and determination. A high IQ only means that the ability is there. It must be tapped and challenged."

And if you want to test yourself to see if you are Mensa caliber, write the American Mensa Selection Agency, Suite 1R, Department KG-2, 1701 West 3rd Street, Brooklyn, New York 11223.

Chapter 7

Identifying Gifted and Talented Learners

A LEADERSHIP PERSPECTIVE

The National/State Leadership Training Institute on the Gifted and Talented responded to requests from educators across the nation for guidance on identification. The institute described identification as the number one priority of local school district personnel. Based on available research and field interviews, the Martinson (1974) report was issued as a starting point for choosing identification procedures.

Martinson (1974) advised that identification plans consider the following topics: (1) what identification can and cannot accomplish, (2) policies for the role of identification, (3) the relative value of various procedures, and (4) various identification approaches.

What Identification Can and Cannot Accomplish

Identification procedures now available can locate most learners of advanced ability and high potential. Location of those learners benefits everyone. Teachers can alter their plans in constructive ways for such students. Parents can better understand and encourage their especially able children in the pursuit of education. Gifted and talented learners can understand themselves better, be aware of their abilities, and foster and maintain positive self-images. Also, identification provides advance notification to guidance counselors and others to take steps to arrange financial aid for higher education.

Identification alone rarely improves learning, however; it does not ameliorate ill health, a lack of motivation, malnutrition, poor parent-child relationships, restricted learning opportunities, or the absence of quality in the school program. It *can* lead to a thoughtful consideration of strategies to reduce, minimize, eliminate, or prevent these destructive impairments to human potential.

Rationale for Procedures: Considerations for Selection

Martinson (1974) suggested a rationale and a series of steps for identification procedures. The rationale is based upon several assumptions and principles that directly guide practice. First, the gifted and talented behaviors to be identified should be specified. The federal definition includes a range of traits, such as general intellectual ability, specific academic aptitude, creativity or productive thinking, leadership, psychomotor skills, and ability in the visual and the performing arts. A poll of 204 authorities (Martinson, 1974) indicated that general intellectual ability, creativity, academic aptitude, and visual-performing arts are the highest priority areas for identification.

A second decision concerns how to measure or otherwise establish accelerated development. Certainly, the Stanford-Binet and the Wechsler tests are excellent indicators of general intellectual ability for many pupils, but actual samples of performance are better indicators of talent for the dance or the graphic arts.

A third consideration, generally well accepted, requires policy statements. It is the acknowledged importance of identification that is (1) begun early in the child's life, (2) continuous (e.g., preschool and all grade levels), and (3) free of stereotypes. It recognizes that a gifted and talented person can be a clean, compliant, motivated, and achieving person; it also recognizes that a gifted and talented person can be rebellious, alienated from the usual, and reluctant to participate. It takes into account that girls can be scientists or that boys can write poetry.

A fourth consideration is the difficulty of locating the gifted and talented in special populations, such as the handicapped, minority groups, and underachievers. This consideration involves the previous ones. If the second and third considerations are of high priority, then in-service training will be available to sensitize persons to functional evidence of ability and capacity.

The fifth consideration may be the most difficult. Martinson described it as the principle of absolute criterion. This principle implies some ultimate limit that is the boundary between the gifted and talented person and the person for whom the standard pace of schooling is appropriate. In operational terms, it requires decisions as to degree of error that can be tolerated. Criteria may be liberal, which may dilute the program, or conservative, which may exclude those who might profit. In our view a sharp and absolute boundary is neither necessary nor advisable. It may, at first, provide convenience and protection for program administrators, but that advantage soon proves to be an illusion when attacked by determined and well-informed parents. A "swinging door" policy, coupled with responsible professional judgment, is better. The child's educational achievements then remain the focus, whether or not in the special program. Parents prefer that, too.

Effectiveness and Efficiency

Martinson (1974) acknowledged the enduring contribution of Pegnato and Birch (1959) in defining the utility of identification procedures to locate gifted and talented learners. The utility of a procedure, or combination of procedures, according to Pegnato and Birch, can be defined in terms of its effectiveness and its efficiency. These dimensions are defined as follows:

$$\text{effectiveness} = \frac{\text{number of gifted and talented found}}{\text{actual number of gifted and talented}}$$

$$\text{efficiency} = \frac{\text{number of gifted and talented found}}{\text{number of persons nominated as gifted and talented}}$$

For example, Pegnato and Birch (1959) reported that in their study, 335 persons were nominated as gifted by reference to group achievement tests. Of this number, 268 persons were subsequently identified as *not* gifted and talented. There were 72 persons identified as gifted and talented, while 19 were subsequently judged to be gifted and talented but not by group achievement data. Consequently, the effectiveness of the procedure was found to be 79 percent, or 72 divided by 91 (e.g., 72 + 19). The efficiency of the procedure was found to be 21%, or 72 divided by 335.

Pegnato and Birch found teacher nomination of mental ability to be 45 percent effective and 27 percent efficient.* Honor roll status (B average) was 74 percent effective and 18 percent efficient. Teacher judgment of creativity was 7 percent effective and 9 percent efficient. A group intelligence test (e.g., the Otis) was 92 percent effective and 19 percent efficient.

Value of Procedures

Martinson's (1974) poll of 204 authorities reported over 90 percent agreement that the individual intelligence test is the best means for identification. By contrast, 64 percent voted for the group intelligence test. It was found that 73 percent favored nationally standardized achievement tests while locally developed achievement tests received a 41 percent rating. It was found that 80 percent held to professional/expert opinion for judgment of creativity,

---

*This finding was under the condition that teachers had received no specific training in identifying gifted and talented pupils. With training and a clear-cut procedure, teachers will be significantly more effective and efficient.

while tests of creativity were recognized by 73 percent. Specific aptitude tests for talent were valued by only 5 percent. Other procedures receiving low evaluations were parent and peer nominations (5 percent), while teacher nomination was rated 70 percent. Demonstrated achievement and evaluation by a psychologist received 70 percent affirmation, while apparent psychological adjustment received 40 percent.

Martinson noted a discrepancy between what educators said they valued and what they did in actual practice. While 75 percent valued teacher judgment, 93 percent used it for identification. Achievement test scores were used by 87 percent in practice, as compared to the 74 percent who valued them; group IQ, 87 percent in practice, as compared to 65 percent valuing; accomplishments and grades, 56 percent in practice, as compared to 78 percent valuing; individual IQ, 23 percent in practice, as compared to 90 percent valuing; and creativity tests, 14 percent in practice, as compared to 74 percent valuing.

Certainly, a variety of procedures do exist, and no one procedure has the confidence of everyone. Teacher nomination and grades carry considerable weight in the identification process. It also seems obvious that the dimensions of effectiveness and efficiency must be continually applied and updated to understand the merits of a procedure or combination of procedures.

Procedures: Advantages, Limitations, and Considerations

Martinson (1974) identified 12 specific procedures that can be grouped into four main clusters: (1) nominations, including those of teachers, parents, peers, or others; (2) personal evidence, including pupil products, student expression, and autobiographies; (3) performance evaluations, including tests and judgments of creativity by experts; and (4) psychometric procedures, including all individual IQ, group IQ, achievement tests and adaptations of those testing procedures. Each has potential advantages and unique limitations.

Table 7-1 contains a resumé of the report of procedures that involve nominations by others. It reflects their relative contributions, especially as included in case history data.

Table 7-2 centers on personal sources of data, i.e., data directly available from the learner. These procedures "work" to the extent that they are opportunities to get information, but persons engaged in identification and assessment must be trained in their use. These sources seem to be valuable as functional evidence of accomplishment.

Table 7-3 summarizes Martinson's analysis of sources about creativity/talent, i.e., performance. Testing has great promise, although it still requires refinement through research. Testing has heightened interest in the nurture of creativity/performance. Experts and judges remain a highly functional source.

Table 7-1 Nomination Procedures in Identification of Gifted and Talented Pupils

Source	Advantages	Limitations	Considerations
Teacher	Teacher participation in screening procedures can be a valuable form of in-service training. Teacher judgment in combination with other criteria can be helpful.	Teacher judgment by itself has been shown to miss gifted and talented learners. Teacher judgments are better at predicting school failure than identifying gifted and talented. Teachers overlook imagination, questioning, and novel solutions as indicators of gifted and talented.	In-service training can improve sensitivity to attributes. Inferences about teacher judgment need to be updated to assess impact of in-service training.
Peers	Pupils list pupils with whom they would like to study.	Gifted and talented persons may conceal their abilities from peers.	This works best in more open environments where all learners have an opportunity to share abilities.
Parents	Parents information about child's interests, hobbies, accomplishments, and sensitivity to others can be valuable case history information.	Educators may dismiss parent data as "pushy." Parents may be unaware of child's abilities.	Parent-teacher conferences should allow time for listening to parents.
Others	Librarians, former teachers, and others can be sources.	Same as those for teacher nominations.	Channels of communication must be opened.

Table 7-2 Personal Sources in Identification of Gifted and Talented Pupils

Source	Advantages	Limitations	Considerations
Pupil products	Evidence of advanced accomplishments is concrete. Products may result from school experience.	The usual problems of subjectivity of adult judgments occur. It may be difficult to discriminate between the creative and the simply unique.	Communication must be established between parent and teacher to be alert to pupil products. Persons must be recruited to render consistent judgments.
Expression of values	Selection of hero-ideals who have had a lasting impact can be an attribute. Essays can be a valuable source.	The usual problems of subjectivity and value conflicts occur.	Expression of values and ideals emerges *only* if there are opportunities for expression.
Autobiography	Hobbies, interests, and expressions of value are revealed. "Early" accomplishments are indicated.	Adolescents may resist the assignment of writing "the story of my life" as an invasion of privacy.	There should be an opportunity to write, tape-record, etc. Personnel should be trained in what to look for.

Table 7-3 Identification of Creativity in Gifted and Talented Pupils

Source	Advantages	Limitations	Considerations
Creativity tests*	Assets and abilities ignored by standard IQ or achievement tests may be tapped. Agreement, or reliability, among judges falls within accepted limits.	Tests may tap only a facet of creativity. Ability of tests to predict eventually creative person still not understood. It is difficult to relate results to specific methods of nurturing.	Results must be combined with other criteria. Data should be gathered to generate knowledge about use.
Judgment of expert judges	Eccentricity can be distinguished from originality. Use of judges saves time of school personnel. Functional evidence of demonstrated accomplishment is provided. Expert may be in "best" position to judge full range of creativity.	Problems of subjectivity may occur.	Experts need to be recruited. Judges need to be oriented to developmental expectations. Judges need orientation toward demonstrated ability or potential.

*Existing tests are more measures of originality and flexible thinking than measures of talent or creativity as these latter terms are most widely understood and used.

Table 7-4 Psychometric Approaches in Identification of Gifted and Talented Pupils

Source	Advantages	Limitations	Considerations
Individual tests of intelligence; Stanford-Binet; Wechsler procedures	Tests are more effective* than group IQ tests. Quality and style of response beyond the more right or wrong are considered. Verbal abilities and motor performance can be identified. Items measure 28 to 54 attributes of Guilford's structure of intellect.	Costs involved are greater than those of group IQ tests. Psychologists may be in short supply. State funding may not reimburse assignment to programs in the gifted and talented. Items (e.g., social situations) may reflect achievement and cultural norms other than innate capacity.	Training of psychologists in interpretation is critical. Awareness of personal influences that affect test performance is critical. Results should be viewed as an estimate.
Group IQ	Cost is low compared to that of individual IQ tests. School success orientation is demonstrated. Person of high verbal proficiency is identified.	Content is pitched to majority of children, not to those with higher abilities. Because of low ceiling performance, procedures do not discriminate among ability groups among gifted and talented. Actual school testing situations must meet test standardization conditions. More training in their use is required than is indicated by test manuals.	Such tests tend to underestimate abilities. It is best used in combination with other criteria. Test can be employed as a screen to locate pupils who should be given individual tests.

*Effective in the Pegnato and Birch (1959) sense.

Table 7-4 continued

Source	Advantages	Limitations	Considerations
Group achievement tests	Cost is low. They are useful in screening. They are appropriate for gross estimate of ability.	Limitations are similar to those of group IQ tests, especially in ceiling effects. Content may not reflect local goals and instructional emphasis. There is a lack of alternative forms for use. Gains in score may be due to chance rather than growth. Content of items may be independent of instruction.	They are best used in combination with other criteria. In-service training in interpretation is required.
Abbreviated tests used in combination	Cost is low. Range of estimate is more comprehensive. They are useful for screening for further study.	Subsequent success not predicted. Tests may miss 40% of existing gifted and talented. Reliability is in question. Short forms may penalize minority group children.	Care in selection as to reliability is essential. Examination of content by local persons is needed. Test should not be accepted at face value.

Psychometric procedures are reviewed in Table 7-4. Tests must be carefully selected; the fact that a test is in print is no guarantee of its quality. Individual IQ tests prove to be the single most supported procedure.

A CASE HISTORY PERSPECTIVE

A Valued Tradition

The case study, sometimes termed case history, is a useful coordinating mechanism for identification. As a product, the case study is a document that summarizes available information and opinions of participants. It may include a record of initial referrals and the results of screening procedures, nominations, personal products, creativity inferences, and/or psychometric procedures. It also notes previous educational experiences and methods of instruction that have been previously used.

The case study can help to identify and certify a pupil as eligible for a school's defined program* for the gifted and talented. The data base should enable an educational team to review a pupil's unique abilities, talents, interests, accomplishments, special needs, and measured attributes. This data base should include the pupil's health, language status, available intellectual stimulation, degree of home stimulation, access to study at home or in the neighborhood, access to mentor at home, responsiveness of the school, attitudes of teachers toward the child, nutrition, attitudes of the school toward learning and human potential, and the pupil's exposure to opportunities.

Martinson (1974) stressed two guidelines for the use of the case history. One is that the gifted and talented can contribute an autobiography and a listing of interests. Second, the psychologists should have access to a review of the factors mentioned earlier prior to testing.

The expense of the case history and its high effectiveness-efficiency are known in a clinical sense. Experts endorse the value of the identification-oriented case study as a means to coordinate and focus decision making for high-quality services. Increasingly, however, case history is being replaced by a more comprehensive procedure. This is the Individualized Education Program (IEP). The IEP includes identification data as one of its components (see Unit V).

---

*An all too common practice is for schools to establish programs first and then identify only those gifted and talented pupils who fit the pre-set programs. Program and identification options should be kept open so they can influence each other and the individual aptitude of each gifted and talented pupil can be matched to the program.

Use of Case History Approach

Identification procedures are a source of distress to practitioners. Objective measures possess an appeal because of their apparent numerical absoluteness and because of the possibility of partial statistical verification; it is difficult to have confidence in human judgments in the face of such concepts as norm, percentile, and quantified grade level attainments that seem to possess such scientific prestige. Educators and parents may doubt their own ability to make identifications based on observation and interview.

A report by Renzulli and Smith (1977) offers an example of practical guidance in use of case history information for identification purposes. Case history data were studied as to their influence on selection. In general, achievement test data were rated highest in influence. Past and present teacher ratings were rated as highly valued. Health, family background, and family ratings were found to have little influence. Peer ratings were found to be influential.

The Renzulli and Smith report was interested in effectiveness ratios (number identified compared to actual number confirmed), efficiency (number screened or nominated to number actually selected), and costs involved in the group test approach and the case history approach. The group intelligence test was used for screening. An individual intelligence test was used as the ultimate criterion for identification of gifted and talented pupils eligible for special education. Three school districts took part in this investigation.

Effectiveness

Criteria of effectiveness were expanded to include ratings of teachers of the gifted and talented as evidence of eligibility for inclusion in a special program for the gifted and talented. Also, effectiveness included the special teacher's assessment of the child's performance in the special program. The data supported the finding that case history procedures identified more pupils for whom the program was appropriate than did the group test screening approach. As an average, the case history approach located 92.42 percent of those subsequently judged as gifted and talented, in contrast to 79.22 percent for the group test screening approach. In operational terms, for every 20 pupils who succeed in a special program, the case history approach would identify 9 out of 10, while the group test screening approach would identify 8 out of 10.

Efficiency

Renzulli and Smith expanded efficiency criteria to include a cost dimension. Consequently, school personnel maintained a record of the number of hours expended, which could be converted into a cost estimate based upon salaries and fringe benefits.

Efficiency estimates were compared for both procedures. The group test screening approach on the average identified 222 pupils; individual testing selected 32. This produced an efficiency ratio of 7.3. The dollar cost for selected student was $119.79, and it required approximately 12 hours to identify each pupil. The case history approach generated 256 pupils for screening with 37 identified, for an average efficiency ratio of 9.3. The average cost per student in dollars was $40.78 per selected student, and an average of 7.5 hours were expended.

Cost Estimates

Cost of services with the group test screening approach versus case history were analyzed and compared to staff involved. For example, the special class teacher in the former spent an average of 97 hours at a cost of $971, compared to 108 hours at $801 for the latter. Administrators in the former spent 94 hours, which cost $1,092, compared to 125 hours with a cost of $91 in the latter. The clerical average for the group test screening approach was 8.6 hours at an average cost of $16; for the case history approach, it was 63 hours at a cost of $62. Psychological services averaged 143 hours for the former with $1,430 in costs, compared to no costs for the latter. Average expenditures for the group test screening procedures involved 373 hours for costs of $3,690. The case history approach involved 323 hours for costs of $1,264.

Helpful Outcomes

Renzulli and Smith (1977) advanced the following conclusions regarding case history approaches:

- Achievement tests coupled with case history performance ratings are highly useful.

- Case history procedures do not yield an unmanageable number of students for screening. Time and cost differences do not support the image of case history review as costly.

- Case history procedures were superior in identification of minority group pupils.

- Teachers of the gifted and talented require extra time to participate in the identification process.

The Renzulli and Smith (1977) report is an example of research applicable to guidance for practice. The use of a screening committee or team appears to be justified, as is the use of a flexible information source. The case history approach has gained a renewed lease on life. The emergence of the Individualized Education Program (IEP) is a prime example.

STRENGTHENING IDENTIFICATION PROCEDURES

That there are still problems to be solved regarding identification procedures is not in dispute. Furthermore, the importance of early identification in the development of high-quality programming is not in dispute. The operational task(s) should focus on strengthening the efficiency and effectiveness of procedures. There is sufficient information available now for the organization of identification procedures, although significant additional breakthroughs would be welcomed.

Possibility of Underprediction

Decisions about selection criteria are compounded by the relative weight that should be assigned to IQ and to grade level estimates inferred from standardized achievement tests. Young-Baldwin (1977) noted that controversies regarding standardized procedures result in two extreme positions: either declare a moratorium on all testing, or retain testing with complete elimination of inequities. Young-Baldwin offered a concrete example that involved 24 persons over a time span from fourth grade through college. It was felt that the life histories of the 24 persons could provide guidance as to the (1) predictive validity of tests, (2) application of tests to culturally diverse populations, (3) effects of instructional systems, and (4) use of tests for grouping.

The sample consisted of 24 black youngsters. At fourth grade, they were selected for inclusion in a special class for the gifted and talented. Admission required an IQ of 130, superior academic achievement, teacher nomination, peer nomination, and personal interview of the prospective pupil. These 24 learners, by contrast, were characterized by a mean IQ of 112 on the Otis Intelligence Test Form Beta EM, and a mean IQ of 123 on the Slossen Intelligence Test. Their mean grade level achievement was 4.9, which was exactly consistent for their grade placement of 4.9. The Stanford Achievement Test (SAT) was the procedure used.

After one year in the special class, the mean SAT achievement was 7.85, although 5.94 would be expected through normal maturation. After three years of enrollment, the mean performance was 10.2, which was nearly three years above chronological age.

It was reported by Young-Baldwin that 21 of the students entered college; they enrolled at institutions such as Tufts, MIT, Princeton, University of

Alabama, University of Michigan, and Dillard University. (The three other pupils had transferred to other districts.) The 21 had been awarded substantial scholarships. Among the *most* notable achievements of the group were these:

- honor roll status at MIT

- finalist at the Notre Dame International Science Fair

- first place in the General Motors Science competition

- completion of high school in three years with a scholarship to study in France

- finalists in National Merit Awards competitions

Young-Baldwin reviewed the accuracy with which achievement and IQ data predicted subsequent success. She concluded that IQ did not predict subsequent achievement success and that achievement test scores only predicted subsequent success on achievement tests. This was especially evident in prespecial class to postspecial class measurement.

A number of guidelines can be inferred from the Young-Baldwin report. It was her thesis that the prediction of future performance from IQ tests underestimates. Achievement subtests (e.g., paragraph meaning, vocabulary) can be more useful indicators of information processing than a global IQ score. Interpretation of IQ scores should take into account known standard errors of measurement. Consequently, an IQ score is not really a two- or three-digit number; it is really a range from a lowest possible score to a highest possible score. (Any reputable test describes its known errors, which are statistically inferred and described by reference to the age of the person as well by reference to subtests.)

Another inference emerges from the same report. The program selection process employed five criteria, three of which were not objective. Therefore, it seems that teacher nomination, peer nomination, and interviews had merit in identification.

Teacher Identification

The ability of teachers to judge superior ability in children has been a matter of continuing interest. The persisting impression is that teachers, as a group, either overnominate or undernominate. The Gear (1978) report was undertaken in response to prevailing research, which has minimized the ability of teachers to identify gifted and talented learners. It was Gear's observation, however, that previous research had sampled teachers without training or preparation in the area of gifted and talented. Gear sought to compare trained teachers with a control sample of teachers typical of the samples of previous studies.

The setting of the investigation was a rural school district located in an economically depressed area. Teacher effectiveness, efficiency, and attitude toward culturally and economically disadvantaged learners were examined by comparing the nomination of learners as eligible for a gifted and talented program by a trained group with the nomination by an untrained group. All relevant variables were controlled. In addition, all 48 teachers (24 control, 24 experimental) were given an attitude survey regarding culturally and economically disadvantaged learners.

Effectiveness was defined as a ratio of the number of gifted and talented learners identified by teachers to the number of those confirmed as gifted and talented. Efficiency was a ratio of confirmed gifted to number of students nominated as gifted. A confirmed gifted and talented person was a learner who was selected by a planning and placement committee. Its membership was composed of a counselor, a teacher of the gifted and talented, a director of special education, a psychologist, and a social worker. Decisions were based on school records, group test data, individual tests, and observation. Any child above the 60th percentile on group tests was given the Wechsler Intelligence Scale for Children Revised (WISC-R). Each team member reviewed pupil data independently so as not to influence one another. The team identified 50 confirmed gifted pupils within the school districts; the mean IQ of these pupils was 133, with the majority in the 130–135 range.

The control group of teachers identified four confirmed gifted pupils per ten confirmed gifted on the average. The trained group identified eight confirmed per ten confirmed gifted. It was concluded that trained teachers were more effective, although no differences existed in efficiency. Attitude toward disadvantaged learners bore no relationship to effectiveness or efficiency. The Gear investigation found that the supposed inability of teachers to be accurate lies in lack of training rather than in an inherent deficiency. It also documents identification as a team process.

Helpful Practices

In 1963, Seashore issued guidelines for teachers, guidance counselors, and program directors regarding the identification of gifted and talented pupils. Her motivation was to place teacher nomination, aptitude tests, achievement tests, and grades in perspective. A parallel incentive was to maximize the usefulness of these procedures in finding difficult-to-locate pupils, especially those in minority groups and those indifferent to school. Her recommendations are affirmed by the Martinson (1974) report. Tactics for strengthening identification can be summarized as follows:

- A program for identification and services must have goals that define the rationale for selection of procedures. These goals should have district-wide endorsement.

- A district should describe its services in terms of what can be done now and what can be arranged in the immediate future. Identification is more useful when the availability of resources is clear.

- No one group should have exclusive control over defining giftedness and talent. All informed sources should be encouraged to make nominations. Final decisions should not be based on a narrow stereotype but on how able pupils can best be served.

- A distinction between potential and demonstrated performance should be maintained. This practice ensures that both cognitive abilities and superior performance, usually described as talent, will be considered.

- Multidimensional procedures are to be preferred to a single criterion procedure. Giftedness comes in many forms and requires many forms of identification.

The first step in identification is the decision to undertake the task. Commitment to the task guides decision making regarding the organization and mobilization of the process and procedures, as well as safeguards and standards of quality to be followed in identification. There has been a tendency to overlook the part that parents might legitimately play in recognizing giftedness and talent in their children and in calling their observations to the attention of school personnel. Also, school practices have tended to look for high achievement and intelligence test results after children are in school, rather than consciously to seek evidences of precocity in preschool behavior.

Chapter 8

Using and Adapting
the Curriculum

SELECTION OF CURRICULUM GOALS

The Nature of Goals

Curriculum can be interpreted in a variety of ways. Educators and parents are familiar with curriculum as a written plan that describes the school's goals and its accountability to its pupils, their parents, and the community's citizens. The definition used here is even more clear and specific: curriculum includes every activity that is deliberately conducted under the direction and responsibility of the school's professional staff.

Wynn, DeYoung, and Lindsey-Wynn (1977) observe that curriculum goals are statements about the purposes of the educational enterprise, e.g., developing literacy skills, promoting self-realization, developing citizenship, training productive workers, building moral attitudes and values, improving intergroup relationships, and promoting international understanding. In short, curriculum goals are statements that indicate the aspirations of the professional staff. When goals are clearly stated, the content and skills that need to be taught in order to direct students toward those goals can be determined.

Goals are usually expressed as outcomes for pupils. These outcomes can be expressed as either short- or long-term performances. The essence of a goal is an expected pupil achievement. The issue of priority is also involved in pupil performance expectations. American education has been willing to emphasize both the needs of the individual person and the needs of the larger society. Four characteristics can be seen in the way Americans phrase educational goals:

1. Outcomes describe expectations of pupil performance.
2. Outcomes aim at immediate (present and current) as well as future performance.

3. Outcomes reflect both learner-centered needs and the priorities of the larger society.
4. Outcomes leave room for creativity on the part of educators by their arrangement of educational services and variety of procedures. (Wynn et al., 1977)

Common Goals of American Education

Given the relative openness of American education, there may be some difficulty in selecting priorities for learners in general, and for the gifted and talented in particular. There are, however, available resources to help identify appropriate goals for all pupils, including the gifted and talented.

Birch and Johnstone (1975) reviewed goal statements of the National Educational Association and the American Association of School Administrators. Despite the diversity of sources, they found common emphases. The persistent themes focus on (1) family life and planning, (2) health and protection from disease, (3) self-realization, (4) communication skills (including literacy skills), (5) science and prudent use of resources, (6) vocational adequacy and consumer awareness, (7) leisure time and recreation, (8) civic responsibility and democratic ideals, and (9) human relationships. Existing curriculum materials cluster around the following common themes (Wynn et al., 1977):

- work-career skills
  - taking pride in work and learning self-esteem
  - respecting and getting along with coworkers
  - gaining information for job selection
  - acquiring skills to enter a specific field of work

- life skills
  - becoming competent in reading, writing, speaking, and listening
  - acquiring the skills of family living
  - managing money, property, and resources
  - using the skills of family living and parenting
  - practicing the ideals of health and safety
  - learning to use leisure time

- social relationships and responsibilities
  - learning the attributes of a good citizenship
  - examining the ideals of a democratic society
  - learning to respect people who think and dress differently

- self-direction
  - maintaining a lifelong desire for learning
  - developing respect for one's own abilities and identity
  - learning to examine and use information
  - adapting to and assessing the impact of change
  - valuing culture and various forms of beauty
  - maintaining wide interest in the forms of known knowledge

Both goals and instructional materials reflect a national perspective. There is more commonality about American education than supposed. The common theme is preparation for adult roles. A balance must be sought between what the individual needs and what society expects from the educational enterprise. Work is emphasized on both sides of this balance. Employers need motivated, competent employees, and individuals must be prepared for vocational productivity that is personally fulfilling.

Sellin (1978) speaks of career development as enabling even pupils of elementary school age to be aware of the variety of occupations that exist. As pupils develop insight and skill in decision making, these skills are transferred to vocational applications. In the junior high school period, these skills are extended to an examination of occupational clusters. The high school period, for most pupils, is the period of either general or specific vocational preparation. Gifted and talented pupils especially need opportunities to explore many different occupations while in the middle and secondary school period. Most gifted and talented pupils should be encouraged to become competent in several vocational fields.

Curriculum Outcomes for the Gifted and Talented

The common goals of education should be the basis for the curriculum outcomes for the gifted and talented students, but the outcomes should be individualized to suit the gifted and talented student's characteristics. Projected curriculum outcomes should balance individual needs with social priorities. These two complementary principles are sound guidelines, verified by experience.

Educators can use the following five qualities as a checklist to test the appropriateness of any curriculum goal statement:

1. Does it allow for a range of pupil performance?
2. Is it relevant for the present as well as for the future?
3. Is it consistent with curriculum outcomes established for all pupils in the system?

4. Does it encourage flexibility and variety as to content, method of instruction, and evaluation?
5. Does it balance individual needs and potential contributions?

Employment of this checklist may well make the educational system less vulnerable to charges of elitism in individualized programming for the gifted and talented. These same five points can also serve as a guide for examining any proposed improvement in educational opportunity for gifted and talented pupils.

APPRAISING THE STRUCTURE OF CURRICULUM

It is unusual, today, to find a school system that does not have curriculum guides for all of its skill and content requirements at all grade levels. Such documents should be adapted and extended to accommodate the educational characteristics of gifted and talented pupils. A variety of resources ought to be employed: (1) textbooks, (2) reference works, (3) expert opinion, (4) the periodical literature, (5) observation of component performers, (6) the pronouncements of organizations and agencies, (7) biographies and autobiographies of eminent persons, (8) preferences of consumers, (9) references to developmental attributes of learners, and (10) surveys of current practice conducted according to defined criteria.

Bloom, Hastings, and Madeus (1971) report a widely accepted procedure for curriculum design. It is especially applicable to curricula for highly able learners. First, it allows for the integration of material from all the various sources. Second, it relates curriculum content to both general goals and objectives. Third, measurement of attainment is tailored to student abilities. Fourth, its measurement procedures can also generate ideas for activities and experiences.

Bloom et al. (1971) termed their curriculum development procedures the preparation of a Table of Specifications (TOS). The TOS, as a product or document, is a grid or matrix that shows the structure of content and the array of objectives. A TOS can be devised by an individual or a group that includes parents, students, alumni, and representatives of the community. The goal in curriculum design is agreement among all concerned regarding the content and skills that should be taught to pupils and in what order or sequence they should be taught.

Objectives

Bloom et al. speak of two types of objectives—cognitive and affective—with skills couched within either of the two. They recommended a taxonomy of cognitive objectives and a taxonomy of affective objectives. They did *not* intend that each and every item of each taxonomy be employed, however. They were emphatic that items should be selected through a consensus of participants and based upon their own priorities. It would seem that objectives should be given a fair share of weight, too.

Structure of Content

Structure is generic. It applies to all content areas, large or small, short or long. Structure includes six elements: (1) terms, (2) facts, (3) rules and principles, (4) processes and procedures, (5) transformations, and (6) applications.

Terms

The specialized vocabulary of the field (e.g., history, dance, biology, mathematics, art) involves defining, recognizing illustrations, recognizing synonyms, and recognizing instances of correct or incorrect uses. Vocabulary is the entry into a field. Vocabulary fluency and flexibility enable the person to store and retrieve information efficiently and to organize concepts in that field. Typically, terminology equates with knowledge in the Bloom et al. sense.

Facts

Whatever information is held to be basic because responsible persons in the field deem it to be fundamentally significant is fact. The student is expected to recall the fact, to recognize accurate versus inaccurate statements of it, and to recall a fact when questioned directly. Examples of facts include names of persons, events, dates, and relevant details of significance. This element describes knowledge and comprehension.

Rules and Principles

The ways in which data are organized into key ideas, schemes, and phenomena (e.g., atomic theory in physics, grammar in language, or cell division in biology) are rules and principles. The student is expected to define the rule, recall illustrations of it, and remember conditions in which it is applicable or inapplicable. For example, "*i* before *e*" is an example of the rule and the "not after *c*" is a condition of exception. This element is basically a recall and recognition type appropriate for knowledge and comprehension in the Bloom et al. sense.

Processes and Procedures

It was acknowledged by Bloom et al. that the use of processes and procedures is not completely covered in the taxonomies. This element of structure refers to a student's ability to use the steps in a process in the correct sequence with accuracy and speed. The student is expected to recall the sequence and follow its steps to completion. It may not be necessary for the student to understand the rationale of a process. For example, a student can calculate a square root without knowing the underlying reason for the process.

Transformations

Founded upon the previous three elements, transformation is the active personalization of instruction by the student. Students transform information, rules, and processes and procedures into their own illustrations. They are expected to recognize new illustrations as appropriate or inappropriate. Examples would be creating a chart from descriptions, turning written description into flow charts or diagrams, or substituting numbers for symbols according to rules or principles.

Applications

The central behavior of applications is problem solving. The student is expected to solve problems that have not been encountered in instruction. It is complex behavior in which the student (1) determines the elements of a problem; (2) selects the facts, rules, generalizations, processes, and procedures that are relevant; and (3) uses the selection to solve a problem. Implied in the Bloom et al. discussion was a fourth step, defining the adequacy of a solution. Within any given field, there are conventions or criteria for judging adequacy.

A Matrix Approach

A grid, or matrix, of outcomes and content can be prepared. A first step is to visualize the learner at the completion of instruction. The second step is to generate items that would be valid assessments of competent completion of instruction. The third step is the selection of items from the item pool. (It should be noted that an item can be a question, observation of the student, a project, etc.). Experienced teachers in a subject field usually agree about 85 percent of the time on processes and procedures, transformations, and applications. Difficulties usually arise over facts versus rules and principles.

There may also be differences in priorities, as people have their favorite facts.

Two additional guidelines are useful. There is no need to complete each cell, so long as participants agree that their product is sufficient to assess overall goals. Second, any item can be applicable to more than one cell; in other words, overlap is acceptable.

The TOS can also be used to relate teaching tactics and student activities for each of the cells. In this way, instruction can be matched to assessment. According to Bloom et al., the effort facilitates reliable evaluation.

An Example

The matrix format can be directly applied to any subject matter or skill area. Wilson (1971) illustrated the application of the TOS procedure to art education. A condensed version is presented in Exhibit 8-1. Inspection of the TOS reflects two modifications appropriate to art education. One is the addition of perceptual outcomes and production outcomes. Another is the condensing of the structure of content into two broad categories. If production were eliminated the result would be an art appreciation (or comprehension) course.

The resulting cells can be completed according to the overall intention. For example, if the American photographer Mathew Brady were selected for study, any number of knowledge outcomes (B) could be generated as to his selection of subject matter (1), use of an art form (2), knowledge of technology (3), and the artistic and historical context of his work (4). A knowledge of the available technology (3) could be combined with context (4) to demonstrate his ingenuity in photographing outdoor scenes under wartime conditions of the 1860s. Generated questions can be classified as B-1, B-2, B-4, and B-3/4. To the extent the student can move beyond recall and recognition questions into personalized interpretations and examples, the student has moved to comprehension (C). As the student moves into production, with its attendant anticipatory planning, execution, and product evaluation, there is a shift toward the higher order abilities of synthesis and evaluation (see Chapter 1).

Again, it should be emphasized that precision and communication are the goals. The TOS procedure is a means to that end; it is not an end in itself. The essence of the procedure is to provide an overall Gestalt of two significant dimensions. The *one* is expectations of and for students; the *other* is the use of content.

Another appealing use of the TOS can be to formalize an independent study or group project between teacher and student(s). This can give both

Exhibit 8-1 Table of Specifications for Student Learning in Art
Education*

	Behaviors			
	Percep- tion	Knowl- edge	Compre- hension	Produc- tion
Content	A	B	C	D
1. Subject matter of art form: objects, events, themes, symbols, allegories, etc.				
2. Art form: film, photograph; painting, drawing, cartoon; sculpture, jewelry, pottery, etc.				
3. Processes: media, techniques, tools, equipment, etc.				
4. Artistic context: artist life forms, art period, reaction fo contemporary critics, significance of style, and use of media and form				

A. Visual-perceptual scanning of works of art. Scanning, or inspection, could be within a work, between two works, or among works.

B. Recall and/or recognition of relevant terms, facts, and/or rules and principles.

C. Relevant processes and procedures, transformations, and/or applications.

D. Student's skill in imitation or skill in an elaboration or original product.

*Adapted from Wilson (1971).

parties a sense of structure for outcomes but allow flexibility for the achievement of those outcomes.

An Elaborate Example

Foley (1971) provides an example of the use of a TOS that illustrates the essence of a TOS. Foley's presentation also illustrates how curriculum design can evolve from references to (1) eminent persons in the field, (2) pronouncements of national societies and organizations, (3) examination of existing curricula, (4) research findings, and (5) examinations of student performance. Foley presents a TOS for writing that is a deduction from the five sources. (In the Guilford sense, it is a classic and competent example of convergent thinking.) His TOS retains the Bloom et al. emphasis upon content and objectives; however, his review of sources led him to amend its elements. The Foley rendition is attractive for both its logic and its applicability for gifted and talented children and youth. In the task of adapting curriculum, the process of Foley would be as helpful as the product.

Exhibit 8-2 presents an adaptation of Foley's recommendations regarding a curriculum for the teaching of writing. The major categories are condensed, although there could be a subset within each of them. The presented TOS is sufficient for illustration, however. The notation system of the TOS allows for communication. For example, D-4 calls attention to the mechanics of writing as applied to student compositions. This notation also allows for task orientation. It must be recalled that the focus of the TOS is upon student performance; it does not describe the teacher's behavior, although it can provide the context for the teacher(s) to assemble resources to assist pupils. For gifted and talented pupils, the TOS can ensure that both basics and elaborations are covered.

Foley (1971) shares examples of sample items that could complete the cells. The examples were drawn from the literature of curriculum and from teacher-made tests.

> Given the topic "Identification of Gifted Students within Minority Groups," compose three paragraphs: (1) one addressed to the editor of the local newspaper, (2) one addressed to the State Association of School Psychologists, and (3) one to the superintendent of schools. After each paragraph, describe how differences in the audience caused differences in the paragraphs. Discuss the rationale for differences and/or similarities.

According to Foley (1971) this item is clearly within the dimension of production (D), since the person must write. It also involves organization (2),

Exhibit 8-2 Table of Specifications for Student Learning in Writing*

Behaviors	Content				
	Ideas	Organi-zation	Style	Mechanics	Words
COGNITIVE	1	2	3	4	5
A. Recall and Recognition					
B. Comprehension					
C. Criticism					
D. Production					
AFFECTIVE					
E. Interest					
F. Appreciation					

A. Terms, trends, classifications of, and methods used by writers.
B. Abilities to paraphrase, interpret, and apply styles used by writers.
C. Critique of content (e.g., organization, elements, judgment, and internal consistency) of examples of writing.
D. Composing one's own first draft and a final composition.
E. Willingness to write and satisfaction in writing.
F. Commitment to the value of writing as a means to express values.

1. Relevance to audience and logic of ideas.
2. Theme and paragraphs relate; emphasis of major ideas is appropriate.
3. Tone appropriate for audience; originality is evident.
4. Accurate use of spelling, punctuation, and syntax.
5. Fluency and variety; balance between concrete-abstract, literal-figural, connotative-denotative; level of usage.

*Adapted from Foley (1971).

style (3), and use of words (5). Consequently, the item could be classified as D-2 + 3 + 5. The reader could confine evaluation to D-5 (e.g., the appropriateness of vocabulary for each audience).

> Locate an example of writing in a professional journal, daily newspaper, news magazine, feature story, or an editorial. Select the four sentences that best illustrate the tone (e.g., informing, alarm, positive, stereotypic, etc.) of the selection as a whole.

The intent of this item is criticism (C) and is directed toward a content objective of style (3). A variation of this item could be to improve a given selection by changing words to modify a tone. Thus, the element would be C-3 and C-5.

Teachers have found the TOS helpful as a master list for reference. For example, file cards can be kept and labeled by letter and number for reference. A teaching file by letter and number also helps with cross references to the assessment and intervention.

A Supplementary Note on Using TOS

Foley's process is instructive for its analysis of issues in the teaching of writing. He noted that writing a clear and effective essay on an assigned topic is an objective of merit. Its instruction and measurement, however, are open to interpretations by writers, teachers, and researchers. The outcome of Foley's resumé was to isolate areas of common agreement and areas of choice.

Agreement is more common than might be expected. One consensus is that effectiveness and clarity in writing depend upon the intended audience. While scientists, administrators, teachers, and authors all write, judgments about the quality of the writing are based on its appropriateness for the intended audience. A second agreement is that all writing is creative. Although writing is audience-centered, it may be intended either to inform or to entertain the audience. Writing can also be a means of expressing personal feelings or experiences. Consequently, it is not appropriate to speak of creative writing as though it were a "subject" or a "content" or "skill." A third agreement is that the choice of words is significant. For example, Mark Twain made the observation that the difference between the right word and the almost right word is the difference between lightning and a lightning bug. A fourth agreement is that writing is judged as to appropriateness of ideas, organization and sequence, and style in relation to its intended audience. A fifth agreement is that affective considerations influence the student's performance.

Disagreements regarding instruction in writing can occur in at least three areas: (1) learning to write through reading appropriate models; (2) using the Guilford exercises, or a conscious thinking approach; and (3) learning to write through writing. The three different approaches involve some variation in instruction. Foley concluded that writing is best learned through writing, provided that it is frequent and is accompanied by precise feedback. In turn, the student should use the feedback and resubmit the product to show that the feedback has been understood. The other two approaches are helpful in combination with frequent writing and feedback. The emphasis of these two approaches can be on learning, through writing, to communicate with an audience or simply to express oneself.

SELECTING CONTENT BY BRAINSTORMING

Both enrichment and acceleration are ways to adapt content to the pace, style, and competencies of the able learner. They are neither methods nor programs, but options. The critical starting point for selection of curriculum is the curriculum of the school district. As with other aspects of educational practice, there is no "best" process or procedure for selecting curriculum content; there are options and combinations of options. Brainstorming is an alternative tactic. Its advocates recommend it as a very direct negotiation between teacher and pupil.

A Brainstorming Approach

Brainstorming is the free association of ideas targeted toward an outcome. The usual sequence starts with the identification of a central concern. The next step is to share ideas, information, and attitudes that relate to the concern. This sharing is conducted in psychological safety; shared materials are not judged as to practicality or even validity. The intent is to generate as many suggestions as possible. The third step is a selection and refinement of suggestions from the shared alternatives. The final step is adoption of a plan for implementation. Brainstorming is solidly grounded in research that has compared group decisions with individual decisions in terms of variety, comprehensiveness, practicality, and other criteria of effectiveness. Group decisions have been found to be superior.

Brainstorming can vary in the time taken and the participants involved. All three steps may be completed within an hour, allowing for the mechanics of recording suggestions and discussion, or the process may be extended over months. Participants may be parents, pupils, teachers, or others. In curriculum planning, the group may be composed only of faculty members, or it may be a mix of faculty and subject matter experts.

Operational Steps

The use of brainstorming as a procedure for curriculum adaptation in the context of education of the gifted and talented has been described by Parnes, Noller, and Biondi (1977). The purpose is to identify the intended outcomes for a unit of instruction that specifies content and behavior of learners.

The first step involves the identification of a unit topic. Within a given time limit, participants freely suggest topics of potential interest. Topics can be drawn directly from existing curriculum or can be expansions of it. Next, participants discuss why the topics, in general, are appropriate. Criteria do not need to be related to suggested topics. For example, personal interest, available resources, currentness, and amount of teacher guidance required could be general criteria.

A second step is refinement of the lists. Parnes et al. suggested adopting a final list of four to five topics and four to five criteria. A simple ranking, round-robin comparisons, or simple majority vote can be used.

The third step is to construct a matrix with topics in vertical order and criteria in horizontal order. A total of 25 cells would be generated (e.g., five topics × five criteria). Each cell would be rated by each participant from 1 to 3, with 1 the lowest and 3 the highest. A tally is then made of the ratings. The topic with the highest ratings becomes the highest priority for further consideration.

The fourth step involves expansion of the topic. Using a brainstorming approach, participants suggest activities or behaviors that they believe would be evidence of mastery of the topic. This list is then refined to a list of five. At this point, considerations of expense, physical space, and maturity of the pupils may be brought in as additional factors.

The fifth step is the construction of a curriculum outcomes matrix. The vertical dimension is the result of Step 4, the horizontal dimension lists the learner behaviors to be accomplished. Parnes et al. recommended the dimensions of Bloom, although alternatives could be used. Consequently, the horizontal dimension could include knowledge, comprehension, applications, analysis, synthesis, and evaluation. The result would be 30 cells (e.g., six behaviors × five activities).

The sixth step is to fill in the cells with activities and evaluations. There is no need to complete every cell. The tactics of brainstorming could apply.

The seventh step involves the pupils with the cells. They develop a plan of work to complete a selected cell or cells.

The eighth step is evaluation of performance, which can involve a range of tactics and dimensions. Dimension includes self-evaluation compared with the external evaluation of the teacher. There also can be feedback from peers. Letter grades are not emphasized; rather, the focus is on the student's intent as compared with the result. The teacher should be interested in the pupil's selection. For example, concentration by the pupil upon knowledge and comprehension may reflect a narrowness of abilities. Some pupils require encouragement to risk more complex assignments.

Chapter 9

Matching Learner and the Curriculum

UNDERSTANDING THE PREFERENCES OF CONSUMERS

The opinions of gifted and talented students and their parents can provide very useful guidelines for practice. A balanced program weighs both the needs of gifted and talented learners and the needs of the rest of society.

A Bill of Rights Perspective

Harris (1976) advanced an educational Bill of Rights for the gifted and talented. He urged that it be understood as a protection for a neglected minority of pupils rather than as a manifesto. The Harris list can be summarized as follows:

- understanding. Gifted and talented pupils need teachers who are informed about human abilities. Decisions about gifted and talented pupils should not be influenced by stereotypes.

- identification. It is urgent that individualized educational intervention be initiated early. Identification should not be by test scores alone; advanced interests, aptitudes, learning preferences, and other functional evidence of actual or potential abilities should be considered. To observe the wide range of superior human abilities requires a wide range of tactics. Moreover, there should be a commitment to locate *all* eligible pupils, not only compliant, highly motivated pupils who are relatively easy to identify.

- creativity/talent. The right to pursue one's capabilities for high performance is associated with the right to have mentors and advocates of proved competence for nurture and modeling.

- leadership. If the developmentally advanced are expected to be leaders, they must experience leadership. Examples of leadership, according to Harris, include consideration, stimulation, autonomy, and selection. Consideration involves viewing the person's solutions as potentially correct, even though they may differ from the usual or intended. Stimulation includes opportunities to wonder during the pursuit of directed outcomes. Autonomy suggests the pursuit of individual interests, both physical and nonphysical. Selection refers to the freedom to pursue truth without conformity. Also involved is the freedom to select from a variety of disciplines that will develop a complete person.

- respect. Valuing the person as an individual comprises respect. Status is not based upon one attribute, such as measured intelligence. Respect encourages success and views failure as a foundation for learning. Respect for potential acknowledges the dignity of prudent risk and the opportunity to create responsive environments.

The Reactions of Pupils

The literature reports a number of insightful views of gifted and talented learners about options for curriculum adaptation.

Independent study, the pursuit of a topic under the guidance of a competent mentor, has long been an option. The topic is usually an extension of the general course of study. It emphasizes information, expansion of research skills, or some combination of the two. Renzulli and Gable (1976) surveyed 196 gifted and talented high school students who had been enrolled in an independent study program for at least one school year. These students had pursued topics under the supervision of either a teacher or a resource room specialist. The format included (1) a proposal to identify a project, (2) approval of the proposal, and (3) mutual agreement between the student and the sponsor. The five factors that led to student satisfaction were:

1. career motivation. Independent study was credited with assisting students in the selection of a college curriculum. An immediate outcome was excitement about school learning and increased ability to evaluate their own work.
2. freedom to pursue interests. Students felt that they had complete freedom to select topics and to determine the depth of pursuit.
3. study habits and thinking processes. Independent study improved abilities to (a) evaluate sources, (b) organize their thoughts, (c) recognize preferred study skills, and (d) develop more efficient study habits.
4. fulfillment of personal objectives. Students welcomed opportunities to exercise individual responsibility. Working on highly personal objectives increased content mastery.

5. self-expression. There was appreciation for the support and interest of sponsors, as well as for the challenge of the experience.

Renzulli and Gable reported an average of 70 to 80 percent positive responses for each of these five factors. Students noted the need for outside consultants and for a focus upon social and emotional objectives as well.

Special self-contained classes and special schools are especially difficult to assess because of their diversity in organization, educational objectives, staffing, and criteria for pupil selection. Bachtold (1974) sampled 56 fifth and sixth graders who were enrolled in a special class ($n = 22$), enrichment in the regular class ($n = 12$), and a learning center model ($n = 24$). For the latter option, children were given time during the school day to pursue a topic of interest under the guidance of a parent volunteer. The standard district-wide curriculum was the source for instructional objectives. The learning center model emerged as the most effective in increasing verbal creativity, as measured by the Torrance tests; the self-contained model was the least effective. Nash (1974) found that a special school was no more effective than a regular school for 66 fourth graders. The advantage of the regular classes was greater socialization.

A 1955 report by Barbe sampled the opinions of 456 graduates of a major work program. It was found that male students had different reactions to the program than female students. This difference was in regard to best liked and least liked features (Table 9-1). Barbe further reported that 74 percent of the

Table 9-1 Reflections of Gifted Students about Their School Careers*

	Rank Order Preferences	
	Male Pupils	Female Pupils
Most Liked Features		
Opportunity to express individuality	1	3
Curriculum differences	2	2
Freedom from regimentation	3	4
Stimulation and challenge	4	6
Classmates	5	5
Foreign language	6	1
Student-teacher relationships	7	8
Small classes	8	7
Least Liked Features		
Attitudes of other teachers and other students	1	2
Lack of contact with other students	2	1
Not enough attention to skill subjects	3	3

*Adapted from Barbe (1955).

women and 61 percent of the men endorsed the program as having made a significant contribution to their lives, and the remainder were not certain. No comments were hostile.

Welch-Brown (1975) studied approximately 100 scientists significantly handicapped by either physical, visual, or hearing impairment. Typical of her sample were a psychology professional (blind), a manager of a computer firm (quadriplegic), and the director of a research division in a pharmaceutical company (deaf). Their careers reflect their struggle to overcome underestimation of their abilities and their perseverence in repeatedly proving themselves. One Ph.D. chemist, for example, was required to take an extra examination after she had completed all those required of her non-hearing-impaired fellow students. A sense of struggle to attain access was a persisting theme. Helpful persons were recalled as those who viewed the impaired person as a human resource to be nurtured rather than as a burden.

Perspectives of Parents

Weiler (1978) has shared her observations about programming based upon personal (parent of two gifted and talented children) and professional (teacher) involvement with one state's approach applied to one school district. The gifted and talented pupils Weiler described were identified by an intelligence quotient (IQ) of 132, teacher nomination, and parent approval, with an absolute limit of two percent of the school population as eligible to receive state aid. The program was initiated for pupils labeled mentally gifted minors (MGMs). Selected episodes from the Weiler (1978) account of programming for the MGMs include:

- Six MGM children in a second grade classroom assembled a house from graham crackers, candy, and icing. The other pupils were working in math workbooks, although they were allowed to watch. The explanation was that the MGM activity was for "qualitatively different" children and was intended to be a qualitatively different study of geometric shapes. Additionally, it was explained that all the children cannot make houses.

- The MGMs went to a computer center and played video display games. The pupils named favorite colors, friends, pets, and possessions which the computer transformed into a personalized story. Upon their return, they shared their excitement with their non-MGM peers.

- A movie, using an EKTA sound camera, was produced, written, directed, and acted by MGMs. The product was shared in a school open house.

- Rockets were built and launched by an MGM group. The activity was scheduled during a physical education class so the non-MGMs could watch.

- While MGMs are enrolled in regular classes, field trips are scheduled exclusively for them. The MGMs have (a) flown to the northern section of the state to study the terrain, (b) gone on a two-day boat trip to study marine biology, and (c) taken a three-day trip to study geology.

- A separate showing of the film, the *Ox Bow Incident,* was scheduled for MGMs. The subsequent discussion was centered upon going along with a mob. The MGMs were also encouraged to role play the mob and to role play the enlightened few.

The Olstad (1978) account, by contrast, is centered in a different school district, but in the *same* state as the Weiler (1978) account. Olstad is also the parent of a gifted and talented child and active in the district's program. She described how her seven-year-old child went from a frustrated, unhappy, aggressive person to a happy, loving, and caring child. The latter traits had been characteristic of the child during nursery school enrollment. She attributed their return to the intervention of the program.

Olstad shared further elements of her school district's program. She noted that the program is based upon the philosophical premise that individualized instruction does not mean treating certain children as if they were somehow better. She noted that IQ is *not* the single criterion for entrance. The learner's work is observed by psychologists, counselors, and administrators. When indicated, formal test results are suspended in favor of performance and observational data. Parents are involved in consent for enrollment. The program in Olstad's district also adheres to the premise that all learners have equal opportunity to achieve an education commensurate with their aptitudes, interests, and abilities. The program is characterized by internal (e.g., teachers, administrators, and parents) and external (e.g., independent consultation) audit.

Olstad (1978) noted that her school district can document that the initiation of a program for gifted and talented learners has had a positive impact for all learners. Examples include:

- Ingenious scheduling that fits in any special activities at the same time creative writing, arts and crafts, career exploration, etc. are scheduled for *all* child learners.

- Program approval by parents and accountability has been extended to all parents and programs.

- Individualized instruction, team teaching, advanced courses, summer enrichment classes, and qualitative substance in subject matter have been extended to all pupils.

- Learning materials, techniques, and experiences designed to stimulate higher intellectual skills and creativity have been extended to all learners.

Lessons Learned

The Weiler and Olstad accounts both closed with lessons learned from their experiences. Weiler observed that the following could be documented in her district: (1) there are substantial numbers of gifted and talented learners who do not qualify for the academic honor role, although they are identified as gifted and talented; (2) teachers evaluate pupils in light of the learner's label; and (3) educational privilege is not earned. The latter results from placement by score without consideration of effort, performance, and aptitude. Parents are thwarted as well, since they learn that their consultation and evaluation is not valued. They learn that complaining is considered ungrateful. School personnel learn to be defensive. Their extreme defense is that 98 percent of the population depends upon 2 percent of the population. Weiler documented that schools learn defensive behavior to charges of elitism. Responses have been to ignore the charge, blast it as a myth, and/or defend it as a necessity.

The obvious lesson learned in Olstad's school district was that the education of all children was improved. It was also learned and documented that (1) to provide for the gifted and talented *solely* because of a supposed social contribution is exploitation, (2) equal education opportunity does not mean sharing a common mediocrity, and (3) equal educational opportunity allows each person to express and realize his or her own special excellence. Olstad noted that her district has learned that the education outcomes most beneficial to society result from programs designed to produce happy, productive, empathetic persons.

Both accounts are instructive. They show that elitism, if it exists, is the result of faulty practices rather than a necessary program consequence and that the pursuit of excellence resides at local levels of education. Both articles also point up the importance of sound quality standards as a foundation for a superior quality of education. The fact that these two parents who reside in the same state have learned different lessons about outcomes makes it apparent that local school systems have the freedom to express their own philosophies, even though they operate under the same state-wide program guidelines.

UNDERSTANDING THE SUFFICIENT CONDITIONS OF LEARNING

Learning is the "work" of pupils. The teacher's role is to adapt expectations and instruction so as to maximize pupil learnings and attainments. As consumers, teachers may be confused by the competing learning theories that vie for their attention. While there is diversity, there are also areas of agreement. For example, most agree that learning is a change in a person's behavior as a result of instruction, imitation, and/or practice. Consequently, learning is purposeful to the person. For children, learning benefits from intervention to maximize its direction and outcomes. That is the main reason for teachers.

The Nature of Learning

Stevenson (1975) summarized agreements among educational psychologists regarding the nature of learning. His conclusions were as follows:

- Children learn from the first weeks of life. Infants and toddlers are responsive and active learners. Vocalization is the foundation for speech and language. Individual differences are apparent; for example, the number of trials necessary before three-day-old infants established a connection between a tone and milk varied widely.

- The research of Piaget has achieved a status equal to that of Guilford and Bloom. The significance of the environment and of increasing readiness has received attention.

- Learning is accomplished through visual, auditory, tactual, and olfactory observation. People and media are significant sources for the child to imitate and model. Social learnings such as interactive behavior and values are outcomes as significant as language and cognitive outcomes.

- Attention influences learning, and children and youth vary in their willingness and ability to attend to sources of information. The former describes motivational factors, such as confidence in one's ability to learn and the interest to persist. The latter involves having clear sensory images, directing one's responses, and selecting relevant features for attention.

- Learning performance can be made more efficient; it is not the passive reception of information. Memory has been found to be especially amenable to intervention through imagery and practice. Imagery is the association of the familiar to the unfamiliar in order to aid recall and retention of learning. Practice is sufficient repetition to move new learnings into long-term memory.

The Stevenson (1975) summary can be further expanded to include the concept that learning is a mediation between the learner and the environment. The environment consists of physical and material resources as well as social interactions with people.

The tasks of learning can be expressed, according to Stevenson, as rate, retention, and transfer. Rate describes the time and number of trials necessary to reach a criterion or expected level of performance. Retention is the recall or recognition of material learned. Stevenson observed that instruction, all too often, stresses recall and ignores retention. Transfer is the application of learning. It can be the use of new information to solve familiar problems or the use of familiar information to generate new ideas, solutions, etc. Transfer is not an automatic function; it can be facilitated through practice. Practice can be the opportunity to observe instances of transfer and nontransfer of learnings.

The Elements of Learning

Stevenson's (1975) conclusions suggest at least three elements of learning: (1) the receiving of learning; (2) the expressing, or demonstration, of learning; and (3) the processing, or mediation, of information, stimulation, etc. between receiving and expressing. A fourth element might be the internal behavior that evaluates consequences, commonly entitled feedback.

Kirk and Gallagher (1979) have proposed a model that accounts for Stevenson's conclusions as well as the learning attributes relevant to educational settings. In their model, learning is viewed as a cycle of (1) environmental stimulation, (2) receiving and perceiving stimulation, (3) processing, (4) expressing, (5) feedback, and (6) decision. Environmental stimulation describes those sources that activate the person's learning elements. Receiving involves perceptions and use of perceptual data; perception is the act of giving meaning to sensory information, such as decoding print symbols to read, knowing the quantity of numerical symbols, and the like. Expressing is the overt action of the person, e.g., writing, speaking, and applause.

Processing, for Kirk and Gallagher, emphasizes memory, association, interpretation, and judgment. It is just as appropriate to substitute Piaget's stages, Guilford's operations, or Bloom's cognitive behaviors. The essential idea is that, when stimulated, the person selects from among available resources in order to respond with accuracy and appropriateness. However, learning does not end with this three-part cycle.

Feedback, the responses of others to one's expressing, can stabilize a response or thwart further similar responses. The absence of feedback creates confusion. Feedback can also be internal satisfaction, and it is a significant source of self-esteem. Data from feedback are usually incorporated into processing for subsequent use to direct or control expressing.

Decision is an adjunct to processing and to feedback. Decisions involve choices of attending, strategies, and criteria for selection of strategies. Decision has an affective component as well, since motivation is involved. For example, the decision to attend to snakes, or not attend to snakes, in a biology class can be highly independent of instructor directives. (Some authorities would include decision as a part of feedback.)

A TOMIC View—A Learner's View

The views of Stevenson (1975) and of Kirk and Gallagher (1979) can be further translated into a more explicit educational perspective. Their discussions can be considered as helpful summaries of learning as viewed by adults engaged in research and teaching. Their discussions can be translated into a model that emphasizes task, organism, motivation, instruction, and criterion. The acronym TOMIC was selected for its ease of retention, an application of the Stevenson (1975) summary regarding the use of images to facilitate memory.

Task describes that which is to be learned, be it a feeling of empathy, a chemical formula, how to drive a car, or an economic theory. It is something that parents, teachers, peers, and pupil deem significant for deliberate and formal acquisition or attainment. Organism is the human being who does the learning. The maturity and readiness of the person should match the task. Motivation is that which influences the person to pursue and persist in the task. It includes all the variables that influence the person to approach or avoid the context and setting of the task. The next element is instruction, which refers to the explanation of a step-to-step procedure to perform a task. That procedure is usually supplied by a teacher. Instruction involves feedback and focus of attention. It can be self-feedback and the ability to appraise one's own performance critically, but it can also be seeking out sources or models for instruction. Criterion indicates when learning has been accomplished, usually by some form of test. Tests that are realistic and lifelike and that measure attainment of the task directly are called criterion-referenced tests. Circumnavigating a block without falling off is a criterion-referenced test of ability to ride a bicycle.

Commentary

However one views learning, a knowledge of its components can be useful in the day-to-day activities of parents, children, and teachers, especially in assessment, planning, and/or evaluation. A learning problem can be defined as a breakdown in one or more of its constituent elements. Decisions about tactics can be referenced to the element(s) involved. Instructional tactics can be related to improved or more efficient performance of the learner. The advantage of the contemporary view of learning is its emphasis upon both the person and the environment.

DECISIONS REGARDING MATCHING

A Central Theme

Matching the learner to the curriculum is a familiar theme to educators. It is a powerful tradition in American education. Serious problems were caused by too literal application of that traditional, unilateral stance, however. The weaknesses and the dangers of that position are now apparent, and it is possible to avoid them.

The traditional match system put all the burden of adjustment on the pupil and none on the curriculum. Each grade was exactly the same for everyone, and each pupil was expected to accommodate to that situation, whether the pupil was beyond the material or whether the material was beyond the pupil. Very few adjustments were sanctioned, except repeating for those pupils who were overwhelmed or double-promotion for those who were bored.

For the contemporary match, the curriculum must be less rigid, more flexible. It is recognized that all pupils are able to learn, but that their styles and paces of learning differ widely. The contemporary match system tends to keep pupils of about the same age together, while encouraging teachers to vary the nature of curriculum content and the rate at which it is presented. The result is a closer fit between each pupil's learning characteristics and the day-to-day content of schooling. At every grade level, the curriculum is varied to meet individual pupil needs and capabilities. The contemporary match obviously puts more authority and initiative in the teacher's hands. It also calls for more public understanding of the increased complexity of the teacher's responsibilities.

Learning Style and Matching

The choice of approaches to match the learner also calls for a knowledge of learning styles. Renzulli and Smith (1978) identified interests and tactics as two principal learning style elements for gifted and talented pupils. Both have direct relevance for motivation and persistence in learning. Interests might be fine arts/crafts, scientific/technical, literary/writing, political/judicial, mathematical, athletic, managerial, business, historical, performing arts, and/or others. Interests can be assessed by direct interview, testimony by others, demonstrated performance, inventories, or observations. Tactics involve both modes of instruction and self-learning procedures preferred by students. Modes include project, simulation, drill and repetition, peer teaching, discussion, teaching games, independent study, programmed instruction, and lecture. Preferences can be assessed much like interests.

Two other dimensions are relevant to interests and tactics. One is a preference for group or individual activities. Another is the interaction of interests and tactics. For example, a given student might prefer a one-to-one discussion regarding historical events, but elect individual projects for scientific/technical interests.

Although not specifically mentioned by Renzulli and Smith, recognition for efforts could be considered another dimension of style. Recognition can be self-approval, approval of teachers and/or parents, or peer approval. Some students may prefer more overt recognition, such as a school performance or mention in the media, awards, or other forms of public acknowledgment.

An Action Model

Maintaining the match between learner and task is a familiar problem to teachers. This dimension can be explicitly related to the needs of gifted and talented learners and the decisions that teachers render. A proposed model that outlines the scope of decisions contains the following elements: *A*ssessment, *C*riteria, *T*ask, *I*nstruction, *O*rganism, and *N*eeds. Assessment describes anticipatory planning and knowledge prior to the introduction of new material. Criteria describes intentions and specifications for pupil outcomes. Task is related to the skills, knowledge, and attitudes sufficient to attain criteria performance. Instruction is the implementation and movement toward criteria. Organism relates to the variables within the person that influence performance. Needs represents circumstances of motivation. As can be seen in Table 9-2, each of these elements has its teacher-centered decisions and its pupil-centered outcomes.

These elements do not define the sequence, but the scope. The overlap between this scope and the TOMIC model is a natural overlap between learning and teaching. Ideally, teachers' knowledge about learning influences their perception about teaching.

Table 9-2 Essentials for Managing and Maintaining a Match Between Learner and Task

Element	Related Teacher Question	Pupil Outcomes
Assessment	Why do I perceive the need for assessment? Why am I interested/how did I become interested? What results do I expect?	Learner is informed of teacher's interest. Learner participates in refining interest.
Criteria	How shall outcomes be stated? How shall mastery be measured? Whom to terminate?	Learner is provided feedback and recognition.
Task	Is the task of merit? Does the task have subtasks? Is the task developmentally appropriate?	Learner participates in selection of task.
Instruction	Do I have sufficient skills? Do I have sufficient resources? Do I have sufficient materials?	Learner willingly participates in instruction.
Organism	Does the learner have prior skills? Does the learner have a preferred learning style? Does the learner possess sufficient maturity?	Learner is informed of responsibilities. Learner is aware of capabilities.
Needs	Does the task have an affective valence? Does the task possess rewarding aspects? Are there other motivational variables	Learner is committed to engage in task.

ELEMENTS OF PLANNING

A lesson plan, regardless of topic, should account for the relevant variables about tasks, the person, and instructional elements. These elements of lesson planning demonstrate commitment to matching and maintaining the match. These elements can be summarized as follows:

- Statement of outcomes is an agenda for the teacher and the pupil that fits into the larger context of curriculum. Teacher expectations would spell out the prescription, and pupil considerations would take incentives for learning into account.

- Motivation details the incentives used by the teacher to secure attention and the means for maintaining attention.

- Readiness involves the ability to recall previous experiences and relate them to unfamiliar elements.

- Elaboration involves relating the familiar to the unfamiliar so that the learner can generalize and apply new learnings.

- Practice of new skills is done in isolation to stabilize performance. Additionally, practice is extended to a variety of situations to promote an internalized criterion of circumstances of application and nonapplication of the new skill.

- Selection of a learning style for skill practice involves method and materials.

- Evaluation is directed toward both pupil and practitioner. For pupil evaluation, information regarding intended outcomes, as well as unexpected outcomes, is gathered. The practitioner will find it helpful to maintain a log for purposes of recycling the benefits of the experience for subsequent planning.

The lesson plan is an important element of individualized education programs and assessment of growth for gifted and talented pupils. A series of lesson plans forms a good basis for review and discussion among professionals interested in the development of a particular able child. The same is true for discussions with parents or pupils about how individualized education programs are being implemented and the kinds and degrees of gains being achieved.

Chapter 10

Managing and Maintaining
the Match

USING NEEDS ASSESSMENT

Describing Needs Assessment

Needs assessment is a well-established psychosocial and psychoeducational process within human service systems. It produces information about the existing level of services within an organization and identifies those being served. The initial emphasis is a summation of what is. The formative aspect of needs assessment is the comparison of the current provisions and programs with known and proved evidence of what should be. Identification of discrepancies fulfills a third dimension, discrepancy analysis, and a fourth component formulates recommendations for eliminating discrepancies. A fifth component may involve the assignment of priorities for recommendations. All of this may be done while another psychosocial process projects what the broader future may be like. With techniques such as Delphi that can be used to estimate future trends (Reynolds, 1973), a prediction of the general nature of the future social climate can be made and specific needs viewed in the light of probable future conditions.

A needs assessment, when completed, is only as valuable as its power to inform and influence. Thus, to help ensure that a needs assessment report will not simply gather dust, the individuals and organizations that wield power and influence over the matter being studied should be deeply and thoroughly involved in designing and conducting the assessment. In this, and in the process used, the needs assessment bears a striking resemblance to individualized education program planning. As the product moves from a submitted report to decision, the tactics of innovation, social action, and the like can apply.

The Process of Needs Assessment

Trezise (1978) summarized the collective experiences of school districts in the organization of a needs assessment for gifted and talented learners. The process originates with a decision that "something" of quality must be done. From this single decision, the process unfolds. The originator is, typically, a parent, a teacher, a principal, a superintendent, an administrator, a school board member, or community advocate. Consequently, a needs assessment can be a single person project or a collective effort. Trezise observed that a collective effort commonly starts with the establishment of an advisory committee. The composition, appointment, status, and mission (e.g., charge) of such a committee are decision points.

The board of education should, by formal resolution, establish a Citizens' Needs Assessment Committee (CNAC). The CNAC should be charged with producing a needs assessment report within 10 to 12 months, or other reasonable time, for submission to the board. It should be clear that submission is *not* adoption, since the board is the legally defined body for policy and legally *cannot* delegate its mandate. The board should commit sufficient funds for clerical assistance, meetings (e.g., mileage, costs), consultation, and other necessities. A person from within the school district should be designated the executive secretary for the committee. Accountability to the board for the product and process would rest with the superintendent. The board would direct the CNAC to survey present practices and compare them with known standards so as to formulate recommendations for consideration by the board.

The superintendent has several tasks, e.g., identification, recruitment, and appointment of the committee membership. Consideration should be given to the balance among deliverers of services (e.g., administrators, teachers), consumers (e.g., parents, pupils, and alumni), and community support groups (e.g., commerce, labor, professionals, PTA). There are no specific guidelines for an ideal effective and efficient composition. Persons should be selected for their commitment, competence, access to information, and belief in the group process. This suggests deliverers and consumers for the most part, with others included according to their presumed contribution of information.* The

---

*It has been the experience of the authors that it is advantageous to separate needs assessment from implementation for reasons of efficiency and effectiveness. Implementation is the transformation of needs assessment into actual operations that may require further board action. For purposes of closure, it may be best to establish an implementation committee later to oversee board decisions. Furthermore, persons may have interests in one area but not the other. It has also been our experience that a committee should be restricted to about 12 to 15 members. This committee can establish task forces to which members could be appointed; a member of the CNAC should be a member of each task force. It is reasonable to expect the CNAC would meet monthly to share progress and to receive reports from chairpersons of task forces, which, in turn, would meet monthly or as needed.

charge to the committee must be structured for clarity of expectations, and the superintendent must keep informed of committee progress in order to help in reducing problems or obstacles to progress.

The committee executive secretary, or coordinator, arranges the first meeting as to time, place, and agenda. The principal agenda items are selection of chairperson, associated chairperson, and secretary. Orientation of the committee members to the tasks is required. Ground rules for decisions must be clarified, especially if the committee divides itself into task forces rather than acts as a committee of the whole. Orientation also includes identification of the contents of the final report. Of critical importance is agreement on a definition of gifted and talented persons.* Details of reimbursement should be clarified. The first meeting should establish group solidarity and common purpose as members share their interests and experiences. A convenient time and place for subsequent meetings should be established.

The first meeting, and subsequent meetings, are successful to the extent that members are confident in their ability to succeed. Board approval and the sanction of a superintendent provide a context; however, clarity is a powerful incentive. Clarity can be achieved through task orientation. If the committee members can visualize and verbalize the structure of their final report, they can continually evaluate their efforts toward fulfillment.

The Product of Needs Assessment

The end product of needs assessment is a final report that should be completed within one year or earlier. The report identifies the number of students served and the adequacy of services. Recommendations are directed toward improvement of services to achieve a level of sufficient quality. The report also contains a review of the procedures used for data collection and analysis. Committee members should be constantly aware that their document can become a powerful rallying point.

Pupil Focus

A first step is the determination of how many students would be considered gifted and talented. The intent is to locate, or estimate, the actual number of such pupils in the school district. Assuming that the federal definition (see Overview) is used, the dimensions of intellectual ability and/or performance are emphasized. For the task of gathering the data, a survey would be

---

*It has been our experience, confirmed by Trezise, that this issue ought not to be bypassed. A committee may view its mission as restricted to academic aptitude alone. It is helpful to review the definition used in the state and/or definitions from other sources. At any rate, the committee should be clear as to its view of who the gifted and talented pupils are.

appropriate. The survey population would be parents and classroom teachers. With orientation, parents do not overnominate, nor do teachers undernominate. Both Trezise (1978) and Brumbaugh and Roshco (1959) advocated a "Child Who ..." technique for the survey. This technique, in checklist format, is a general screening for an estimate of potential gifted and talented learners. Example items are found in Exhibit 10-1. An alternative would be to request teachers to nominate students in light of the federal definition. This provides a rough estimate that can be expected to be approximately 70 to 80 percent accurate; that is, it may overestimate or underestimate by 20 to 30 percent. It is essential, however, to study the list of identified gifted and to see if it contains proportions of boys and girls and proportions of minority students equivalent to those in the total school population. If not, further identification steps should be taken to remedy the disproportions.

Focus on Present Services for Pupils

Located pupils are assessed as to their present level of services. Trezise noted that it is *not* necessary to interview each or every pupil. The committee can select 20 percent for inquiry. The sample should be representative in regard to grade levels, sex, and socioeconomic status; in addition, representation of schools within the districts should be balanced. The following items can be used to assess the pupil's current educational status:

- What is the grade level of assignments completed?
- What is the cognitive level (as per Bloom) of class discussions?
- How are advanced interests and/or skills accommodated?
- Are advanced level experiences/projects available?
- Are supplementary materials that are on advanced levels and appropriate for interests readily available?
- Are independent study and competency-based examinations available for the student?
- Are there opportunities for students of common interests to collaborate with one another?
- How does the pupil perceive his or her progress in school?
- How does the pupil describe his or her one wish for the school program?
- What activities does the child do outside of school that could be in-school activities?

Exhibit 10-1 Example of "Child Who" Survey Technique

Directions: Think of the pupils under your direction/supervision. The following items are designed to help you think about these learners. Beside each item write the name, or names, of learners whose names come to mind. Think of the items as a nomination similar to a political convention.

In my opinion a child who:

Item	Name(s)
1. is the best student	
2. has the largest vocabulary	
3. has original ideas	
4. is followed by his or her classmates	
5. is most scientifically oriented	
6. is able to judge his or her work	
7. is the biggest nuisance	
8. is highly motivated	
9. is highly popular with other children	
10. is advanced in academic areas	
11. has parent(s) who are concerned about their child's enrichment and educational progress	
12. is sensitive to the needs of others	
13. is interested in questions of right and wrong	
14. is able to role play with flourish and attention to detail	
15. is interested in collections and hobbies	

- What extra cocurricular activities does the school sponsor? Is the pupil enrolled? Why not?

- Do all pupils have opportunities for cross-grade clubs, special projects, etc.?

- How frequently does the pupil use the school library and/or media center and/or educational resources center? Why? Why not?

- How does the school arrange for visitation to points of interest in the community?

- What cooperative arrangements does the school have with community recreational and cultural sources?

The central purpose is to identify any gap between the pupil's capability and the extent of challenge.

Focus on Policy and Practice

The preferred practices identified by Reynolds and Birch (1977) could be adapted to fit examination of current policies and practices within the district. Trezise (1978) shared an adapted version developed for use in Illinois. Furthermore, Newland (1976) has advanced pertinent questions as well. Representative sample items are summarized in Table 10-1. Local CNACs should be encouraged to formulate their own personalized items.

Needs assessment is undertaken to provide guidance for program development and evaluation. Its spirit is genuine inquiry. It is nonjudgmental and does not engage in fault-finding or criticism of the past. Needs assessment generates information that must be managed and put to constructive use. Most appropriately, it forms the foundation for recommendations.

TRANSLATING NEEDS ASSESSMENT

Understanding the Task

The task, or goal, of needs assessment is to generate information and proposals for action. Ideally, the action will be implementation, which implies an orderly plan that is a systematic, logical, and rational outgrowth of the data available from needs assessment.

Warren (1955) and Wolfensberger and Glenn (1975) offer models for translating needs assessment data into recommendations. A recommendation serves as a goal, usually stating the persons to be served and under what

Table 10-1 Assessment of Policy and Practices

Dimensions	Example Items
Administration and coordination	Does the school have written policies regarding the education of gifted and talented pupils?
	Does the school have written policies regarding the identification and individualized planning for pupils?
	Does the school have a written policy regarding coordination of program elements and coordination with other school programs?
	Does the school have a written and formal plan for the evaluation of its efforts?
	Does the school maintain a listing of its pupils and have records available for periodic review and revision?
	Does the school have policies regarding adequate and orderly funding?
Identification	What policies exist for the participation of psychologists, social workers, and others in assessment?
	What criteria are used for assessment and individualized planning?
	Have staff received training in using the criteria?
	Have staff been oriented toward understanding the attributes of gifted and talented pupils for identification and nomination?
	Does the school have a systematic, flexible plan for continuous identification?
	Are teachers encouraged to report behavior and achievement of worth for identification?
Curriculum	Is there a written curriculum plan in the school district?
	Are the goals and objectives stated with sufficient clarity to measure and assess pupil performance?
	Do pupil performance data enable the pupil to advance through goals and objectives more rapidly or at an early age?
	Is there regular appraisal of the curriculum as to its adequacy for gifted and talented pupils?
Instruction and instructional support	Does the school make books, articles, journals about gifted and talented pupils readily available to teachers?
	Does the school have a support system for innovation, such as technical assistance, in-service training, or consultants?
	Are teachers encouraged to try experimental approaches to meet individual and group needs?
	Are teachers encouraged to observe other teachers and/or programs for professional development?
Instruction	Does the school have policies for flexible scheduling for pupils and/or facilities to enable pupils to pursue interests and content?
	Are pupils given opportunities for in and out of school activities consistent with individualized goals and objectives?
	Are trips, projects, and activities undertaken toward fulfilling individual goals and objectives?
	Are facilities, materials, and guidance available for independent study?
	How are teachers recruited and assigned, and by what criteria?

Table 10-1 continued

Dimensions	Example Items
Resources	Are there legal provisions in the state to regulate / guide practice? How are these provisions implemented? Does the state department of education have a responsible person / position / administrative unit to oversee legal provisions? Have state resources been accounted for?

circumstances. A proposal is an elaboration and expansion of a recommendation. The proposed action elaborates the intended service description and identifies the (1) initiator of service, (2) provider, (3) funding source, (4) intended data, (5) evaluation, (6) population, (7) type of service, and (8) priority. Gallagher (1978) endorses this method of translation. He observed that programs are often conceived in haste, without consideration of all components, and oriented only to the short range (e.g., one year); usually consider only direct instruction-classroom factors; and neglect evaluation as well as support services.

Stating Recommendations

According to Wolfensberger and Glenn (1975), recommendations are stated in a context of values and beliefs about services. They should direct attention to the need for decisions, without necessarily proposing specific solutions. For example, suppose a needs assessment committee conducted a survey of school policies and practices regarding identification. It was found that able pupils were known to teachers and principals at junior high levels, but that fewer pupils had been identified at elementary and senior high levels. Furthermore, district policy did not allow for pupil personnel services (e.g., psychologists, social workers, nurses, guidance counselors) to be extended to gifted pupils per se; such services could be made available only if the pupil were manifesting conflict in schools. The need for recommendations about identification is obvious.

Applying the Warren (1955) criteria that a recommendation must take population and circumstances into account, the following could be advanced:

A central source of identification should be established for gifted and talented pupils and their families. Identification should involve actively seeking all pupils who may be in need of services and delivering appropriate services to them. It is imperative that all families, teachers, school personnel, and community agencies are alerted to the importance of *early* identification and intervention.

Although this example is not a complete response, it does reflect how a recommendation can identify a problem area and target attention on it.

Stating Proposals

Given the recommendation for an entry point that is targeted toward nonschool sources, a proposal could be generated. Exhibit 10-2 illustrates the components of an action statement. It is, by *no* means, a complete solution. For example, it would be necessary to address school staff. Furthermore, there is no reason why pupil personnel services has to be *the* unit. The entry point could be handled by a variety of strategies.

A Further Note on Translation

Translation actually involves three phases: (1) gathering data, (2) generating recommendations, and (3) advancing proposals. A fourth phase could be implementation of proposals, and the fifth would be assessment and evaluation of implementation. In practice, the first two phases could be accomplished by a needs assessment committee within one year, assuming cooperation and sufficient sanction. Depending on the clarity of recommendations, the third phase, could require an additional year. These time periods do not preclude initiative by individual teachers and/or principals. However, in establishing a comprehensive program of substance and permanence, care in long-range planning creates a helpful context.

UNDERSTANDING EDUCATION PROGRAMMING

Elements of Programming

Interest and experience in education of the gifted and talented are neither new nor novel. What is new is the sense of urgency regarding improvements in the quality of education for more gifted and talented youngsters in the context of individualized education for all learners.

An enduring question for educators and parents is the identification of elements necessary for establishing and maintaining a high-quality program. Lucito's (1963) schema builds on a sound outline of the necessary and sufficient conditions that must be considered by decision makers. The Lucito resumé, consequently, remains a useful vehicle around which to organize educational programming, planning, delivery of services, and evaluation.

Exhibit 10-2 Example of an Entry Point Proposal Generated by Needs Assessment

Description
    The school district needs to seek cooperative relationships with families and community as entry points to services for gifted and talented pupils and to work together on generating referrals and eliminating gaps in sources of referrals.

Type
    The establishment of entry points for gifted and talented pupils would be new for the school district. It would require expansion and revision of existing pupil personnel services.

Population
    The entry point service will/would be available to all pupils.

Initiator
    The school board should endorse the principle of early identification and the principle of an orderly entry point.

Provider
    By board action, the director of pupil personnel services should be directed to establish and publicize the availability of an entry point.

Target Date
    The entry point should be in place within one school year.

Funding Source
    Existing budget should be expanded. Exploration of state sources for pupil personnel services reimbursement should be undertaken. Exploration of federal sources should be considered.

Evaluation
    An increase in the number of referrals from parents and community agencies will be considered partial evidence of success. The director of pupil personnel services will be expected to formulate a program evaluation plan to be submitted to the superintendent and school board.

Priority
    This proposal is assigned a high priority for implementation.

Lucito described an education program as a written, formal, and deliberate plan for organizing and mobilizing resources on behalf of learners. In general terms, programs for the gifted and talented have concentrated upon (1) identification, (2) provisions, (3) procedures, and (4) problems/challenges. As has been noted earlier, identification involves the location of pupils whose behavior or potential performance meets stated criteria. Although the exact criteria vary from school district to school district, any plan or program describes its criteria for eligible learners. Educational provisions are the adaptations of standard practices and written policies for dealing with gifted and talented learners. Moreover, provisions are best arrived at through group decisions that merge the views of administrators, board and community, policymakers, teachers, parents, and other participants. Education procedures cover stated objectives, as well as tactics and strategies. Problems include issues that identify the constraints and facilitators in program operation.

The Nature of Provisions

Educational provisions should be rooted in the goals of the program. Goals offer guidance and direction. Pronouncements of professional or parent organizations, government commissions, and agencies can be useful sources for goal statement ideas. State and local boards of education are also potential sources.

There is temptation to radicalize goals, to dismiss the regular curriculum totally in order to justify "special" programming. It is sometimes felt that, if goals are "good" for all other children, they somehow cannot be good for the gifted and talented. Lucito suggested, as did Birch and Johnstone (1975), using standard well-established educational and social goals, such as self-realization, economic usefulness, civic responsibility, and human relationships, and translating those goals into detailed objectives for gifted and talented students in order to balance group concerns and individual needs. Moreover, these goals emphasize subject matter and skills. Acceptable special education provisions require a broadly endorsed statement of aspirations, and this approach helps to ensure that any endorsement is openly arrived at and thoroughly understood.

Provisions must allow for different rates of learning (cognitive development). Educators should maintain close communication in order to share ideas. For example, extracurricular activities are the most commonly found adaptations for able children and youth at all levels of education, and it could be valuable to share information on these activities. Acceleration is another procedure common at all educational levels. Competency examinations for advanced placement is a college level tactic that has been increasingly evident in elementary and secondary schools, as has independent (guided or directed individual) study. The seminar as a community of scholars need not be restricted to college settings. These options are important discrete provisions, but they are *not* a program. They are means to ends and should be components of all programs.

The Nature of Procedures

Educational procedures are ways of teaching or instructing. A program must include a section that explicitly treats the various ways instruction is to be conducted and provides a rationale for each. For instance, if discovery is a recommended teaching procedure, the program should make clear why and when it is to be employed. Actually, such an overt statement provides greater professional and scholarly freedom. Almost inevitably, parents and the community recognize that, while they should know how teaching will be done, teachers should have wide latitude and encouragement to adapt, adjust, and create teaching approaches that match the many-faceted personalities of their charges as well as possible.

In general terms, we commend process approaches referenced in Guilford's concept of operations (see Chapter 1). Subject matter concerns are focal in forming concepts (as opposed to accumulating random facts), increasing information, and widening interests. Similarly, instructional procedures can be keyed to the Bloom taxonomy (see Chapter 1) for both cognitive and affective content. The emergence of Piaget's work on moral (e.g., responsibility) development, the Bloom et al. analysis of affective outcome, and the theory of values clarification reflect expansions of this dimension. Also present in affective objectives is the strong theme of responsible and responsive leadership.

Constraints on Program Development

The 1980s are relatively free of the major constraints on program development that were prevalent in the last two decades. Contemporary parents and professionals are not so plagued by the confusion, cross-purposes, conflict, and lack of adequate information. There are still some disagreements and major problems of cost, but power struggles and role confusion seem to be at an all-time low. Everyone agrees that more trained personnel are needed. Perhaps most important, advocate parents are more organized. Several states have mandated special education for gifted and talented young people; federal support has grown stronger. The social-psychological climate seems to be one that removes constraints and encourages development.

The emergence of evaluation as a decision-making tool during the 1970s is also reassuring, because it allows for continuous monitoring. Evaluation also recognizes a decision as a starting point, not an end point. Consequently, evaluation procedures and process confirm that well-considered decision and selection from among informed opinions can prompt action. Moreover, investigations now tend to concentrate on common attributes, especially the influence of accelerated rate and increased capacity on development and adjustment. Also, it is becoming clearer that costs need not be excessive. Quality of education need not be confused with quantity of dollars, although the two are related in that fundamental programs require support.

Power struggles for program control between departments of regular instruction and departments of special education appear to have been settled. Special education now tends to provide administrative coordination, but calls upon all the school's resources. As far as day-to-day teaching operations are concerned, it appears accurate to say that the team concept has gained favor since the 1960s. This means that the learner's regular class teacher and the parent are the essential unit. Resource personnel from special education serve to support their efforts, not to struggle for dominance.

In the recent past, too, the role of parents has been clarified. Parent permission and endorsement are required for special programming. Parent education procedures have emerged to help parents (1) promote their child's continuing achievement and motivation, (2) urge legislative support of programs, and (3) serve as a support group for other parents. Moreover, the tactics of social action are resulting in a mutual trust between professionals and concerned citizens.

A Model for Priorities

Educational programming for the gifted and talented evolved through a series of breaks with the constraints that might interfere with maintaining programs of quality. Good quality requires matching, maintaining, and managing (Fig. 10-1).

Learner and curriculum should be matched, as learning conditions and teaching tactics should be matched. Matching means to couple, to equate, to pair, to harmonize, to balance, and to keep pace. It relates to individual psychoeducational goals and to societal needs.

Maintaining the match is a prime task for teachers. The Reynolds and Birch (1977), Sellin and Birch (1980), and Whitmore (1980) references and the discussion in Chapter 1 provide helpful sources. Maintaining means to continue, to persevere, to keep up, to retain, to sustain, to assert, and to perfect.

Figure 10-1 A Model for Educational Intervention

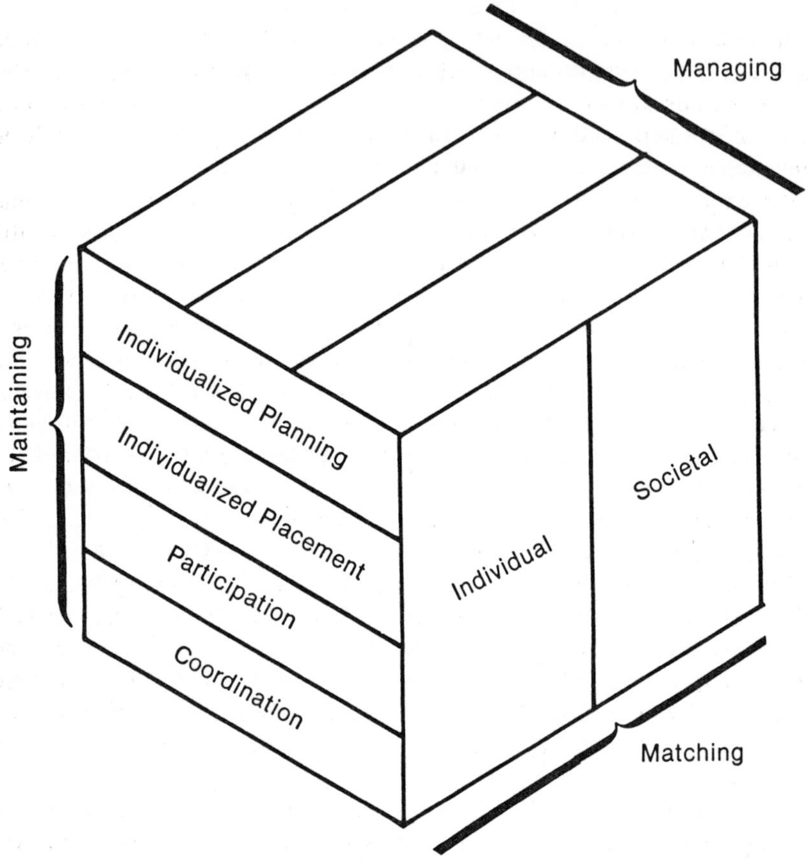

Managing, as used here, means to administer, to control, to direct, to handle, to be orderly, and to arrange. The theme of this element is to support teacher, pupil, and parent. It relates to programs, policies, and resources.

Summing Up

In this unit, priorities in educational programming for gifted and talented pupils were identified and defined. These priorities can be viewed as a translation of the attributes of such pupils into educational practice.

IDENTIFYING GIFTED AND TALENTED LEARNERS

Identification refers to those procedures used to locate gifted and talented for inclusion (enrollment) in individualized education programs. Identification is the certification of eligibility. It means that the pupil *needs* certain kinds of specialized education. Assessment necessary for individualized education programs goes beyond data needed for identification.

Procedures should be selected on the basis of a definition of gifted and talented learners. Procedures can be judged as to their effectiveness (a ratio of number identified to actual number) and efficiency (a ratio of number found to number nominated). They can be grouped as nomination, personal sources, measures of creativity, standardized tests. Teacher nomination is a widely used method. Expert opinion is a favored way to judge talent or talent potential in artistic and/or performing arts. The case history also has validity in identification. It has been found to be effective, efficient, and of reasonable cost. The concept of the Individualized Education Program has expanded the utility of this tactic (see Unit V regarding the IEP). The difficulty with standardized tests is that these procedures can seriously underpredict performance. Nominations are helpful supplements.

Teacher judgment/nomination can be effective and efficient despite the false stereotype of the teacher as nominating only the sweet-smelling, washed, and compliant. With training in the full range of attributes of gifted and talented pupils, teachers identify 80 percent of gifted and talented, compared to the 40 to 50 percent rate prior to training. Individual IQ tests have about a 90 percent rate. The use of a variety of procedures would ensure close to a 100 percent rate.

Identification is strengthened to the extent that it is undertaken in the context of goals and in the context of present and future services. Identification of students is fundamental, but it is of little value without a program of good quality to match.

USING AND ADAPTING THE CURRICULUM

Curriculum describes the deliberate and formal intentions of a school or teacher to fulfill social mandates and to attend to the needs of individual pupils. It consists of what, by design, is taught in school.

Goals communicate standards of pupil performance for both the immediate and the long-range future. Clarity of goals can maximize teachers' freedom to pursue their own creativity in methods. Common goals of American education emphasize career-work, life skills (including literacy), self-direction, and personal-social relationships (including citizenship). Selection of goals for the gifted and talented should be based on the structure of the regular curriculum content, take individual and social outcomes into account, and reflect accurate understanding of the attributes of the gifted and talented.

Curriculum content can be organized according to a Table of Specifications (TOS), which facilitates communication and outcomes, selection of activities, and measurement. It can be a format to structure independent study and group projects; it can enable educators to describe content expectations. Content of curriculum can also be generated by brainstorming. This procedure is used either when the teacher is confident of his or her command of content or when more active involvement of pupils is desirable.

MATCHING LEARNER AND CURRICULUM

Consumers of services, pupils, and parents are useful sources for planning and feedback as to program goals and outcomes. A Bill of Rights for the gifted and talented could be described as protection and/or opportunity for understanding, identification, talent development, leadership, and respect.

Studies of pupil reactions suggest that special services do not necessarily create feelings of elitism among the pupils; this is the reaction of others. Pupils perceive special services, or adaptations, as helpful in career motivation, freedom for interests, improvement of study skills and habits, self-expression, and fulfillment of personalized objectives. Males and females report differences as to aspects of services, however, so responses to program evaluations should be separated by sex. Handicapped gifted persons report a greater struggle to overcome attitudes than to overcome difficulties in content.

Parent testimony reflects the concept that high quality of individualized education for *all* pupils is a necessary condition for services for the gifted and talented. The practices of schools more often create elitism than do attitudes arising within pupils. School districts respond differently to the charge of elitism. Some dismiss the charge as unfounded; others are willing to examine their practices.

Learning theory can be a direct source of guidance for teachers. Learning, which is a purposeful change in behavior, involves rate, retention, and transfer. The elements of the learning cycle can be understood as stimulation, receiving, processing, expressing, feedback, and decisions. It is these attributes of learning that the teacher must consider in adaptation.

Elements of the sufficient conditions for learning can be understood as task, organism, motivation, instruction, and criteria. This describes the learner's view of learning. Learning styles of gifted and talented pupils can be understood as preferences. One choice may relate to interests; another, to instructional mode. Preference for individual and group activities is another. A fourth is preference for product recognition.

Maintaining the match requires thought and planning. Elements of planning include decisions about assessment, criteria, task, instruction, organism, and needs. One example of matching and maintaining is a tool known as the lesson plan. Elements of a lesson plan, deduced from the role of learner and of teacher, include outcomes, motivation, readiness, development, practices, activities, and evaluation.

MANAGING AND MAINTAINING THE MATCH

Needs assessment is a first step toward establishing a foundation for the development of a high-quality program. Needs assessment is a systematic study of the present level of services that is to be used as a basis for a subsequent initiation of services. It is designed to locate eligible pupils and to survey their current status and needs. Both sources (e.g., services/resources and pupils) are the means for declaring goals and objectives.

The goal of needs assessment is to produce a product, a final report. At a minimum, the report should describe (1) pupil populations, (2) present level of services, and (3) policies and practices in force. The action-oriented portion of a final report is its recommendations and proposals, which translate gathered data into statements to be considered for action. The purpose of a recommendation is to direct attention to a valued action. Recommendations are stated in the language of "should."

Recommendations are the context for proposals, which include the following elements: (1) description of service/provision, (2) type, (3) population(s) to be served, (4) initiator, (5) provider, (6) target date, (7) funding source evaluation, and (8) priority rating. Proposals, in turn, translate into implementation of one or more of the following: program, provisions, and procedures. A program is a written document, or plan, to adapt or modify curriculum for particular pupils. Procedures describe tactics, especially those of teachers.

The translation of needs assessment into endorsed programs must take into account certain constraints and/or obstacles: (1) disagreement among experts, (2) insufficient knowledge, (3) differing values of education, (4) high costs, (5) power struggles, (6) lack of urgency, (7) role confusion, and (8) lack of trained personnel.

Enrichment

IDENTIFYING GIFTED AND TALENTED LEARNERS

1. In your own words, describe the differences between effective and efficient identification procedures. Which, in your opinion, is more important—effectiveness or efficiency? Defend your choice.

2. Review the Seashore guidelines regarding identification. Find out to what extent these guidelines are used in your school district. Are others used? Share your findings.

3. Suppose you had to testify before a policy-making board regarding identification. In a ten-minute presentation, what points would you make regarding the role of teachers? Why would you choose those points?

4. Suppose you were to write a three-page article for (a) the state chapter of the American Civil Liberties Union, (b) the local chapter of Concerned School Psychologists, and (c) the school district newsletter. How would your outline structure differ regarding identification? Why?

USING AND ADAPTING THE CURRICULUM

5. Select any two textbooks or one text and an encyclopedia. Find a topic common to both sources. Does the content reflect a consideration for the common goals of American education? Which ones? Can you think of reasons for omission? Could you specify ways of improvement?

6. In the same situation as in No. 5, prepare a Table of Specifications regarding the content and outcomes. Could you extend outcomes into analysis, synthesis, or evaluation? What relationship do you notice between these "higher" functions and the basics?

7. Could you develop a Table of Specifications for Chapter 2? How did you decide upon the content and outcomes? Share your prospectus with others. Another option could be to write a 30-item multiple choice test. What agreements do you notice with others? Are there loadings or concentrations on either content or outcomes?

8. Consider the tactics of identification. How could brainstorming be used to generate a curriculum for in-service preparation of teachers? Share your results.

9. Consider Foley's (1971) Table of Specifications for writing. How could this table be helpful in the improvement of *your own* professional writing?

MATCHING LEARNER AND CURRICULUM

10. Consult teachers' manuals (two or three) and select a common topic. What elements, or parts, are found in common? How do these acknowledge the TOMIC and/or the ACTION model? What provisions for learning style are acknowledged?

11. In the same situation as in No. 10, what elements of lesson plans in these sources acknowledge a Bill of Rights for the gifted and talented?

12. What weight, in your opinion, should be given to consumer opinion? What implications did you draw from this discussion?

13. How could you transform the essential (in your opinion) features of learning and teaching into a poster(s) to influence parents, teachers, board members? Share your product(s).

MANAGING AND MAINTAINING THE MATCH

14. Determine if a needs assessment has ever been conducted in your district. Secure a copy of the final report. Interview its participants. Compare and contrast your findings with the content of this unit. Share your insights.

15. Select three sheets of paper (8½ × 11). Divide each sheet into four parts. Prepare a coat of arms for a matcher (on one page), for a manager on another, and for a maintainer on another. Share your drawings.

16. Review the prototype. Briefly rewrite the article to describe a woman of the same age who heads the purchasing department of a major supermarket. What tactics of matching, managing, and maintenance would account for the different (not necessarily better) outcome? Share your insights.

Describing Quality Education

SYNOPSIS

High-quality programming is often confused with frills or attractive extras. Excellent education has nothing about it that is unnecessary, however; it has only the essential attributes of individualization and the means to implement them.

Program evaluation is a helpful tool for building and describing quality. Evaluation is the organization of information for decision making. It sets forth the language and concepts necessary to develop, maintain, and assess program outcomes. The intent of this unit is to identify proved standards under which sound programming for the gifted and talented functions. It serves as a guide for educators, who must remember that *programs become vulnerable without solid evidence to justify continuation.*

KEY IDEAS

High quality is necessary to regulate and reward sound policy and practice. Quality programs have a number of attributes. These can be expressed as systematic versus accidental, continuous versus disjointed, flexible versus rigid, and anticipatory versus defensive. Evidence of excellence can be found in programming for all gifted and talented pupils in all content and skill areas for all age levels. The initiation of modifications for selected learners is a starting point, not the ending point.

Excellence in programming for gifted and talented learners requires consideration and respect for the competencies of regular class teachers. The substance of high-quality services rests, in part, on the availability of free and appropriate in-service education prior to the introduction of new programs and provisions. Respect for teachers is a form of advocacy that runs interference for teacher and pupil.

Quality begins with clearly defined education. The press of events can obscure the necessity for describing practice. Teachers are viewed as the foundation for high-quality programming. Attributes of effective teachers are known and understood. The availability of alternatives that pupils, parents, and teachers can choose is a sign of quality if the alternatives are individually prescribed for the pupil. Documentation for program claims is another attribute of quality.

Managing and maintaining high-quality programs can be likened to a confederacy on behalf of able learners. This confederacy involves declared support for innovation. Goals and objectives of the program can be useful tools for matching the means to the ends. Evaluation comprises both processes and procedures for gathering and interpreting information to formulate decisions for program improvement. Accountability is responsible stewardship of resources directed toward attainment of aspirations.

A PROTOTYPE

Chronological age need *not* be a barrier to effective participation in planning, or improving the future. The Yourtowne schools have implemented this principle for their Basic Scholars.

The Future Is Now for Yourtowne

YOURTOWNE, N.B., WIRE SERVICE RELEASE: The future can be grim. Uncertainties over fuel supplies, unrest over alternative energy sources, economic and employment projections do not always inspire security.

But for a group of about 100 Basic Scholars, the study of the future can be both exciting and educational. These secondary students are participating in Project 2000 A.D. This project is a participatory effort of community leaders to plan for the future of the county.

The Yourtowne Public Schools assumed the task of integrating efforts of the students and of the parent committee of Project 2000 A.D. Student participants were drawn from public and nonpublic schools in the county. The Human Services subcomponent of the Basic Scholars Program has served to organize the students.

These students work in concert with the parent committee and serve as its principal staff for research and development and to monitor public opinion. These students report to the parent committee on findings and implications of findings. They also make regular reports to community organizations as well as to students in their high schools.

The Basic Scholars have recruited students from outside the Basic Scholars Program to participate. Public polling has used a Delphi technique. Delphi studies compare what is against what might be. This comparison can provide guidance as to unmet needs.

The Basic Scholars have named their task force "Futuristics 2000 Task Force," which, in turn, is organized into study committees on specific issues. The group is preparing a preliminary report based upon its polling and analysis of public opinion.

Glimpses of the future were shared by the students at a school assembly at Hubert Humphrey High School. Highlights of their findings by study committees were:

Education

- disapproved of teachers becoming obsolete
- approved of maintaining extracurricular activities
- approved of competency exams for students but not for teachers
- approved of students being allowed to move at their own pace regardless of age

Energy

- Sun, wind, alcohol, and biomass conversion are familiar to the public.
- Use of organic waste (biomass conversion) was the most favored.
- Solar energy was not perceived as feasible because of the area's almost constant cloud cover.

Transportation

- Railroads were perceived as the most feasible for freight hauling.
- A monorail appeared feasible provided fuel is available.
- Electric cars and promoting walking and cycling were endorsed.

Housing

- Underground dwellings could save considerable energy.
- Multifamily housing should be more widely considered.

- There should be greater publicity regarding the pros and cons of insulation.

Safety and Security

- approved of raising the speed limit
- disapproved of raising the age for driving and of lowering the drinking age
- had mixed reactions to capital punishment

Intergovernmental Relations

- There was opposition to either a metropolitan or consolidated county government.
- Mass transit was the only intergovernmental function to be approved.

Economic Development

- Unemployment, inflation, and new job sources were perceived as high priorities.
- Alternative sources of governmental income such as lotteries, off-track betting, and the like were of interest.
- Tax benefits, donation of city owned property, and a nationally oriented media campaign were seen as means to attract new industry.

While the project and its coordination are intense, it is a tribute to the Basic Scholars and their sponsor, Phyllis Hammer, for perceiving their competence as an integral part of future planning. It is also a tribute to the ways in which learning can be expanded beyond the classroom.

Chapter 11

Defining the Educational Context of Quality

THE MEANINGS OF EDUCATION

Any discussion of high-quality education must be anchored in a fundamental agreement on what is meant by education. Newland (1976) observed that the lack of a definition thwarts initiation of programs for gifted and talented persons and even contributes to their termination. A philosophy of education provides a rationale for practice, decision making, and evaluation for highly able learners. It must be grounded in an integration of beliefs and knowledge about the social and individual context.

Education is usually subject to one of three interpretations in the public mind. When it is equated with the public schools, education refers to buildings, staff, teachers, and budget. Education can also be viewed as all that influences, or shapes, a person's behavior; this is often termed *inculturation* (Mason, 1960). Third, education can mean the formal and deliberate instructional tactics of trained and competent persons, which have special implications for gifted and talented pupils.

American education is characterized by regard for the individual (psychoeducational) and regard for the social order (socioeducational). Philosophies of education, in a democracy, vary as to (1) definition of the balance between the social and individual welfare, (2) conceptions of the "good" social order, (3) view of individual aptitude and motivation, and (4) advocacy of teaching mode.

The Needs of the Individual and of the Social Order

In very general terms, Newland's views can be understood as an endorsement of formal and deliberate education of, for, and with gifted and talented persons, designed to balance the individual's need for self-fulfillment and

177

society's need for its human resources. Mason and Newland agree that both purposes (i.e., individual and social) of education are fulfilled through physical comfort, psychological stability, vocational adequacy, and social relationships. For example, physical and mental health require adequate nourishment, shelter, and appropriate sexual expression. Vocational adequacy presupposes the skills and knowledges sufficient for career success. Social relationships involve status and recognition by others; the alternatives are loneliness and dominance by others. Psychological stability requires a sense of security associated with personal confidence and a sense of purpose. Growth is the expression of creativity, curiosity, and pursuit of novelty. Attainment is the feeling of personal direction and responsibility.

Describing Education

Viewing education as teacher-pupil interactions directs attention to the use of experience to interpret the present and to increase the ability to direct and manage the future. For that reason, particularly, it seems preferable to think of education as the *formal and deliberate efforts of competent persons to enable learners to structure and manage experience so as to achieve balanced social and individual needs.* An expanded definition might be that education is the organization of subject matter and skills by teachers to stimulate intellectual operations and learner responses so that students might acquire and value physical comfort, psychological stability, vocational adequacy, and social relationships.

Motives for Programming

The operation of free, tax-supported education in the United States has been motivated by a national belief in and desire for a balance between social purpose and individual fulfillment. According to Kirk and Gallagher (1979), these general motives do not necessarily support the kind of individualization gifted and talented persons need. They point to the possible limiting effects of (1) egalitarianism, (2) universal education, (3) decentralization, and (4) social confidence.

Egalitarianism reflects the American ideal of equal education opportunity. Unfortunately, this ideal is too often translated as though equal means identical. The same education for all means poor education for those who are atypical, however. It is only recently that equality has come to be viewed as education equal to the individual's unique capacities.

Universal education means education available to everyone and required for everyone. In the history of American education, the mandatory age for school attendance has been progressively increasing. For example, in the early years, only third grade education was required. It increased to sixth and eighth grades by World War I. Most states now require attendance until ages 16 to 17. During this time, there has been a sharply increased awareness of pupil diversity, which has created a demand for alternatives in curriculum. Even so, the need to spread the benefits of education to everybody has slowed moves in the direction of differentiated education.

Decentralization gives the power over education to the individual states in the United States. Formal schooling is a national (or federal) responsibility in most countries of the world. The premise is that education is so significant that it requires a broad perspective and coordinated planning. By contrast, not only is American education a responsibility of the states, responsibility is usually further delegated to local school districts. One result is that nationwide coordinated effort and leadership are difficult to achieve. On the positive side, no school district is pressed into a common mold; there is freedom for individual initiative and innovation.

Social confidence reflects an attitude. Citizens who believe that resources are available to solve problems have a corollary confidence in their social institutions. When confidence in social institutions is lessened, there is a greater need to place confidence in persons. The latter has been an incentive for programming for the gifted and talented, as in the beginning of the race to explore space. When people are sanguine about the superiority of their culture's technical, artistic, scientific, and humanistic social institutions, however, there is less incentive to invest in the special education of leaders. That attitude can deter rather than foster the development of gifted and talented individuals, young or old.

THE SUBSTANCE OF QUALITY

Written documents such as school newsletters, yearbooks, alumni mailings, annual reports, budget requests, curriculum guides, and catalogues are used by schools to convey and describe the quality of their services. Bender (1975) compared these types of documents to advertisements and speculated as to how the Federal Trade Commission (FTC) might view such publications according to truth in packaging criteria. Although the tone was light, the Bender discussion is a thought-provoking perspective regarding quality.

Bender identified six areas that informed consumers could examine in printed material produced and distributed by schools: (1) accreditations, (2) claims and representations, (3) admissions, (4) preparation, (5) fees, and (6) disclosure. Parents, pupils, and the public might also examine these areas in gifted and talented programs.

Accreditation denotes approval by a recognized private organization or governmental unit. One evidence of quality in human services has been the willingness of an agency to be inspected by competent "outside" evaluators. Some schools claim membership in an organization. Some convert a limited approval to a blanket endorsement of *all* its component programs. Schools should be willing to document their claims to endorsement and the circumstances under which the accreditations apply, if they do, to programs for gifted and talented pupils.

Representations allow potential consumers to judge for themselves how well a program fulfills its mission. Bender identified four important factors in making such a judgment. The way in which the program is regarded by its current and past consumers is one. Reports of evaluations from alumni and higher education admission records could provide documentation. Faculty qualifications would be a second basis for judgment. Written records of staff competencies and role expectations should be available for inspection. Facilities are a third dimension, and their use and arrangements for their use should be described. A fourth element that should be examined is the nature of services. For example, do high school counselors actually communicate with and assist gifted and talented students with admissions to higher education institutions? Comprehensiveness may be claimed, but do services apply to all grade levels?

Admissions should reflect clear criteria. A test would be the uniformity with which criteria are applied. For example, it may be said that one criterion for admission to a gifted and talented program is an intelligence quotient (IQ) of 130, but that this criterion can be waived if there is sufficient documentation of outstanding performance or other estimates of potential. Inspection of records, however, might reveal that only the IQ is used.

Preparation refers to the program's role in fulfillment of occupational competence. For example, an advanced placement course should really mean that introductory courses will be waived upon college entrance. Course selection, enrichment activities, etc. should further occupational goals.

Fees involve costs to parents and/or pupils. A program may be perceived to be free to participants; however, hidden costs may later be discovered. For example, a music program may be seen as an enrichment service, but the parents learn afterwards that they are expected to furnish the uniform, buy the instrument, and arrange for "private" lessons by the music director. The parent of an elementary pupil may believe that an accelerated math program is available at the central high school. Only later does the parent learn that the costs of transportation and materials are their costs. Bender observed that the existence of costs is *not* the issue; the issue is suggesting "free" and then deferring explanations.

Disclosure is the match between declared goals and results. The rate of attrition from a program and reasons for it should be available to prospective candidates. Furthermore, what is expected of the student should be specified in advance, and statements of objectives must include criteria for their evaluation.

School documents are increasingly being viewed by regulatory agencies and the courts as contractual agreements. The standards that have regulated the private sector of education are being applied more and more frequently to public sector education. One implication is that schools must document self-proclaimed excellence and results. Tactics of evaluation and of the Individualized Education Program (IEP) are useful for documentation (see Chapter 6). The Bender guidelines support and reinforce ethical and honorable practices, since evaluative tactics serve to guide and improve services. Parents, students, participating teachers, and mentors will have little dispute with programs for gifted and talented pupils if their suggestions are welcomed and addressed.

A FRAMEWORK FOR QUALITY EDUCATION

The National/State Leadership Training Institute on the Gifted and Talented (1978) described a framework of high-quality education as follows:

> The hallmark of education for the gifted and talented is careful planning of individual opportunities for advanced learning which are suitable to exceptional minds and talents. Such education enhances development; it does not restrict or postpone. It accommodates the school to the students, rather than the reverse. In short, it recognizes the child's right to learn.
>
> Under special conditions, the public schools can competently provide for gifted and talented children and youth. Such special conditions could be: (1) well designed identification processes; (2) awareness and commitment on the part of school administrators as to the needs of the gifted and talented; (3) staff orientation and training to assist in identification and to support special services for them; (4) adequate human and material resources, including trained teachers, to meet the children's needs; (5) differentiated experiences and activities parallel to these needs with process strategies to carry out such provisions. (p. 2)

The institute (1978) listed essential activities for school districts in support of their framework: (1) planning and assessing needs; (2) securing stable funding; (3) informing policy makers regarding needs, including legislation; (4) maintaining awareness of current information; (5) providing in-service training for teachers; and (6) evaluating programs.

A RANGE OF OPTIONS

The options available to school districts for education of the gifted and talented are expanding. Each option must be studied to determine its benefit to the pupil and the program's capability to deliver. Selection of options at the school district level may be a compromise between available resources and pupil needs, as expressed in the IEP. A valuable outcome of the IEP process (see Unit V) and of needs assessment (see Chapter 10) is the documentation needed for subsequent improvement.

Maul (1978) has listed various alternatives of merit used in the public schools. Her concepts can be fitted into two interrelated groups of strategies: (1) those initiated by a teacher within the regular class and (2) those organized by a responsible program coordinator. Both emphasize matching learner and curriculum, and both need the assistance of the regular class teacher. Also, in both instances, the program coordinator consults with the pupil's teacher.

Available Alternatives within the Regular Class

Maul's (1978) variations are available, or are potentially available, to the pupil's regular teacher; they are summarized in Table 11-1. Each is based on an agreement between the pupil(s) and the teacher. Both parties clearly understand their responsibilities and expectations. Use of these strategies also affords opportunities for guidance and consideration of values. Procedures for scheduling of released time and for visitations must be established. The principal and/or program coordinator can be helpful in this area, as well as in the evaluation of the outcomes of these options.

Multiclass and District-Wide Alternatives

Other strategies involve larger spheres of cooperation. The same care must be taken with respect to individual prescription for the pupil, arrangement of schedules and resources, and evaluation. These options could be greatly facilitated by a program coordinator. The options that prevailed until recently are summarized in Table 11-2.

The alternatives of either the full-time, segregated special school or the special class in a regular school are "historical" options rather than valued options today. There has been an increasing emphasis on what the pupil does (program) rather than where the pupil is (place). Programs are now being implemented in the context of regular class attendance, with few exceptions. More and more special teachers seem to be deployed as consultant or resource teachers, advising and teaming with regular class teachers in elementary, middle and secondary schools.

UNDERSTANDING THE ATTRIBUTES OF QUALITY TEACHERS

Curriculum and Anticipation of the Future

Maker (1975) examined research to find the various roles involved in teaching gifted and talented pupils. Curriculum adapter was one of the roles identified. The most needed adaptations of the regular curriculum were those

---

Table 11-1 Examples of Individualized Education for Gifted and Talented Pupils Available to the Classroom Teacher*

Descriptor	Attributes	Pupil Benefits
Independent study / research projects	Learner studies, an advanced content area and / or advanced uses of research methodologies.	Standard curriculum is enriched. Acceleration may result if product can be used to waive requirements.
Accelerated units of study	Commercial sources and / or faculty developed Tables of Specifications can be introduced such as statistics within a regular math unit.	Student is freed from doing more of the same and allowed advanced study within his or her own competence.
Team teaching	Teachers arrange their schedules so as to be available to students with specific interests. Availability could be addressed to seminars, lectures, demonstrations, and / or visitations.	Pupil(s) are in early contact with appropriate role models. Teachers do not have to be all things to all people; they are free to pursue their strengths.
Mentor	Competent volunteers, parents, lay persons, teachers agree to meet for regular periods for specific purposes with gifted and talented pupil(s).	Student is introduced to a new field of interest, or student's special interests are defined and stabilized.
Service projects	Students are engaged in activities of service to others within and external to the schools. Pupils may be engaged as tutors, teacher aides, tour guides, production assistants, etc.	Opportunities for leadership and the satisfactions of service are provided, and career choices may be stabilized.

*Adapted from Maul (1978).

Table 11-2 Examples of Cooperative Arrangements*

Descriptor	Attributes	Pupil Outcomes
Multiage grouping	Pupils are grouped together within reasonable age spans based upon common interests. Emphasis is upon the standard curriculum for enhancement of skills. A leader, or head teacher, schedules the use of human and material resources.	Contact with psychological peers allows for stimulation and mutual encouragement.
Clustering	Pupils attend a cluster/magnet school that serves a designated geographical area. Typical practice is to schedule two one-half day sessions with a qualified teacher who has four groups per week with the remainder of time devoted to consultation. Regular teachers are involved in pupil instruction. Sometimes this method is termed *Resource Room*.	Outcomes are similar to those of multiage grouping. Minicourses, workshops, and seminars may be used. Method may be helpful in sparsely populated districts.
Special talent center	This method involves, usually, a central facility that houses a program devoted to some grouping of interests. Pupils spend most of their time within the regular school setting. Area vocational technical schools may be used. Institutions of higher education might sponsor such centers as well.	Opportunities that might not otherwise be available to pursue interests are provided, and use of resources is maximized.
Itinerant teacher	A qualified specialist travels on a scheduled basis from assigned school to assigned school. The itinerant teacher usually spends one day per week in each school. Time is spent with groups defined by age, grade, readiness, interests, etc. to pursue projects. Regular teacher is responsible for the standard program.	Opportunities are provided to interact with a helpful role model and to pursue interests not normally covered in the standard curriculum. Interaction with highly motivated students is another benefit.
Consultation	Emphasis is upon consultation with (not dictation to or domination of) the teacher of each identified pupil. Consultation centers upon the preparation, implementation, and evaluation	

Defining the Educational Context of Quality 185

Table 11-2 continued

Descriptor	Attributes	Pupil Outcomes
	of the pupil's Individualized Education Program. The consultant may also provide appropriate inservice opportunities as requested/needed by the teacher.	Student has the opportunity for an appropriate and individualized education that fulfills the Individualized Education Program.
Mentor	Needs of a pupil are matched with a competent role model who may/may not be an educator.	Benefits are similar to those described for mentor in Table 11-1.

*Adapted from Maul (1978).

that encouraged creativity, an understanding of value systems, the development of skill at acquiring knowledge, and the ability to make sound predictions. These are summarized in Table 11-3. Teachers were urged to examine their existing curriculum content in light of those attributes. For example, the study of American history can be an opportunity to prepare for the future. The *Mayflower Compact* can be studied by recreating the circumstances to show how the need for the document arose from events. The creativity of these new settlers in adjusting to new conditions and agreeing to regulate

Table 11-3 Curriculum Adaptations for Futuristic Attributes

Theme	Characteristics of Successful Adaptation
Creativity	Learning alternatives for interpersonal relationships
	Learning alternatives for earning a living
	Learning to protect oneself from an alien environment
Values systems	Understanding the process of valuing
	Understanding why persons hold different values
	Understanding and resolving conflicts in values
	Acknowledging the values of others
Acquiring knowledge	Learning to locate information
	Sorting relevant data from the superficial
	Applying knowledge in proper context
	Coping with obsolete information
	Avoiding misleading and erroneous information
	Recognizing the need for continuing learning
Prediction	Anticipating the consequences of present actions
	Pre-planning actions to solve problems
	Increasing reaction time to new events
	Learning procedures necessary to regulate technology

their behavior can be illustrated. The compact itself sets forth a system for valuing participatory democracy. Pupils can examine the content and the theory base of the compact. The utility of the document to predict subsequent events could be another area for application.

The quality of a curriculum may be judged, in part, by the accuracy with which the educational experience enables the gifted and talented pupil to anticipate and predict the future. Maker's features of creativity, values, knowledge, and prediction can certainly be influenced by teachers as they work in the context of whatever curriculum is in use in their schools.

Attributes of High-Quality Teachers

Bishop (1976) reported the opinions of gifted and talented students about their teachers. The students were drawn from a pool of participants in a statewide honors program, and each was asked to nominate his or her "best" teacher in high school. That yielded 109 teachers, called the Identified Group (IG). Bishop then identified persons who had been teachers of those participants, but who had not been nominated. These, called the Validity Sample (VS), numbered 97. Additionally, 30 teachers from the IG sample were randomly selected for in-depth interviews. Bishop's purpose was to compare the IG group with the VS group to discover differences and similarities between the two. The VS served for verification. Specific comparisons were made as to:

1. personal and social traits
2. educational philosophy
3. classroom behaviors and practices

Bishop found that teachers in the IG group had a mean IQ of 128 as measured by Wechsler Adult Intelligence Scale and scored especially high on verbal abilities. Verbal interests were also reflected in the IG group by their greater membership in book clubs, high rates of magazine subscriptions, and greater use of library facilities for personal use. Other evidence of the verbal-intellectual interest of the IG group was that their desire to increase their own intellectual growth was given as one reason for their choice of teaching as a career. They also had maintained continuous enrollment in college courses beyond college graduation.

Achievement motivation was a significant variable. Teachers in the IG group had higher grade point averages in professional courses and in the subject matter courses of their teaching specialty. They frequently reported that they had enjoyed school as students and that they had been encouraged to select teaching as a career. On the Edwards Personal Preference Schedule they scored higher on items related to needs to (1) do their best, (2) accomplish a difficult task well, (3) be able to do things better than others, and (4) accomplish tasks that require skill and effort.

Personal variables that did *not* reflect differences were age, sex, and number of years of teaching experience. Experienced teachers and beginning teachers were equally represented. Nor were there any differences with respect to marital status, degree held, institution attended (e.g., public versus private, teachers' college versus liberal arts), course work preparation, and extent of association with professional associations.

The IG sample reflected more positive attitudes toward the gifted and talented; they strongly preferred teaching such pupils. The VS group were more likely to reject this type of assignment and state preferences for teaching average, slow learning, or retarded pupils.

Perceptions of the role of a teacher were assessed by requesting the teachers to write brief essays describing effective and ineffective episodes. The IG group were concerned about (1) motivating students to study, (2) motivating students to want to think independently, and (3) instilling an interest and appreciation in their subject matter and learning in general. The VS group, in contrast, were interested in subject matter attainment; they saw effective and ineffective teaching in terms of pupil achievement.

Classroom practices were assessed by analysis of the reasons that the gifted and talented pupils nominated a particular teacher. Frequent descriptors were (1) stimulation, motivation, and inspiration; (2) presentation of subject matter in an interesting manner; (3) encouragement of interests and participation; (4) enthusiasm for the subject/course; and (5) demonstration of interest in the pupil as a person. Teachers in the IG sample were also described as responsible, systematic, business-like, and organized in their behavior. The VS teachers, by contrast, were described as evasive, unorganized, slipshod, and routine.

Bishop suggested that these findings have implications for teacher preparation programs and for selection and assignment of faculty. It was his conclusion that such assignments should not be made as rewards for seniority or as a way to vary the work of teachers who usually teach average and retarded children.

Chapter 12

Developing High-Quality Programs

COMMON QUESTIONS ABOUT STARTING PROGRAMS

Often the parents, teachers, and school board of a local district wish to do "something" about the community's ablest children, but no one is certain how to proceed. Trezise (1976) identified the questions that most perplexed school personnel who wished to start local programs. Based on these questions, Trezise recommended that the first step would be to determine if there is a state plan that either specifies requirements or provides guidelines. If so, such a plan should clarify many questions about (1) philosophy of education of the gifted and talented, (2) definition of the population to be served, (3) staff requirements, (4) certification, (5) in-service training, (6) funding, (7) program options, and (8) the state's expectations regarding performance objectives.

State plans ordinarily allow and encourage adaptation to local circumstances. They can be especially helpful to local district program planners in:

1. managing learning when the pupil leaves the regular program for a part of the day only to discover the teacher expects "missed" work to be made up.
2. identifying criteria for program enrollment, such as (a) achievement scores, (b) group intelligence quotient (IQ), (c) individual IQ scores, (d) teacher nominations, (e) parent nominations, (f) cumulative records, (g) performances and products of the pupil, (h) self-reports, and (i) creativity tests.
3. clarifying the responsibility for determining eligibility of pupils when, as is often the case, the obligation is lodged in a selection committee.
4. specifying the role and membership of an advisory committee. Such a committee could recommend a local definition of gifted and talented pupils, the age levels(s) at which to initiate programs, extensiveness of

189

the first steps, the proportion of all pupils to be enrolled, curriculum emphases (e.g., arts, academic, science), behavioral goals (e.g., leadership, critical thinking, creativity, academic skills, and broadening of interests).

5. achieving congruence among definitions of gifted and talented learners, identification procedures, and program content.

6. specifying evaluation criteria for program effectiveness. Programs sometimes falter and fade because vague expectations make evaluation impotent.

7. selecting organization for instruction options. *This, today, usually means identifying or creating ways to ensure the appropriate individualized mix of curricular and extracurricular enrichment, plus age and subject acceleration.*

8. obtaining funds and staffing. Trezise favored state reimbursement for the salaries of consultants and other support persons rather than funding based on a gifted and talented pupil "head count" or on a count of "hours in program" or on program approval for "units." Better still than reimbursement is advance funding. Consultants should be eligible for joint state-local funding, too. Other reimbursable costs ought to include in-service training, planning grants, and "seed money" for a first year start-up. Other expenses would best be allocated from the local district budget.

9. providing in-service training. Such training would include (a) attention to the literature on the gifted and talented student, (b) comprehensive planning for the school district, and (c) "change agenting" skills to improve staff capabilities for implementation strategies.

Trezise's (1976) resumé certainly should, if updated, expanded, and applied in local terms, help to minimize confusion. Attention to these nine questions should be repaid in permanence, substance, and stability of program.

ORGANIZING FOR INNOVATION

Starting Points

Ward (1962) pressed for psychoeducational and psychosocial perspectives on the planning and organization of programs for gifted and talented pupils. He was among the earliest to note that acceleration, ability grouping, enrichment, and independent study are descriptors for administrative arrangements or procedures; they do not describe the program. The intent of administrative procedures and policies, according to Ward, should be to facilitate and nurture the sound education of gifted and talented pupils. Consequently, program options ought to be adapted to pupils rather than the reverse. Barbe (1965), too, observed early that arguments regarding the relative merits of enrichment versus acceleration or ability grouping versus mixed groupings neglect a central issue. These options are the means, not the ends. Also, as Reynolds and Birch (1977) urged, individualization in the regular class should have first priority. Attention should be directed to the nature of learning environments and the processes involved in achieving favorable outcomes for individual pupils, not to relatively meaningless expressions (Sellin & Birch, 1980; Whitmore, 1980).

Lanza and Vassar (1972) advocate looking to the unmet needs of gifted and talented pupils as the most justifiable starting point for development of programs. Programs that are initiated without regard to the needs of pupils have very short histories. For example, a district may launch a "course" in computer science without any survey of student needs, interests, aptitudes, and readiness. Then, a year or two later, everyone wonders what happened to the original enthusiasm. Instead, Lanza and Vassar suggest that program objectives should be derived from an assessment of the nature and needs of the pupils to be served. Furthermore, they are quite specific in their advocacy of parent involvement. They also advanced the point that it is essential to balance the program intentions in regard to age levels, subject matter, and performance areas.

Key Features

Renzulli (1975) reported a survey and analysis of key features of high-quality programs based upon an opinion survey of recognized authorities. He deduced 16 common features from his literature search. This list in turn was submitted to a panel of 21 experts, whose task was to assign rank order priorities to the 16 features. The 21 persons had been nominated by their peers as the most qualified to respond to this type of task. Statistical evaluation of the data revealed consistent agreement among the panel members, which was interpreted as validating the existence of key features.

Several items surfaced as high-priority features in the opinions of the panel of experts. Table 12-1 contains the seven highest priority features. Table 12-2 summarizes two types of information: those features rated by the panel and those submitted by the panel but not on the original list.

The report is notable for its neutrality. For example, the text merely states that the panel selected the teacher as a key feature most frequently. The sponsoring agency must specify its own criteria for role definition and related

Table 12-1 Key Features of Programs for the Gifted*

Feature	Rank Values	Rank**
Teacher	274	1
Curriculum	240	2
Student selection	220	3
Statement of philosophy and objectives	208	4
Staff orientation	200	5
Plan of evaluation	139	6
Administrative responsibility	125	7

*Adapted from Renzulli (1975).
**It must be emphasized that all seven features are essential to a sound, high-quality program.

Table 12-2 Useful and Helpful Additional Features of Programs for the Gifted*

Features of Usefulness	Rank Order of Features
Guidance services	95
Ability grouping / acceleration	92
Special equipment / facilities	73
Use of community resources	50
Early admission	41
Community interpretation	40
Supplementary expenditures	35
A program of research	25

Features of Helpfulness	Number of Vote ($n = 21$)
Community support for quality education	10/21
Morale and esprit de corps	9/21
Student assessment and reassessment	9/21
Student performance evaluation and reporting	10/21
Interpretation to parents and selected students	9/21
Small and flexible groups	13/21
Pupil interpretation / recognition	13/21

*Adapted from Renzulli (1975).

qualifications. Although the report does not identify specific curriculum objectives, it does urge that objectives be identified. The chief value of the Renzulli report is that it identifies a manageable universe of the features to be considered by prospective participants. The list of features can be used as a checklist for participants to order their priorities, inventory their resources, and establish first steps for action.

UNDERSTANDING THE TACTICS OF INNOVATION

Innovation, as used here, means the introduction of change within a system for the purpose of improving services. The person who engages in this process is known as an innovator or a change agent. Innovation (or change agentry) is called for in substantial amounts if comprehensive, enduring programs of high quality are to be widely and successfully initiated.

Background for Innovation

Much useful knowledge and skill concerning tactics and strategies of innovation have been accumulated. This body of procedures and information can be used to start and guide social action, innovations processes, and community organization. Change agentry or innovation often begins with the mobilization of resources (human and material) in a purposeful, organized effort to achieve an outcome of proved worth on behalf of a person(s) who would not otherwise be able to effect change. It involves planning and selection of tactics that are democratic, persuasive, honorable, and respectful of human dignity.

The Nature of Influence

The literature of change agentry isolates five common elements of the process: (1) sources of influence, (2) the impact of actors, (3) the design of a plan, (4) selection of tactics, and (5) permanence of change.

Influence is a form of power; it can be employed to alter the behavior of another person or group. There are two broad types—authority and prestige. The former is vested and sanctioned by a title, a job, or position and confirmed by law or policy. Prestige, in contrast, is informal; a person or group earns influence through competence, representation of constituents, friendship patterns, warmth of personality, or experience. Effective change agentry uses both sources of influence. In certain instances, change agentry originates with a power base in prestige, and agents seek to secure authority for programs for the gifted and talented. In other instances, a person of authority may mobilize the support of persons with prestige to gain the widest acceptance of the proposed gifted and talented program.

The Actors of Innovation

The three actor roles are termed: legitimizer, active participant, and change agent. Legitimizers are persons of authority who can exercise the veto. Their opposition, resistance, or apathy can be fatal. Legitimizers are susceptible to influence, however, and give meaningful support if favorably inclined. Persons with prestige can also be legitimizers, since they can often influence persons of authority. Active participants are persons who believe in the proposed plan and are willing to furnish the time, skills, and resources necessary to help execute program objectives. They can be volunteers; they can be paid staff. Such persons are influential by sanction or by endorsement of persons with either type of influence.

The change agent is the informed and convinced person, or nucleus of persons, who provides leadership, sense of mission, and encouragement to sustain effort. The change agent(s) organizes planning, involves the actors, mobilizes tactics of change, monitors process, and seeks out resources. Skill and motivation characterize the change agent.

Routes of Influence

The change agent recognizes that influence can flow down or up. It can be a jet stream or a trickle. The change agent also recognizes that influence can be regulatory or consultative and that both dimensions require flexibility. These sources are depicted in Figure 12-1. The trickle-down approach views change as emerging from policy makers of authority and prestige. Legitimizers become important first considerations. This approach *may be* effective when there is a tradition of centralization of policy formulation. The trickle-down approach depends upon a regulatory, formal system for operation.

The trickle-up approach is illustrated by grassroots movement. It recognizes that an initial effort can spread with a ripple effect. It does not ordinarily emerge from a well-defined base; it seeks to diffuse its influence into the widest possible spheres. Most useful in decentralized systems, it employs the tactics of infiltration and consultation to achieve change.

Neither of the sources is "good" or "bad." They are only different approaches. As Figure 12-1 suggests, regardless of approach, the teacher and the learner occupy center stage of interest and importance.

It is sometimes tempting to envy states and even nations with legislative mandates. Such mandates do not guarantee progress, however, since the vigilance of change agentry is required in any event. Experience demonstrates that persuasion by example, consultation, and open negotiation are the most valued approaches to acceptance and permanence for programs on behalf of the gifted and talented.

Innovation as a Significant Role for Teachers

The innovator's options for bringing about change may include modification of (1) student behavior, (2) parents' attitudes, (3) the resources and staff

Figure 12-1 Routes of Influence

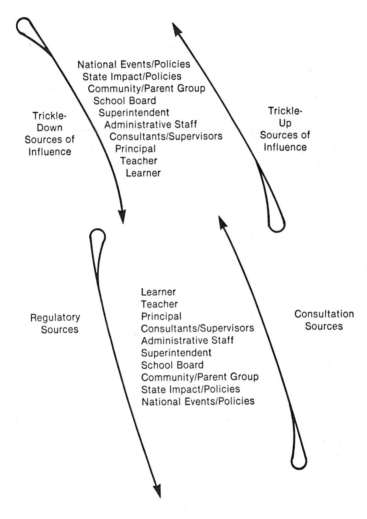

National Events/Policies
State Impact/Policies
Community/Parent Group
School Board
Superintendent
Administrative Staff
Consultants/Supervisors
Principal
Teacher
Learner

Trickle-
Down
Sources of
Influence

Trickle-
Up
Sources of
Influence

Learner
Teacher
Principal
Consultants/Supervisors
Administrative Staff
Superintendent
School Board
Community/Parent Group
State Impact/Policies
National Events/Policies

Regulatory
Sources

Consultation
Sources

of a school district, (4) policies of the school district, and (5) personal performance. Maker (1975) observed that one attribute of the successful change agent on behalf of gifted and talented pupils is the ability to generate alternatives that are valid modifications of an existing situation. Some teachers accept that role readily.

Innovation as Problem Solving

An innovation is usually the product of change. Figure 12-2 displays a scope and sequence model in the application of problem solving to produce innovation or change. According to Maker, the steps might best be viewed as interdependent stages. Figure 12-2 can also serve as a model for describing progress. The sequence could be summarized as follows:

1. Identification of a Concern

When confronted with a significant discrepancy between what is and what should be, the innovator acknowledges a personal responsibility to initiate change and to undertake the process. At this level, specificity is not required.

Figure 12-2 A Model for Innovation in Programming*

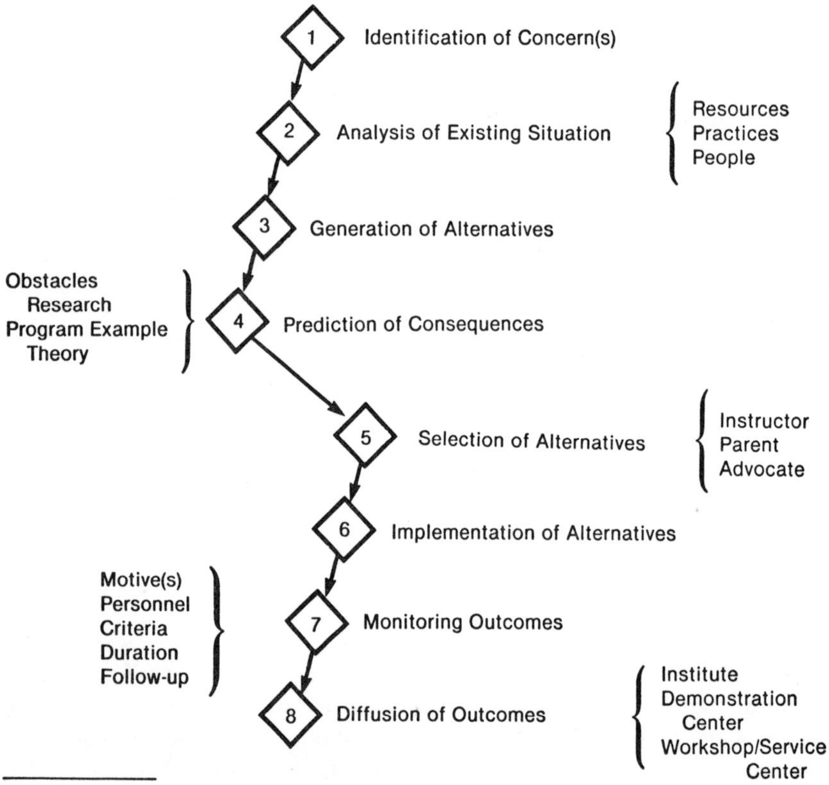

1 Identification of Concern(s)

2 Analysis of Existing Situation
   { Resources
     Practices
     People

3 Generation of Alternatives

Obstacles
Research
Program Example } 4 Prediction of Consequences
Theory

5 Selection of Alternatives
   { Instructor
     Parent
     Advocate

6 Implementation of Alternatives

Motive(s)
Personnel
Criteria } 7 Monitoring Outcomes
Duration
Follow-up

8 Diffusion of Outcomes
   { Institute
     Demonstration
     Center
     Workshop/Service
     Center

*Adapted from Maker (1975).

2. Analysis of Existing Situation

Formal and informal investigations unearth persons who are potential helpers. Some have the influence to motivate others; some have the authority to allocate resources. Others are willing to commit time, effort, and skills to carry out assignments. A few may combine all those virtues. The problem is sufficiently defined and clarified in this stage, too, so key expectations are made plain and outcomes for accomplishments can be charted.

3. Generation of Alternatives

The people from Step 2 are involved in the production of possible solutions to the concern highlighted in Step 1. It is helpful to produce a variety of possible paths to a solution. Premature criticism may blunt the open creativity needed at this point. These steps can be the product of needs assessment (see Chapter 10) also.

4. Prediction of Consequences

During the prediction stage, alternatives are subjected to examination, criticism, and refinement. Each alternative is weighed in terms of scientific supporting evidence, expert opinion, and practical experience. Potential obstacles are considered.

5. Selection of Alternatives

Maker (1975) suggests that alternatives can be grouped according to style. The parent style implies nurture, the advocate style suggests a partnership among participants to effect change, and the instructor style reduces problems to task elements and appeals to rationality. An alternative that depends heavily upon advocacy may be best. Maker is correct in the observation that teachers have too often been viewed as objects to be changed rather than as sources of change and reform. To involve educators, many of them teachers, as advocates could be the most fruitful alternative.

6 and 7. Implementation of Alternatives and Monitoring Outcomes

Implementation and monitoring are combined since their content is similar. The description of an alternative, in its most elegant form, includes goals expressed as criteria for success and resources to be assembled to overcome or bypass potential obstacles. Possible motives, sources of influence, and incentives for change are detailed. An agenda, or time line, can be helpful both for planning and for progress reports. Finally, provision for amendments and follow-up activities is made.

8. Diffusion of Outcomes

Moving one or more of the alternatives into action is the diffusion stage. It is evident that each step builds on the ones before it. If each step is a solid one, the foundation has been laid for a sound program structure for gifted and talented pupils.

Tactics of Innovation on Behalf of the Gifted and Talented

Three different tactics for innovation are the institute, the center, and the workshop. It was Maker's observation that educators of the gifted and talented must be drawn from the ranks of those already engaged in teaching, and each of these three alternatives operates on that premise.

The summer institute usually has its major impact on attitude rather than skill. Teachers who have attended institutes are more likely to (1) develop class interest centers, (2) offer a local district version of the institute to colleagues, (3) make proposals for special education projects for gifted and talented pupils funded from outside agencies, (4) modify subject matter curriculum for gifted and talented students, and (5) individualize instruction for gifted and talented pupils. There are three activities in an institute approach that appear particularly helpful: (1) self-assessment by participants that parallels values clarification procedures; (2) opportunities for direct contact with gifted and talented pupils, as in practice teaching; and (3) modeling. If the institute sponsors practice what they preach, modeling is done in forms such as small and large group instruction, minicourses, multioptions for evaluation, guided independent study, and activity-oriented learning.

A demonstration center facilitates observation of high-quality, illustrative practices. It is also a resource for visitation and inspection. Benefits derived from demonstration centers are similar to those found in the institute approach, namely, an increase in gifted and talented pupils served, more sophisticated proposals, diversity in program options within one school district, and up-grading of curriculum content. It has been difficult, however, to transport the excellent practices of centers into the home district in either the same or an adapted form. The difficulties of matching the model center exactly to the circumstances of a particular local school system are evident. Assistance of the center staff is needed if "new" practices are to be incorporated into an existing school structure.

The workshop approaches were likened by Maker to a service center approach. Consultation and technical assistance are provided to the district staff on site. The assistance can be provided by one person or a team. A team composed of a "talent bank" committee is usually favored. Positive outcomes from workshops include wider involvement of teachers in training and wider adoption of practices. Success in this approach appears dependent upon (1) endorsement by top administrators, (2) released time from teaching or other duties or paid additional time for participants, (3) gifted and talented pupils and parents as participant-consultants, and (4) skill of workshop leaders in organizing local resources.

In summary, carefully planned tactics of change can influence modifications of practice. Regardless of approach, greater empathy toward the gifted and talented individual results from this kind of deliberate intervention. However, adoption and implementation of new practices remain the key issues. University or college instruction, model centers, and in-service consultation and workshops have their place. The task for research and evaluation is to achieve a greater fit between tactic and intended audience.

Innovation forcefully compels attention to the principle that teachers are not objects to be manipulated. Maker's review is a vivid reminder to agents of change to respect individualization of approach for gifted and talented persons. This same respect and individualization should be evident for teachers.

Sustaining Beliefs

Innovation requires persistence in the face of apathy and resistance. Consequently, it is well to reflect on certain beliefs that have sustained agents of change. These may be stated as follows:

- Change is possible.

- Alliances are helpful.

- Be for a cause, not merely against the present situation.

- Equate change with extended opportunity, removal of inequity, and affirmation of rights or privileges.

- Offer positive incentives, not threats.

Discouragement must be resisted, of course, and remembering these points may help to renew both enthusiasm and resolve. Also, in change agentry, there probably are no minor successes. Even the slightest movement in a preferred direction can be highly significant. Sometimes shifting the position of one log unlocks what had seemed an immovable jam.

Chapter 13

Developing a Confederacy for the Gifted and Talented

AN OPEN SYSTEM

The obstacles that impede educational programs for the gifted and talented can be identified and overcome. The need is to create an open system for service delivery (Uhler, 1977). Such a system would be the opposite of the "two box" system that has developed in many countries, with special education in one box and the rest of education in the other box (Reynolds & Birch, 1977).

Closed systems are separate from the rest of the school system; they are in the schools, but not of the schools. The isolation and compartmentalization of the program establish territorial claims. Domination is by a tight group of "insiders." No other individuals or groups are allowed to, encouraged to, or sanctioned to participate. Parents are expected to rubber-stamp specialist-teacher decisions. The closed system very often is based on the idea that a good program for gifted and talented children can have little in common with "ordinary" education.

An open system, in contrast, is a confederacy for the gifted and talented. Talents, abilities, and skills both internal and external to the educational community are tapped. The open system is built on the lessons learned from the careers of eminent persons such as Leonard Bernstein, Winston Churchill, John Dewey, Thomas Edison, Albert Einstein, Helen Hayes, Ernest Hemingway, Martin Luther King, Jr., Pablo Picasso, and Babe Ruth, who shared a common history of *early* affiliation with a capable and nurturing adult. They were allowed freedom to pursue worthwhile interests and experienced early success. Schools with open systems reach out for help from all educators and community members to join in implementing rich lessons in the life experiences of individual gifted and talented pupils.

The formal internship was one example cited by Uhler (1977). In this context, internship means a mutual venture among a school representative, a student, and an adult in a specialized occupation. The curriculum content is made up of guided and independent research and development projects that are conducted in close harmony among the three participants. It focuses upon occupational roles and responsibilities. Examples of appropriate pairing are the art student with a commercial illustrator, the biology student with a veterinarian, and the math student with the civil engineer. It is possible to formalize internships on local levels, too.

Exploratory partnerships are more informal than internships. The goal is to establish an interaction with an adult of similar interests and aptitude. This option calls for evaluation by the educator, the learner, the parent, and the adult. Its outcome, too, should be enhancement of experience and enrichment of knowledge and understanding.

Mentoring calls for the systematic use of gifted and talented pupils as mentors and assistant teachers for all sorts of people within the school and within the community; a service dimension is built into the program. Professional educators instruct gifted and talented pupils in teaching methods that they (the pupils) then employ under teacher supervision. These methods, for example, could be related to literacy skills for age peers and younger pupils. As with other options, there would be monitoring, evaluation, and goals to be pursued. In this way, others benefit from the skills of the gifted and talented learner, while the social responsibility and humanistic dimensions of the gifted and talented learner are enriched.

All of these options should be used in a way that allows the gifted and talented learner to earn academic credit toward graduation. Credit could either be given in substitution for standard courses or granted for electives. In any event, the professional educator would have a central role in management of the options.

SUPPORT SYSTEMS

Defining a Support System

Consultants, supervisors, coordinators, directors, and allied nondirect service roles are worthwhile only to the degree that they help teachers and pupils. According to Gallagher (1978), the support system should be based upon (1) consultation rather than regulation, (2) orderly activity rather than random exchange, (3) collective planning rather than imposition, and (4) verifiable recommendations rather than transitory fads.

The Gallagher exposition is helpful both to the individual charged with program direction and to the individuals serving as advisors. The theme is that a support system ought to supply an organized means for maintaining high-quality services:

> The objectives behind support elements are simple enough to define: to generate, transform, and deliver valid ideas and skills to the people who deliver direct educational assistance to children and their families. (p. 134)

Those in support systems ought to know their consumers' ideals, needs, ideas, and competencies. Since the motivation for excellence most often comes from individual teachers, a measure of the effectiveness of support services is the extent to which the individual teacher's desire for excellence can be incorporated into policy decisions. Moreover, the support system ought to deliver individualized assistance to its consumers through in-service training.

Elements of a Support System

Gallagher listed four elements of support systems for the educator: (1) research and development, (2) demonstration, (3) personnel preparation, and (4) technical assistance. Research and development originate with the discovery and/or location of knowledge and culminate with the synthesis of the knowledge into products and/or skills. These activities usually begin in higher education settings or in research and development units within school districts, intermediate/county districts, or state departments of education. Demonstration is the illustration and evaluation of results obtained from research and development. A higher education facility may use a laboratory school as a demonstration center; during the 1960s and 1970s, some public schools were designated as demonstration centers. During demonstrations, further verification and refinement of practice take place.

Personnel preparation can be both pre-service and in-service. More and more, such preparation is becoming a collaborative effort between institutions of higher education and school districts. At pre-service levels, preparation involves instruction and internships supervised by master practitioners in local settings. In-service preparation can lead to continuing certification and advanced degrees. In any event, the provision of internships (full-time under supervision) or externships (on-the-job supervision) is essential. The interaction between these institutions of higher education and school districts is a source of strength through cross-fertilization of ideas.

Technical assistance is systematic consultation with short-range training objectives. It is not uncommon, for instance, for higher education faculty members to share their know-how with public school colleagues. More typically, the person responsible for the gifted and talented program will be charged to (1) assess a faculty's needs for assistance based upon direct interviews/observations, (2) organize tactics, and (3) evaluate consequences. Technical assistance is effective and helpful to the extent that teachers see improvement in day-to-day instruction by consciously modifying previous practice. Consequently, teachers must be involved in the planning and operation of technical assistance. Furthermore, teachers, as part of their commitment to high quality, should demand technical assistance. Otherwise, school resources may too easily be diverted into other functions.

Gallagher (1978) reminds us that technical assistance is organized service designed:

> to improve the competence of educational service delivery personnel by increasing their management, organizational, or program skills; and/or their available information relative to their multiple skills of educational service delivery to students. (p. 139)

Helpful tactics for improvement can include *at least* the following:

- a talent bank. The bank account is an inventory of the skills, judgments, and experiences of the faculty and staff. This inventory can also include names and special abilities of personnel and resources outside the educational community.

- memorandum of understanding. This is a written communication between the parties giving and receiving technical assistance. It spells out the agreements on what (e.g., workshop, visitation) will be delivered, under what circumstances (e.g., credit/noncredit, in-school, paid or voluntary), for how long, and criteria for determining when assistance is no longer needed.

- evaluation. This begins with some form of needs assessment and ends with a determination of whether and to what extent the needs were met. The main task of technical assistance is to deal with the educator's concerns until they are satisfactorily resolved.

Translating Knowledge into Action

The overall purpose of a support system is the translation of knowledge into action. In the language of evaluation, support systems should have impact; in operational terms, support systems should make a positive, constructive difference to teachers and pupils. Gallagher (1978) uses a model to identify five stages of translation. The person responsible for the gifted and talented program in a school system can use the stages as a checklist. Table 13-1 traces

Table 13-1 Stages in Translation of Knowledge into Practice*

Stage and Its Descriptor	Characteristics of the Stage	Assessment Questions
I. Discovery of knowledge	New facts, ideas, and concepts about learners, practices, or service systems are generated. Previous information may be affirmed.	Where is the information available within the region or the school district? Who has access to it?
II. Knowledge applied to target group	Stage I data are applied to learners and their families by scientists with competence and knowledge about gifted and talented persons.	Who has conducted the research? What confidence can be placed in their results?
III. Generation of systematic programming for the gifted and talented	Stage II results are applied to the specific needs, developmental levels, and problems of the gifted and talented under controlled circumstances.	What materials, products, and/or skills were verified?
IV. Field testing	Stage III results are tested in realistic settings. Evaluation is adequate to demonstrate validity to practitioners and policy makers.	How do these results work in our district? Who could use them?
V. General adaptation and/or adaptation to the field	Verification from Stage IV is sufficient to produce common agreement for wide adoption. The new is transformed into common, or formal, practice.	Does the information exist in our district? What evidence exists to identify its use?

*Adapted from Gallagher (1978).

a pathway of translation encountered in the process of innovation. Stage I discoveries do not march smoothly toward Stage V, however. The main barriers are breakdowns in communication among the participants within each stage. In addition, any inattention to evaluation leaves doubts about validity.

It is obviously helpful if there is a trusting relationship and a professional fellowship among those who seek improvement. It can be mutually beneficial to institutions of higher education and local school districts to cooperate in Stage II, III, and IV processes because they would both have early access to complementary sources of information about improvement. The model can be helpful for assessment of the knowledge and practice currently in place, as well as for identification of future needs.

Funding

A major barrier to support services is inadequate funding. Money is usually channeled toward direct services to pupils. Gallagher and many others agree that financial incentives are essential if support services are to promote quality and furnish a continuing knowledge base for implementation. Subsidies should be available from state and federal sources, as well as from private sector sources, for support services.

BUILDING PROGRAM AND BUDGET

The Context

Because of the competition for state and/or federal grants, ends (goals) and means (resources) must be closely examined. All program costs, from start-up to evaluation, can best be justified if there is early attention to these questions. Furthermore, the maintenance of high quality requires attention to results, including the cost/quality interaction. Many tools are available to educators and to school systems to guide and shape rational decision making. Common examples are Management by Objectives (MBO) and Program-Planning-Budget Systems (PPBS). The initial promise of these budgeting systems sometimes evaporated because their advocates failed either to communicate or to demonstrate their potential for helpfulness.

Spillane and Levenson (1978) recommended MBO, wherein resources can be matched to goals. The process can be especially helpful in defining the relationship of "special" programs for the gifted and talented pupils to the overall context of general education. In their description of the MBO process, several attributes emerge. MBO is a team effort; participants include teachers, parents, staff, students, and members of the community. Second, MBO is characterized by clear, written, and measurable goals and objectives. Third, MBO is characterized by positive incentives to its participants. Finally, MBO requires careful assistance for its participants. Every school budget has its "item number series." For example, all control office expenses may be coded 100, instruction (including teachers' salaries) 200, supplies and equipment, etc. 300, and so on. MBO makes it possible to understand and relate resources (especially the dollar cost of time) to the aspirations of the district.

The Elements

A goal, according to Spillane and Levenson, sets forth a broad, long-range ideal. An objective is a short-range, measurable achievement, one of the steps by which a goal is attained. For example, to improve reading levels would be a goal, while to improve reading levels by three months at third grade would be an objective. Goals would be applicable throughout a district; objectives would be applicable in either particular buildings or particular programs.

MBO is intended to maximize freedom, autonomy, and creativity. Although the process calls for a certain common adherence to goals, objectives can vary. Spillane and Levenson described one district in which the goal was to design instruction according to the diversity of individual student learning styles. Within that school district, one school chose to institute individualized assessment to guide teaching tactics, while another school emphasized open classroom processes with peer-assisted learning. Both schools declared their objectives and shared their results.

Incentives are resources provided to participants so that they can pursue goals. Two types of incentives have emerged in school practice—the minigrant and the block grant. Usually five to ten percent of the school budget, or some fixed amount per teacher or per building, is set aside. Individual teachers can petition for support to implement their own projects up to a fixed amount. A block grant is awarded to an individual school for a special purpose. In each instance, the participant(s) are required to specify objectives and means of evaluation. Grants of either type allow for purchase of material as well as the part-time employment of persons with special skills. This is a positive step in the direction of decentralizing authority in school systems, a direction that has much to commend it.

Team effort requires orientation, which should involve the following basic steps:

1. After needs assessment and consultation with teachers and the public, the board of education declares district goals, which then become a matter of public record. Budget requests by principals and program directors are submitted in line with goals. This procedure matches resources to goals through auditing numeration, a code for showing which funds relate to which goals.

2. The office of the superintendent specifies administrative and staff responsibilities for goals, also based on consultation with teachers and with the public.

3. Goals and objectives are set for each school, and the principal is delegated the responsibility of supporting staff goals and objectives.

4. Control office resources necessary to implement school goals and objectives are specified and requested.

5. A plan of work as to time line, activities, and evaluation criteria to achieve objectives is prepared, again with faculty and parent participation.

A Plan of Work

In planning for talented and gifted children and youth, the preparation of objectives may be more difficult for administrators than for teachers, who are accustomed to declaring intentions through lesson plans. The plan of work becomes an opportunity for orientation. In general terms, orientation to the MBO process is helpful to understand the types of objectives related to management and the types of measurement. Worthy administrative objectives include routine maintenance (e.g., the running of the school), problem solving (e.g., solving conflicts, resolving a dilemma), innovation (e.g., introduction of a new approach), and personal development (refinement, improvement of job-related skills).

In one sense, objectives define the needs of teachers and how they use time in routine tasks, problem solving, innovation, and/or personal and professional improvement. Objectives can be stated and measured in at least two ways. The quantitative way involves numerical gains on an objective criterion; the qualitative way rests more upon judgments of superiors, peers, and participants. Both are important.

The plan of work can be logged by a work sheet that states the what (goal), when (target date), and how (activities). These work sheets make up a kind of continuing journal so that a final accounting is not deferred until the last moment.

Spillane and Levenson (1978) cited numerous applications of the MBO system to education of the general school population as well as to education of the gifted and talented. Their examples were keyed toward the role of the principal as a resource for either innovation and/or problem solving.

A pair of examples illustrated the use of work plans to fulfill objectives. One teacher who developed a proposal for a minigrant first described his goal to demonstrate his ability to record and relate student performances and learning styles. In the indicator section, he described his activities in keeping student records of performance and of student preferences for learning. Evaluation was to be through the ratings of his peers regarding the adequacy and scope of his records.

One principal used a different format for a block grant. She organized it into indicators (sources of concern), objectives (target accomplishments and target dates), and an action plan (activities to be undertaken). Her evaluation criteria were as follows: (1) Am I meeting objectives? (2) Should indicators be amended? (3) Should objectives be changed? and (4) Is the central office helpful to the school in achieving goals? Faculty ratings and central office staff ratings were used for evaluation.

Funding Considerations

The costs of a program vary from district to district. This variance depends upon the nature of the program, adequacy of school resources prior to initiation of the program, and types of provisions selected for implementation. As a rule of thumb, the costs of a program for gifted and talented pupils should fall between those of speech correction services (largely an itinerant teacher/specialist type of program) and those of programs for specific learning disabilities (largely the shared responsibility of the regular class teacher and a resource teacher). An important variable of cost to the district is the availability of state and federal funds. A very influential factor is the district's method of budgeting and of sharing costs, for this can make a program seem costly or inexpensive, depending upon which accounting practices are used.

Correll (1978) prepared an analysis of costs for programs for the gifted and talented. The analysis divided costs into three categories: (1) present resources, (2) start-up costs, and (3) maintenance costs. The present resource category covered the general education resources available to the school district. For example, if a school district already has a comprehensive library with trained librarians, then these costs are incorporated into existing budgets. Otherwise, funding would be required. Some school districts have a memorandum of agreement for sharing reference resources, consultation about acquisitions, and/or personnel. Such an agreement could involve the resources of an institution of higher education, as well as a public library. School districts that participate in student teaching/internships have access to the resources of that institution.

Other examples of available resources include: (1) pupil testing, (2) guidance and counseling services, (3) abundant supplementary learning materials, (4) teachers informed about and competent in individualized education, and (5) competent instructional consultation/supervisory services. These provisions are often already part of the general budget.

Start-up costs were identified by Correll as administration and individualized assessment. Administrative costs relate directly to the identification of gifted and talented pupils and to the translation of psychoeducational assessment data into individualized programs. Moreover, coordination is involved in maintenance of recommendations and plans, and it is centered on the types of priorities described in Unit III. Arrangements for in-service training and consultation should be instituted for participating teachers. Relationships with parents should also be established.

The administrative function can be performed by the creation of a full-time position or by designation of this responsibility to a staff person. Individual psychological examinations are also a consideration, and it is necessary to ensure that staff members sanction and support this activity. Both of these areas would be appropriate budget items for the gifted and talented program. (In principle, however, it is preferable to distribute these functions over several staff positions rather than to set up positions solely for the coordination of the program for gifted and talented pupils.)

It must be decided whether the maintenance costs of the programs for the gifted and talented will be considered separate budget allowances or included within the general budget fund. Regardless of the decision, there are at least seven cost categories: (1) administration, (2) supervision, (3) consultation, (4) teaching, (5) instruction, (6) pupil services, and (7) program evaluation.

The costs of administration were defined by Correll as the time required of the superintendent and principals in planning, implementation, and maintenance. She estimated that the first two stages would have a cost figure of 5 to 10 percent of central office staff and 2 to 3 percent for maintenance. Principal time would be 20 percent for the first two stages and 10 percent thereafter. These estimates could be charged to the gifted and talented program.

Supervisory personnel costs are difficult to establish, since such persons may be considered central office staff. For example, the music supervisor may be listed as a member of either the central office staff or the department of music. These types of supervisory services are available to all teachers. Correll recommended that no more than five to ten percent of cost should be charged to the special program, but the logs and equipment-sharing records should produce an exact figure for accounting purposes.

Consultant costs should include all consultants' salaries and district travel expenses. This would be a direct cost to the program. However, the use of a full-time consultant should reduce the costs of administration and supervisory services. Teaching costs include expenses for in-service institutes, tuition and scholarships for teacher preparation, and travel to demonstration centers, conferences, and workshops.

Instruction, it is agreed, focuses on facilitation and direct enhancement of the abilities of the gifted and talented pupil, whether through an internship, in directed study, or in any other learning situation and whether conducted by regular or special teacher or both. Examples of direct, allowable costs include teacher aides, outside consultants, special courses, transportation, and special materials or equipment. It is to be hoped that such equipment or materials would be available to *all* pupils; if so, this cost would become part of the regular budget to a proportionate degree.

Pupil costs involve identification, assessment, evaluation, and counseling. If the school has minimal or no provisions for these services for all pupils, then this area becomes very expensive for the gifted and talented program. The thrust of this service is to support individualized education programs. Correll recommended about three percent of the total cost estimate for program evaluation.

Goal Orientation

An example of program objectives for gifted and talented pupils was developed by the Bureau of Special Education, Pennsylvania State Department of Education (1973). The document's statements could be recast into five broad goals: (1) identification, (2) parent relationships, (3) community relationships, (4) program responsibilities, and (5) school district responsibilities. These goals and their related components are summarized in amended form in Table 13-2.

These goals offer a degree of structure on which further elaborations could be based. Obviously, this listing could be modified or extended. Perhaps more important, the Correll (1978) and the Spillane and Levenson (1978) discussions could be used to (1) generate measurable objectives, (2) fix responsibilities for implementation, (3) describe related activities, (4) specify evaluation criteria, and (5) assess needs for revision and modification. This list can also provide guidance for budget and resource needs on both district and individual school levels.

Table 13-2 Management Goals for Individualized Education of Gifted and Talented Pupils

Major Goal	Component Goals
Identification	1. The school will test referred pupils for school readiness, yearly achievement, academic ability, occupational preference, and other relevant matters.
	2. The school will share test results with parents.
	3. The school will ensure that parents fully comprehend the results of testing.
	4. The school will identify gifted children of kindergarten and prekindergarten levels.
	5. Identification will be followed by implementation of an Individualized Education Program.
Parent relationships	6. Parents will be involved in the planning and implementation of educational activities.
	7. Parents will attend regularly scheduled meetings with other parents of children enrolled in the program.

Table 13-2 continued

Major Goal	Component Goals
	8. Parents will be given literature regarding the education of the gifted and talented.
	9. Parents will be provided with written descriptions of the district program.
Community relationships	10. The school will invite institutions of higher education to assist in education of gifted and talented pupils in content areas.
	11. The school will cooperate with colleges and schools of education in the education of gifted and talented pupils.
	12. The school will help community agencies identify the weekend, summer, and afterschool needs of gifted and talented pupils.
Program responsibilities	13. The program will make use of individual alternatives such as acceleration and enrichment.
	14. The program will meet the standards and guidelines of approval established by the state department of education.
	15. The program will be available to elementary pupils as well as secondary pupils.
	16. The program will balance performance, cognitive outcomes, and affective outcomes.
	17. The program will declare goals with reference to the school curriculum and each pupil's Individualized Education Program.
	18. The program will emphasize opportunities for gifted and talented pupils to be of service to others both inside and outside the school community.
	19. The program will assist regular class teachers with gifted and talented pupils.
	20. The program will involve community experts, including parents, to serve as mentors.
School district responsibilities	21. The school will make its materials and library resources available to gifted and talented pupils.
	22. The school will regularly evaluate the program.
	23. The school will arrange for participation of gifted and talented pupils in cocurricular activities.
	24. Guidance services will be extended to gifted and talented pupils.
	25. Guidance services will include social, emotional, and physical needs.

Chapter 14

Understanding the Impact of Quality Programs

Impact, in part, refers to the effect of the program upon learners. A program for gifted and talented persons has varied effects upon participants and nonparticipants alike. Attention to impact is evidence of proper concern for high-quality education for everyone, gifted or otherwise. The process and procedures of evaluation have their value as helpful resources to appraise the consequences of program operations.

THE NATURE OF EVALUATION

According to Cooley and Lohnes (1976), evaluation can be understood as a process to gather data in order to make intelligent decisions regarding continuation, revision, and improvement of services. They suggested that the process and procedures of evaluation can be understood through examining the why, who, what, when, where, and how. An understanding of these six elements should lead to a grasp of the design and implementation of evaluation projects.

Elements of Evaluation

Why evaluate? It could be to fulfill requirements of funding. In some states, local school districts are expected to conduct year-end assessments of pupil performance. Certain state, regional, or local educational agencies operate on zero-based or sunset budgeting systems that put time limits on program operations. Renewal is conditional upon proved impact of the program. A second motivation for evaluation is the belief that decisions should be based on verifiable information and that order can be achieved by pursuit of declared goals. A third reason grows out of the realization that it is not enough to verbalize commitment to high-quality education. An index of quality must be established through objective, replicable assessment.

Who is an evaluator? According to Cooley and Lohnes, an evaluator is a person trained in the social and behavioral sciences of education. Background preparation may include philosophy, psychology, sociology, and research and statistical inference. The evaluator is required to organize, to manage, to adhere to ethical standards, and to relate to diverse populations. As a professional, the evaluator operates between two distinct populations. One is composed of innovators and disseminators; the other, school boards, administrators, teachers, parents, and learners.

What is an evaluation? Cooley and Lohnes (1976) defined it as:

> a process by which relevant data are collected and transformed into information for decision-making. . . . Evaluation is successful insofar as the information it generates becomes part of the decision-making process in education. (p. 3)

What is evaluated? Typically, evaluators concentrate equally on curriculum, instructional methods, and use of materials. The evaluation may be in process for one or two years, or it may be a continuing process for the life of the innovation.

Who uses evaluations? There must, of course, be a client. In this case, the client is the public, represented by a board of education. The client pays for the services of an evaluator in one of two ways. A full-time evaluation director may be hired by the school system, or an evaluator may be employed as a contracted consultant.

The eventual beneficiary of evaluation is the learner, since evaluation is used to improve the management and maintenance of quality. The ethics of evaluation requires that the emphasis be on facts, not on what employers want to hear. This necessitates objectivity. Another ethical matter is the evaluator's willingness to disclaim competence for a particular assignment if not prepared by training or experience to carry it out.

The when, where, and how of evaluation often involve compromises. Evaluations are conducted according to what is available within actual school buildings with pupils, staff, and teachers. It is usually difficult to control for the effects of extraneous influences.

Evaluation involves the analysis of relationships among many variables. It depends on statistical inferences generated from four domains of influence: (1) the initial characteristics of learners; (2) the context, or environment, of the implementation; (3) instructional practices; and (4) the outcomes or attainments of the pupils. The process of evaluation requires compromises between ideal conditions and less than ideal realities. Compromise tends to affect the generated data, and the resulting limitations must be understood.

Consensus in Advance

The evaluator must arrive at a consensus with the client. Consensus, or agreement, is needed before an evaluation is undertaken if subsequent results are to be meaningfully used for decision making. Cooley and Lohnes point out that answers to the following questions are necessary prior to organizational agreements:

1. What are the purposes of education? (In this case, for gifted and talented children and youth.)
2. What are the rules of evidence? (How are facts verified? What makes a statement about the program for gifted and talented pupils believable?)
3. What are the requirements of decisions? (Who decides? Who decides who decides?)
4. What distinguishes a finding from an interpretation? (How is wishful thinking about gifted and talented children's accomplishments separated from reality-based information?)
5. What are the assumptions, viewpoints, and information that prompted the evaluation? (What does the gifted and talented child program document say about this?)

These questions involve choice and negotiation. Agreement in advance will increase the likelihood that evaluation information will produce actions.

The language of evaluation must be precise in order to facilitate communication among participants. The essence of evaluation is the comparison of intentions with obtained results. Decisions are intended to improve practice through action.

A MODEL FOR EVALUATION

Provus (1971) and Stufflebeam (1971) took the same position as Cooley and Lohnes (1976) in their emphasis upon the evaluator as a mediator between the contractor for evaluation services and those affected by its findings. All agree that it is a function of evaluation to assist in decision making.

Provus advanced a discrepancy model that emphasizes a comparison of intentions and obtained results. Discrepancies between the two alert participants to the need for action. Stufflebeam advocated a decision-making model with greater attention to the use of data. Both approaches have their adherents within the field of education for the gifted and talented. Both have had a major influence upon the preparation of evaluation specialists, upon standards of practice, and upon funding agencies' requirements for evaluation

Both Provus and Stufflebeam point out that evaluators serve as consultants, with the first step being to agree on what is necessary for conducting an evaluation. The outcome of this prearrangement, according to Provus (1971), is the design of a plan for evaluation. Agreement should be reached regarding design, installation, process, product, and comparison. The design is the agreed upon plan for the evaluation. Typically, needs assessment identifies the required dimensions of design. Installation concerns the circumstances and actual operation of the program. Process is the term for the attributes of pupil performance to be studied and the means by which they are studied during the evaluation. Product refers to the reports and recommendations that result from the evaluation.

Stufflebeam (1971) proposed a model that attempts to relate decisions to program. He speaks of interactions between four types of decisions and four types of program operations. The decisions relate to (1) planning, (2) structure, (3) implementation, and (4) recycling; these are balanced against four operations: (1) context, (2) input, (3) process, and (4) product. Stufflebeam's interactions can be shown as a matrix such as the one presented in Table 14-1. It appears from this table that the language of evaluation varies, but there is agreement as to overall purpose. The constructs (what is done) may well be more important than the terms. Consequently, the tactics of evaluation can be understood as:

1. establishing the context of quality in which the program will operate, typically labeled mission statement
2. identifying the existing resources and attributes of participants that are starting points, typically labeled input
3. monitoring the actions of participants toward the goals of the mission, usually labeled as process
4. analyzing results, usually labeled outcomes, expressed in performance or products
5. making recommendations inferred from the interactions of the preceding four elements, usually described as impact statements

Evaluation is based on a trusting relationship because of a mutual desire for improvement. Its impact is to inform and provide a rational basis for decisions. Evaluation is a planned partnership.

Applications to Education for the Gifted and Talented

Evaluation is an honored tradition in the history of education for gifted and talented pupils. Costanzo-Sorg (1979) summarized the published work on evaluation as applied to programs, large and small, for gifted and talented

Table 14-1 A Matrix for Planning and Conducting Educational Evaluation*

Operations	Decisions			
	Planning (Goals and Objectives for Accomplishment)	Structure (Procedures and Resources to Be Installed)	Implementation (Introduction and Maintenance)	Recycling (Reactions to Attainments and Results and Impact)
Context: needs assessment, results, mission statement, assumptions, constraints, facilitators, etc.	Consistent statements and policies and commitment to evaluation.	Secure consent and endorsement of participants; secure insights of participants.	Initiate program and evaluation procedures as agreed upon schedule.	Revise to achieve consistency as needed.
Input: pupil attributes, staff resources, material and physical resources, costs, receptivity, etc.	Selection of appropriate tactics of measurement to assess available sources of input.	Schedule inservice training for participants, parents, and students.	Ensure that resources are in place and available as required.	Examine comprehensiveness of input variables.
Process: activities, instruction, experiences, reactions, tactics, etc.	Selection of procedures to introduce and inform about evaluation tactics.	Arrange for incorporation of participant insights.	Monitor to ensure schedule and commitments are met.	Review adequacy of activities associated with gathering and using data.
Product: outcomes matched against context and input.	Evidence of availability of data sources; use of objective data and qualitative data.	Assess credibility of intentions among participants.	Assemble and assess data as agreed; prepare progress reports and final reports as needed.	Make decisions regarding continuation and improvement.

*Adapted from Stufflebeam (1971) and Costanzo-Sorg (1979).

learners. Her review concluded that the tactics and purposes of evaluation advocated by Cooley and Lohnes (1976), Stufflebeam (1971), and Provus (1971) are widely used by specialists in the education of gifted and talented learners. She paid particular attention to evidence of high quality in evaluation.

Consumers of evaluation were advised by Costanzo-Sorg to apply five criteria to reviews of reports or plans. First, the purposes and intentions of evaluation should be consistent with the means employed for the evaluation. Procedures should be reliable in the statistical sense of yielding stable results that can be attributed to the program rather than to measurement errors. Objectivity requires control of human perceptions and investment; the use of independent observers can be helpful. Relevance denotes the relationship of results to the larger context of operations. It also means that a total program or curriculum, not a fragment, is considered. Finally, credibility must be considered. Consumers must judge the applicability of reports to their own situation. Attention to detail and ongoing involvement of consumers will enhance confidence in the final reports.

Evaluators were advised by Costanzo-Sorg to be open and willing to evaluate their own performance. Pertinent questions could include: (1) Did I seek improvement in services to children and youth? (2) Did I insist on advanced planning to secure the necessary consensus? (3) Did I use sufficient and varied sources of data? (4) Did I relate procedures to goals and maintain consistency? (5) Did I provide sufficient in-service training or orientation for participants? and (6) Did I insist on sufficient time for program operation? Appropriate answers to these questions enhance credibility.

ACCOUNTABILITY AND EVALUATION

Dimensions of Accountability

Accountability and evaluation have become watchwords for both special and general education programs at all levels of education. Federal grants have increasingly required applicants to devote as much attention to evaluation concerns as to program goals and activities. Management systems from business and commerce have been adapted for the administration of educational programs. Management has grown into a distinct professional role with status equal to that of the more traditional role of research. Concern about the scarcity of financial resources, coupled with increasing financial outlays, has resulted in closer examination of the cost/quality ratio in educational practices. Examination of educational practices in relationship to costs and results seems likely to continue.

Educators of gifted and talented pupils recognize that their willingness to examine practice is part of a high-quality program. They also see that the use of the Individualized Education Program (IEP) provides a natural context for the examination of practice. To welcome accountability, however, is not enough. There are pitfalls and traps to be avoided. For example, Hedges (1979) illustrated that achievement test data can be manipulated to show significant gains even though there has been no change in practices. A comparison of pre- and postinstruction scores as the sole criterion for performance misses the essential purpose of the effort. Hedges noted that, in some districts, individual schools are ranked on the mean performance of their pupils. He expressed amazement at the general failure to recognize that, with such procedures, 50 percent will automatically be below average, regardless of actual quality.

The central purpose of accountability, according to Hedges (1979), is that data should provide feedback to faculty. Cammeron (1978) affirms the view of accountability as a means to improve instruction and the quality of services. In this sense, accountability and evaluation supply a rational basis for decisions. In the context of gifted and talented education, Cammeron observed that accountability should guide educators, not dominate or intimidate them.

Cammeron concluded, as did Raybin (1979), that curriculum should be the central focus. If the curriculum documents the goals and objectives that the school holds for students, it follows that evaluation provides both the procedures and process for monitoring how those goals and objectives are attained. As with other aspects of practice, Hedges, Cammeron, and Raybin speak similarly of accountability as a tool and as a means toward an end. All three agree that accountability serves to inform and leads to improvements.

Raybin advanced the concept of minimum essentials for faculty participation in the evaluation of curriculum goals and content. The minimum essentials constitute a floor, not a ceiling. The faculty, both regular teachers and those concerned particularly with giftedness and talent, should determine and agree on a reasonable and attainable package of common expectations so that any pupil can expect fundamental similarity, regardless of instructor. For example, a high school faculty involved in a junior level U.S. history course may adopt a general goal of helping the student to understand that an event of little note at its time may have far-reaching consequences. Events such as the invention of barbed wire, the importation of rabbits into New Zealand, enactment of Prohibition, and the sale of Alaska could be discussed to attain this goal. Raybin's minimum essentials concept was not meant to perpetuate a straight-jacket, rigid curriculum. Teachers would be free as to teaching techniques, use of materials, expansion of goals, and use of additional content.

The relationship of the minimum essentials concept to accountability is that, in an evaluation, pupil performance is studied in relation to the circumstances associated with the performance. Consequently, evaluation of alternative means to achieve common expectations can be conducted without pitting teacher against teacher.

A Model for Management

Individualization of instruction and establishment of quality programming for gifted and talented learners can be viewed as integrating information and deriving implications. Kirk and Gallagher (1979) considered these activities a series of action steps that can serve as an inventory for the internal monitoring of program operations:

1. nurture: the prevention of failure. It is the school's task to identify its community resources that further gifted and talented pupil potential. This calls for cooperative work with health and social service agencies to maintain a biological, medical, and cultural environment that allows human ability to flourish.
2. identification: the procedures and criteria by which a pupil is located and certified as gifted and talented.
3. assessment: the transformation of identification data and of relevant personal data into a profile for subsequent steps.
4. prescription: setting goals and objectives. As with assessment, the information can be used both for individual guidance and for program guidance.
5. instructional management: the educational relationship between learner and educators. This step refers to the daily ongoing activities to fulfill prescriptions.
6. implementation: the services, resources, equipment, scheduling, and other things required to support and facilitate the educational relationship.
7. monitoring: both pupil and program evaluation. This dimension provides the substance for revision, redesign, and improvement.

In actual practice, Steps 2 and 3 may be combined and the sequence of Steps 4 and 5 reversed. It is the scope that is significant.

The six questions often associated with the lead paragraph of a news article, i.e., why, who, what, when, where, and how, can help bring individualization of instruction for gifted and talented pupils into focus. These focal action points are areas that require decisions. (Note that these same useful questions helped Cooley and Lohnes bring the concept of evaluation into sharper focus.)

These dimensions of activities and decisions are cast into a matrix in Table 14-2. This chart provides an overview of the interactions among decisions and program elements.

One function of the matrix is to structure an inventory of the user's own knowledge about the education of the gifted and talented. The 36 cells have been filled in as an example. A second outcome could be to inventory the written documents, resources, and practices of the school district.

Inspection of the matrix shows familiar, essential attributes of programming: (1) aptitude treatment interaction, (2) behavioral manifestations, (3) correlates of performance, (4) performance objectives, (5) Individualized Education Program, (6) Table of Specifications, (7) acceleration, (8) enrichment, (9) sufficient conditions for learning, (10) summative approach, and (11) formative approaches to monitoring.

Summing Up

DEFINING THE EDUCATIONAL CONTEXT OF QUALITY

The phrase *the needs of the individual* can be more than a cliché. Educational psychology identifies human needs as (1) physical comfort, (2) psychological stability, (3) vocational adequacy, and (4) social relationships. These needs describe both individual and social purposes of education. Education has been defined as the formal, deliberate efforts of competent persons to enable learners to structure and manage experience so as to balance their social and individual needs.

Motives for quality programming for able learners have their origins in the social and cultural context. Motives based on egalitarianism, universal education, decentralization of education, and social confidence have proved to be both obstacles to and facilitators of high-quality programming. The substance of quality can be understood through documentation. Six areas are identified as indicators of quality: (1) accreditation, (2) representation, (3) admission, (4) preparation, (5) fees, and (6) disclosure. The substance of quality can also be understood as a framework in which (1) the school accommodates the learner and (2) the central role of teachers is recognized.

Quality programs have a variety of tactics for individual pupil accommodation: (1) independent study, (2) accelerated units, (3) team teaching, (4) monitoring, and (5) service projects. Multigrade and districtwide tactics include: (1) multiage grouping, (2) clustering, (3) talent centers, (4) itinerant teachers, (5) consultation, and (6) mentoring.

Excellent teachers of highly able pupils enable their pupils to anticipate their future roles. These teachers are perceived by their pupils as organized and systematic. Such teachers are of all ages, teach in all content areas, and

Table 14-2 A Matrix for Management

Decisions	Planning Activities			Instructional Activities		Evaluation
	Identification	Assessment	Prescription	Instruction	Implementation	Monitoring
Why (rationale)	Identification is designed to structure program goals, to define pupil attributes, and to serve as a form of outreach.	Assessment of relevant data leads to the maximum aptitude intervention interaction, which is maximized by inclusion of cognitive, affective, educational, and performance data.	Data allow adaptation to the individual's needs; goals focus on task orientation of participants; precision of performance objectives structures pupil performance.	Instruction is matched to aptitude and situation to maximize performance.	The teacher pupil interaction requires support; support services maximize the ability of teachers to nurture.	Evaluation structures decisions for improvement; attention to pupil and program permits rational decision making.
Who (responsible person)	Nominations are made by teachers, parents, pupils, principals, and program coordinators.	Psychologist and/or social worker, parents, teachers, pupils, and program coordinators make assessments.	Parents and teacher must give endorsement; program coordinator manages support services.	Pupil fulfills responsibilities agreed upon with classroom teacher.	Program coordinator is resources manager.	Evidence of participation by appropriate persons and evidence that participation has been helpful are required.
What (content)	Teachers and/or parents must complete referral forms, and parents must complete	Individual IQ test, formal achievement tests, description of behavior manifesta-	Goals are expressed as annual goals and translated into as performance objec-	Table of Specifications is matched to assessment and prescription.	Table of Specifications is matched to assessment, prescription, and instruc-	Evidence of conformity to procedures and evidence that procedures have been

permission forms for assessment.	tions, and description of correlates of performance are needed.	tives.		tion.	helpful are needed.
When (origin and duration) — Nominations should be processed any time during the year and decisions rendered within 60 days.	Within 20 days after initiation, assessment is completed.	Within 20 days of assessment, prescription is completed.	Within 20 days of assessment, instruction is initiated.	Within 20 days of assessment, implementation is initiated.	Evidence that time lines have been met, identification of obstacles, and an annual review of pupil and program outcomes are needed.
Where (settings) — Identification takes place within natural settings (e.g., home, classroom), and conditions appropriate for formal testing.	Time and place are convenient to parents and classroom teacher.	Time and place is convenient to parents and classroom teacher.	In-school, out-of-school, and community options are used.	In-school, out-of-school, and community options are used.	Evidence that settings and options appropriate is examined.
How (procedure) — Tactics and techniques of screening are referenced by program goals and definition.	Tactics of aptitude intervention are used in compliance with criteria of effectiveness and efficiency.	The tactics of the Individualized Education Program (IEP) are used, and a Table of Specifications (TOS) is established.	The IEP and TOS are extended into instructional options of acceleration and/or enrichment.	Resources are matched to sufficient conditions of learning.	Tactics of summative and formative evaluation are used.

may be either male or female. Effective teachers are openly committed to education of the able, first to the pupil's interests and concerns and second to subject matter as a vehicle for motivation.

DEVELOPING HIGH-QUALITY PROGRAMS

Planning and organizing programs for the gifted and talented reaffirm the principle of accommodation, or matching pupil to curriculum. Authorities agree on seven distinct features that should be considered for planning: (1) teacher/staffing, (2) curriculum, (3) student selection, (4) statement(s) of philosophy/objectives, (5) faculty/staff orientation, (6) plan of evaluation, and (7) administrative responsibilities and accountability.

Innovation is the use of influence(s) upon actors, a process that involves the mobilization of resources to achieve an outcome of proved worth. The role of change agent can be assumed by any informed person. Such a person is characterized by an inner sense of responsibility. The role of change agent can be discouraging, however. It is helpful to remember that change is seldom instant or easy.

Using tactics of innovation involves the process of problem solving. Tactics of innovation have included (1) the summer institute, (2) demonstration center, and (3) workshops. A principal lesson from the comparison of these tactics has been to respect the integrity of persons to be influenced. Teachers are not objects to be manipulated; they should be valued partners in the design and execution of in-service efforts.

DEVELOPING A CONFEDERACY FOR THE
GIFTED AND TALENTED

Managing and maintaining program quality can be viewed as a confederacy for the gifted and talented. Schools must be open to community and family influences. The tactic of purposeful mentoring facilitates this openness and makes its possible for the school to form new partnerships and expand its resources.

Funding of programs is a significant consideration, since innovation requires fiscal support. This support could be directed toward (1) discovery of knowledge, (2) applications of knowledge, (3) systematic programming, (4) field testing and verification, and (5) adaptation to wider populations. The match between goals and budget can be achieved through a rational process of relating ends and means.

The costs of programming for gifted and talented learners depend upon district budget policies regarding office costs, instructional costs, and the like. Moreover, the nature of services already in place influences the amount of start-up costs. Areas of direct charge to the gifted and talented program could include costs associated with (1) administration, (2) supervision, (3) consultation, (4) teaching, (5) instruction, (6) pupil services, and (7) program evaluation.

UNDERSTANDING THE IMPACT OF QUALITY PROGRAMS

Impact is judged through the relationships and/or effects of constituent program elements upon one another. Evaluation has emerged as the preferred procedure by which to gauge impact. Evaluation can be described as answers to why, who, what, where, when, and how. These elements suggest its scope. A model of matrix for evaluation of programs can be used to illustrate how these elements could be applied to (1) planning for identification, assessment, and prescription; (2) considering instructional tactics and implementation; and (3) selecting evaluation strategies.

Users of evaluation reports can apply reasonable criteria to assess the adequacy of results. These criteria include (1) internal consistency, (2) reliable measurement, (3) relevance to educational context, (4) objectivity, and (5) credibility.

Evaluation is not confined to total programs alone. Individual teachers can apply these tactics to their class situations. A proper common focus for evaluation and accountability is the examination of curriculum. A strategy of minimum essentials can be used.

The technicalities of innovation, management systems, evaluation, and accountability can obscure the pursuit of quality. The central concept of quality should be the willingness to document program aspirations and claims. The tactics of innovation, management systems, evaluation, and accountability are means to the end of documentation. These tactics can be understood as responsible stewardship.

Enrichment

DEFINING THE EDUCATIONAL CONTEXT OF QUALITY

1. In your own words, describe in two or three sentences three attributes of quality in education. Select one for emphasis. Share your choice with others. What one key attribute emerges from this discussion?

2. Suppose your school district were going to plan a campaign to raise taxes by one mill on behalf of gifted and talented learners. What claims for excellence could be advanced? What examples of documentation would be required in support of your standards of excellence?

3. Suppose you were the parent of a gifted child who was destined to solve one of the world's serious problems by age 30. Describe the desirable attributes of your child's teacher. Share your results. Are the attributes different because of the problem selected?

4. Survey your school district regarding the variety of alternatives used for gifted and talented learners. How many different options exist? Can you deduce any reasons for their popularity?

DEVELOPING HIGH-QUALITY PROGRAMS

5. What values and beliefs about innovation do you personally support? What circumstances within your experience and/or your preparation generate your beliefs?

6. What roles do you believe parents, pupils, and community members should play in the process and tactics of innovations? What do your beliefs convey about participation?

7. Suppose you had the funds to hire a change agent. Write a job description entitled *Wanted—Change Agent for Able Learners.* Prepare a 75- to 100-word advertisement. Share your copy with others. What common elements are present? What elements are dissimilar? Combine into an advertisement of common agreement.

DEVELOPING A CONFEDERACY FOR THE GIFTED AND TALENTED

8. Examine your school district's budget for the previous year. Is program budgeting or management by objectives used? Are priorities evident for able learners? How does the budget reflect priorities?

9. Develop an outline for a plan for funding for a quality program for gifted and talented learners from kindergarten through 12th grade in your school district. Suppose your only constraint would be that full-time, segregated, special classes were held illegal by your state courts. What budget categories would you propose? What goals would you assign to these categories? How would you evaluate goal outcomes? What costs would you assign to general budget and to a separate account for your program for the gifted and talented? Share your plan. What circumstances conditioned your recommendations?

10. Propose an outline or strategy for assessing the in-service needs of regular class teachers in regard to quality education for the gifted and talented. What dimensions would you select for emphasis? Test your survey with several colleagues. Share your findings.

UNDERSTANDING THE IMPACT OF QUALITY PROGRAMS

11. Review a federally funded project outside your school district. If possible, obtain the proposal and the final report. Describe the match between goals and assessment of outcomes. Can you pinpoint the use of tactics of evaluation described in this unit? What decisions about school practice were taken as a result of the project?

12. Select two articles about similar topics on education of the gifted and talented. One topic should be related to research; the other, to evaluation. Compare the two articles as to tactics and results. Which of the two was more helpful to you? Share your insights.

Understanding and Using Individualized Education Programs

SYNOPSIS

The Individualized Education Program (IEP) has gained popularity and acceptance as a concrete, valuable aid for teachers. It focuses on the individualization of instruction to meet the needs and learning style of a single person. All learners learn different things at different rates, in somewhat different styles, at different levels of motivation, and at different depths of acquisition. Individualization is an acknowledgment of the futility of uniform expectations, which neglect the uniqueness of the learner and the creativity of the educator.

Several states now require or encourage the use of the IEP in gifted and talented education programs. Many other states recommend similar documentation for individual gifted and talented pupils. The use of the IEP is modeled after that prescribed in Public Law (Pub.L.) 94-142 and in its regulations as they appear in the *Federal Register*. On May 23, 1980, the Office of Special Education (OSE) of the U.S. Department of Education issued a policy paper entitled *Individualized Education Programs (IEPs)*. That paper updated and clarified the purposes and functions of the IEP requirement. The following adapted excerpts from the policy paper (p. 3) would be relevant to IEP use or to similar systematic planning for gifted and talented children:

The IEP provision has two main parts (a) the IEP meeting(s)—at which parents and school personnel jointly make decisions about a child's "program," and (b) the IEP document itself—which is a written record of the decisions reached at the meeting. The overall IEP requirement, comprised of these two parts, has a number of purposes and functions:

1. The IEP meeting serves as a communication vehicle between parents and school personnel; it enables them, as equal participants, to decide jointly upon what the child's needs are, what will be provided, and what the anticipated outcomes may be.
2. The IEP itself serves as the focal point for resolving any differences between the parents and the school, first through the meeting and second, if necessary, through the procedural protections that are available to the parents.
3. The IEP sets forth in writing a commitment of resources necessary to enable a child to receive needed special education and related services.
4. The IEP is a management tool that is used to ensure that each child is provided special education and related services appropriate to his or her special learning needs.
5. The IEP is a compliance/monitoring document that may be used by personnel from each governmental level to determine whether a child is actually receiving the free appropriate public education agreed to by the parents and the school.
6. The IEP serves as an evaluation device for use in determining the extent of the child's progress toward meeting the projected outcomes. (The law does *not* require that teachers or other school personnel be held accountable if a child does not achieve the goals and objectives set forth in his or her IEP.)

There is no single required or best format for the IEP, but there are clusters of characteristics, such as goals, objectives, implementation strategies, necessary resources, and specification of evidence of goal attainments. The IEP has great promise as a rallying point for persons committed to deliver high-quality education and related services.

KEY IDEAS

Pub.L. 94-142 provides a model of personalizing education for gifted and talented learners. This model employs the IEP as a vehicle for personalization of education. The IEP promotes program quality by requiring that certain conditions be present before the IEP can be used. In addition, the IEP can operate only if suitable conditions are maintained.

Assessment is a critical component in the IEP process. While identification procedures are used to certify eligibility for services, assessment procedures are used to obtain information to guide the teacher's action.

The regular class teacher is a central person in the formulation of the IEP and its implementation. In addition to meeting the requirements associated directly with the IEP, teachers must also serve as consultants to parents, pupils, and peers, and as resource persons for high-quality programming.

The core capabilities that teachers must have include professionalism and instructional competencies. This common body of practices is necessary to provide a sound context for individualized education of the gifted and talented and of all other pupils as well.

A PROTOTYPE

The Yourtowne Model

What typical qualities should be present before any school system can assert that it has an acceptable program for gifted and talented pupils? The following are six fundamental characteristics:

1. comprehensive, covering preschool through higher education
2. continuous, available for the pupil's entire school career
3. balanced, including equal opportunity to work in all curricular and extracurricular areas
4. participatory, involving regular and special teachers, pupils, parents, and community resources both in decision making and instruction
5. flexible, adaptable to changes in school and pupil conditions
6. individualized, encouraging instruction based on close matches between pupil characteristics, what is taught, and how it is taught

The description of Yourtowne that follows illustrates verified key themes of programming. Several very relevant details have been omitted, however. The description does not enumerate the various in-service activities that helped prepare the town's teachers and administrators for their special roles. It does not tell how individualized pupil plans were drafted and approved. Other essential elements, like a means of evaluating the outcomes of the operation, are missing. This prototype is a structural outline on which programs can be built.

EDUCATION PROGRAM COMPONENTS

The Yourtowne design for the education of gifted and talented pupils has a major component and four subordinate components.

The Major Program Component: Basic Scholars

The main component, which includes the other four, is called the Basic Scholars Program. This component is open to all pupils who earn achievement test scores and subject grades high enough to qualify. It is also open to all pupils with high intelligence quotients (IQs), even though their school grades may not qualify them. The latter pupils must indicate that they wish to improve their grades, and their teachers must agree that the pupils are making sincere efforts. After being nominated by their teachers, parents, and their school principal, pupils become part of the Basic Scholars Program with the approval of the program coordinator. The Basic Scholars Program is open to everyone, kindergarten through 12th grade, who meets the requirements. It is not compulsory, however; students who qualify are not required to be part of the program.

The Basic Scholars Program focuses on skill and understanding in reading, language, and mathematics at every grade level. At least one of the following criteria must be met for admission to the program:

1. standardized achievement test scores in mathematics, reading, and language averaging at least 25 percent above the norm for the pupil's grade
2. report card grades in the top 10 percent of the class in mathematics, reading, and language
3. individual test IQs of 125 or more

The objectives of the Basic Scholars Program are (1) to encourage students to increase their reading, writing, and mathematics understanding and skills; (2) to motivate students to qualify for the Basic Scholars Program, and (3) to guide students who are already Basic Scholars into one or more of the other four components of the activities for the gifted and talented in Yourtowne's schools.

The Four Other Program Components

The other four program components are Special Interest, Advancement, Talent Development, and Human Service. Basic Scholars may add one or more of these four or may limit themselves to the Basic Scholars component. They may move into or out of these four supplemental components during the school year with approval of the teachers, parents, principal, and program coordinator. A pupil who falls below and remains below the Basic Scholars standards for two consecutive report periods, however, is removed from the supplementary components. Also, the pupil's continuation in the Basic Scholars Program is reviewed with teachers and parents.

The Special Interest Component

Opportunities for pupils at all grade levels to pursue learning beyond the range of usual class activities are provided in the Special Interest component.

Elementary pupils in the regular curriculum, for instance, ordinarily study the denominations of U.S. coins and bills, and learn to make change. A Special Interest study, however, could take a Basic Scholars elementary pupil into the history of money, the functions of banks, or the fluctuations of the U.S. dollar on international exchanges. Similar possibilities for Special Interest study in all aspects of the curriculum are plentiful in both elementary and secondary schools.

Special Interest work is encouraged under the following conditions:

1. The Basic Scholar has completed all regular assignments satisfactorily.
2. The time taken by the Special Interest study does not interfere with completion of continuing regular class work (though it may require being away from the regular class group occasionally).
3. There is professional guidance and monitoring of the pupil's Special Interest study available from a teacher or other school staff member.
4. The quality of the Special Interest work is evaluated and reported to the pupil and to parents.

Each local elementary and secondary school usually has a number of publications for teachers, pupils, and parents that give suggestions for Special Interest projects in mathematics, history, writing, science, literature, psychology, government, communications media, and other curricular fields, as well as in extracurricular fields. This component also deals with career implications of student projects, as do all the other components.

The Advancement Component

There are two parts, age-grade advancement and advanced standing in subject matter, in the advancement component. There are always some children who ought to have the opportunity to attend some or all of their classes with older pupils. The work of Basic Scholars is reviewed at least once each year by the school principal, their teachers, and a school psychologist to determine whether it would be advantageous to arrange a partial or complete age-grade acceleration schedule. Parental approval is necessary for any such move and the pupil's own feelings must be considered.

For advanced standing, arrangements are made through regional colleges and universities to implement existing procedures, such as those monitored by the College Entrance Examination Board. Each Basic Scholar's work and achievement records are reviewed at least annually by the teachers and the school's counselor to determine whether any should be recommended for an advanced standing course or courses. As in all other program plans, parental approval and fulfillment of the four conditions for Special Interest work are required for age-grade advancement or advanced standing.

The Talent Development Component

The intent of the Talent Development component is to discover and foster talent potential among pupils. Some talents show themselves at an early age. Many great musicians were performing at age eight, nine, or ten and were composing significant works while in their teens. Some talents, such as those that involve extraordinary motor skills and stamina (swimming, acrobatics, figure skating), reach their peaks in the teen years. Other talents, such as creative writing, tend to take longer to mature. The Yourtowne approach (1) offers encouragement to talent where it is noticed and (2) includes in-school activities that identify and guide talent. The encouragement phase operates as follows:

- Art, music, physical education, and writing teachers are asked twice each year by principals to supply the names of children in all grades who show outstanding promise or very high present capability in the performing and creative arts.

- Parents are asked to indicate which of their children are studying privately in the creative and performing arts.

- Principals and/or counselors work with each such child to ensure that the schools' facilities are being used to encourage these children.

- Principals and/or counselors have built information banks of resources that might be available to give scholarships in the performing and other creative arts. They share what they find with parents, pupils, and teachers.

The augmentation phase of this component operates in every school in kindergarten through 12th grade. Each pupil who shows signs of talent is encouraged to develop it. The child is put into contact with someone from the school or the community who will further the child's special skills, abilities, and understandings.

The Talent Development component is monitored in regular meetings of a school-system-wide task force of teachers, augmented by parents and by performing and creative arts teachers. The coordinator of the gifted and talented programs convenes that task force and works with it.

The Human Service Component

Basic Scholars gain experiences in helping others through the Human Service component. It is an in-school operation in which Basic Scholars learn new and advanced skills of social and vocational importance while they work as volunteer assistants to members of the school system's faculty and staff. In order to take part in this component, Basic Scholars must meet the same four conditions that are required to take part in the other components.

The coordinator of the gifted and talented program determines, in conferences with pupils, principals, and teachers, the nature and scope of service assignments in each elementary and secondary school. It is not free labor to be used indiscriminately. An essential part of each such assignment is that it has:

1. educational objectives of value that match the needs of the Basic Scholar assigned
2. clearly defined and challenging responsibilities
3. a definite beginning and ending time
4. professional guidance from a school faculty or staff member
5. an evaluation that is shared with pupil and parents

Some such activities are being successfully carried out in every Yourtowne elementary and secondary school. Secondary and elementary students serve, for instance, as teachers' assistants in class work and tutoring. Others prepare bibliographies in the library. This service component capitalizes on what must be done, adds other important service opportunities, and ensures that scholars have practical experiences in applying what they know.

PUPIL ACTIVITIES

The Yourtowne five-part program is designed to maintain gifted and talented pupils in their regular classes. It is not a "pull-out" program, i.e., pupils are not withdrawn from regular classes at specified times to be with a special teacher or with other gifted and talented pupils for certain periods each week. Also, the program does not call for transporting pupils to centers for certain activities. Of course, pupils leave their regular classes from time to time, but it is always with the teacher's approval and after they have met the conditions of participation in each of the components.

There are some groups of gifted and talented pupils who meet and work together. These are informal groups of Basic Scholars, however, and the group meetings arise out of some mutual instructional need or other program purpose. Thus, the groups are expected to form, change, reform, and disband when the needs change.

STAFF AND RESPONSIBILITIES

It is the responsibility of the principals to establish and maintain the components of the gifted and talented education program in the schools over which they have authority. They consult with the program coordinator to ensure that each school's program, while to some extent unique, is also consistent with school-system-wide guidelines.

In each school, one teacher and one librarian are identified to give joint instructional leadership to the gifted and talented program in that school. The librarian serves as a continuing resource person for Basic Scholars and their teachers. Special attention is given to the location and dissemination of instructional materials for the Basic Scholars. Depending upon the size of the school, the two leaders are allocated one or more periods per day to consult with other teachers and to provide minicourses for in-service continuing education for other teachers.

Program coordinator and assistant coordinator are staff positions. Their purpose is to ensure consistent and continuous development of gifted and talented education system-wide. They provide guidance and offer consultation to the operating staff. They are also responsible for maintaining smooth interactions between this program and all the rest of the school system's operations.

These two staff members are essential to program success. They organize and operate a systematic and continuous in-service education effort in all the schools. They collect data on all gifted and talented pupils. To a very large extent, principals use the coordinator and assistant as resource persons to keep informed about the details of the program as it gets underway. Liaison with other educational, business, and community agencies is also their responsibility. In short, full staffing of these positions from the outset has a most significant bearing on the achievement of program stability and effectiveness.

Yourtowne's Board of Education believes that a sound and workable design for the education of gifted and talented children and youth is now in place in the community's elementary and secondary schools. The board and the superintendent say it is not a "fancy" program, but one that is solid, with all of the essentials that these pupils need for appropriate education.

The program and its related components did not burst forth full-blown. Its sense of direction emerged from the efforts of many persons, whose open and thorough efforts resulted in wide acceptance. The major steps in program implementation were found to include, but were not restricted to, the following:

- obtain board of education approval
- appoint program coordinator and staff
- orient principals and teachers
- identify Basic Scholars

- prepare IEPs for Basic Scholars
- identify teacher/librarian instructional leaders at schools
- establish community advisory group(s)
- plan in-service training for leaders
- conduct in-service training for leaders
- introduce four other components formally
- set up evaluation schedule for Basic Scholars
- report regularly to board of education and community

Persons associated with special education for gifted and talented students recognize that it flourishes best when viewed as a part of the whole educational system. They know that all pupils profit from individualized and specialized work, not just those who are gifted and talented. They realize, too, that the interest and participation of regular class teachers, specialists, principals, and all parents and pupils are needed to do any educational job well and that a program for gifted and talented pupils cannot remain a good one if the school system does not keep elevating its sights for all of the pupils in all of the schools (Sellin & Birch, 1980).

Chapter 15

Providing a Rationale for Individualized Educational Planning Programs

THE PRECEDENT OF PUB.L. 94-142

In certain states, individualized education programs for gifted and talented pupils are required by law or by state regulations. The task of compliance with such a mandate is mainly one of organization to prepare an individualized education program (IEP) for *each* identified gifted and talented pupil. In other states, teachers and parents still must persuade responsible officials that the IEP merits attention and support as a foundation for high-quality services for gifted and talented pupils.

The idea of the IEP is not new; it is within the tradition of the case study approach. What is new is its widespread application. Pub.L. 94-142 mandates an IEP for each handicapped pupil in the United States. There are no exceptions. States that require an IEP for gifted and talented pupils model their requirements after those of Pub.L. 94-142. There is a good supply of information about the IEP's application to gifted handicapped pupils. Aside from the Pub.L. 94-142 precedent, there are numerous justifications for using the IEP concept for all gifted and talented pupils. In fact, some suggest applying the IEP concept to all pupils (Reynolds, 1978).

Mortinger (1979) shared an example of an IEP criterion approach that he applied to student writing. As a teacher of elementary school age children, he was attracted to the premise that the reason for a pupil's "poor" performance may be that he or she does not know what is expected. In this premise, pupil aptitude does not refer to innate abilities, but to the various ways pupils understand directions. Pupils vary in their need for clarity about what the teacher's expectations are.

In Mortinger's example, a very able ten-year-old boy was found to write with originality. However, the pupil's content was marred by poorly formed letters and stilted sentence structure. It was obvious to Mortinger that it would be useful to give this boy directions to write in a more legible manner and to write more varied sentences. Accordingly, it was planned to introduce objectives of:

1. letter legibility, defined as letters placed on lined paper, uniform in size with other letters, and shaped as to standard cursive form
2. sentence variety, defined as the absence of connector words such as *and, but, therefore*
3. sentence structure variety, measured by the average length of sentences (in words) contained in writing samples

The intervention was to last for 18 daily 15-minute sessions. Before starting the intervention, five days were spent in obtaining writing samples in order to establish current performance standards. After five days, it was established that 40 percent of the pupil's writing contained illegible letters. With instruction in standard cursive form, the pupil's rating dropped to zero.

Intervention was then begun. By the tenth session, it was established that 74 percent of the pupil's sentences were of the same length. The pupil was directed to rewrite so that no one story contained all sentences of four to five words or all sentences of between 21 to 27 words; the pupil was to vary the number of words. By the end of the 18 sessions, only 25 percent of his sentences contained the same number of words. It was established that 91 percent of the pupil's sentences began with *and* or *but*. With direction to eliminate these introductions, the pupil's rating dropped to 35 percent.

Mortinger's report is instructive for several reasons. First, the student was not simply enrolled in a creative writing course with the hope that he would improve. Second, specific data relevant to the performance of the pupil were gathered, and instructions were tailored to focus pupil attention on particular writing behaviors. Third, feedback was designed to show the pupil whether expectations were being met. Fourth, specific criteria for success were clear in both the pupil's and teacher's minds. Fifth, the teacher established a sequence for priorities and did not attack all three at once.

Certainly, this kind of example is applicable to all pupils, not only to those who are gifted and talented. Both the process and the procedures have been used successfully with pupils who have a variety of learning rates and styles. The special point about this illustration for gifted and talented pupils is that these learners can often be taught early in the school years to design their own instruction, following that model or other models. Thus, guided independent study can be initiated early and can become more independent sooner with gifted and talented pupils, if they are deliberately given insight into the process and procedures used by their skills teachers.

PRIOR CONDITIONS FOR INDIVIDUALIZED PROGRAMS

There is enough experience with IEP implementation as defined by Pub.L. 94-142, to show that certain background conditions are essential for it to work. According to Cole and Dunn (1977), the essential lesson from one state's experience is that the processes and the procedures employed by each school district in collaboration with parents and pupils must be organized.

Goals and Outcomes of the IEP Process

One outcome of engaging in the IEP process is legal compliance with federal and state provisions. This calls for conformity to legalistic criteria by which the adequacy of an IEP is assessed. These principles originated in the protection of equal educational opportunity for handicapped and minority group learners, but they now protect equal opportunity for gifted and talented pupils, too, in many localities. *Least restrictive environment* is most often interpreted to refer to the setting of education. Alternatives that maximize normal school situations are preferred. *Appropriate education* is achieved by matching education and services to the aptitudes of the learner. *Nondiscriminatory assessment* means the use of procedures that are educationally relevant and take suitable account of individual differences in background and status. *Positive presumption* is a view that human potential is dynamic and evolving, not fixed. In practical terms, it means that all pupils are considered able to improve through teaching. *Due process* involves the inclusion of parents, or other advocates, and pupils in decision making, when appropriate. This principle implies that parents must be informed prior to action and circumstances that justify intentions must be defined. Moreover, endorsement must be secured, and persons involved are to be informed as to appeal procedures in instances of disagreement. *Informed consent* is a further refinement of due process. Endorsement by parents and other participants must be obtained without pressure, and persons are free to appeal decisions. Usually, this principle is applicable to parents and their advocates.

These principles are certainly applicable to the IEP process for the gifted and talented. They could be expressed as goals for IEPs for the talented in the following way:

> An Individualized Education Program for a gifted and talented pupil is the product of nondiscriminatory assessment that defines the most appropriate education in the least restrictive alternative founded upon positive presumption of the learner's potential. The development of the plan and its content conforms to the criteria of due process and reflects informed consent by its participants.

In operational terms, a clear outcome of the IEP is the translation of identification and assessment data into the prescription of individualized education. Identification, as an outcome, should result in a census that accounts for each gifted and talented pupil within the school district. This census provides primary data for estimating current and future needs for resources. With information on the numbers of pupils, requirements for personnel, equipment, materials, aids, and travel can be reliably projected. Compliance and the establishment of a program census require both organization and in-service training.

Organizational Aspects for IEPs

Cole and Dunn (1977) hold that each school district should specify what it intends to do to help parents and teachers develop IEPs. The Council for Exceptional Children (1977) suggests that each school district's statement should include (1) school district responsibilities, (2) participants to be included, and (3) a definition of the scope of the IEP. The district's chief responsibility is to initiate and conduct meetings for the design, revision, and evaluation of each pupil's IEP. Cole and Dunn press for a statement of board of education policy and a public endorsement by the superintendent to show that it is a serious matter. The minimum cadre of participants in IEP construction includes the parents, pupil's teacher, and a representative of the general education system. Other personnel may attend as requested. The scope of the IEP includes statements of goals, objectives, and services for the pupil, based upon personalized assessment. The IEP also specifies services and explains how performance will be evaluated.

The minimum elements that teachers, school officials, and parents must organize if the IEP concept is to be applied to gifted and talented pupils are identification, assessment, planning, product, implementation, and evaluation. Also, it is necessary to reach agreement on the processes of participant involvement.

Assume that a needs assessment has identified the desired pupil-related objectives and program goals. Also, assume that the curriculum of the district possesses sufficient clarity and flexibility to be adapted to individual pupil needs. In this case, identification involves informal observations and analyses of the pupil's in-school, home, and community performance. The information gathered in the identification phase may prompt either the teacher or the parent to propose a more formalized assessment.

Assessment, in this context, is an extension and amplification of identification. It is conducted with the knowledge and endorsement of parents. (State laws or regulations may require formal assessment by a certified psychologist to supplement teacher and parent judgments.) Assessment serves at least two functions. It provides certification of the pupil's eligibility for special educational services and for modification of general educational practices. It also establishes the pupil's current educational levels and indicates the pupil's aptitudes and interests.

Assessment is a participatory process. It is part of the communication between school and home that occurs prior to the scheduling of an IEP meeting. The product of this meeting is a written plan.

A continuing aspect of implementation is evaluation of outcomes stated in the IEP. These organizational elements are depicted in Figure 15-1. This figure identifies the steps in the process and suggests responsibilities for the faculty and staff of the school district and for the parents.

Special Concerns about Tests and Testing

The intent of Pub.L. 94-142 and its IEP component highlights the need for sensitivity in assessment procedures, according to Abeson and Zettell (1977). Their views coincide with those of the Council for Exceptional Children (1976). Both call attention to the limits of formal, norm-referenced testing procedures. It is not that these measures should be abandoned, but rather that their appropriate uses should be identified and more confidence placed in teacher judgment. This understanding would be another very important prior condition to the development of IEPs.

Understanding the Limitations of Testing

Standardized tests are useful only within the limits of the objectives stated by their publishers. Common abuses of interpretation are failing to match the program to the measurement and ignoring the setting of measurement.

An analysis by Jenkins and Pany (1978) illustrates the match between program and measurement. They compared the content of five standardized achievement tests with the content of five standardized reading series. They were interested in the match between first and second grade achievement as reflected by assessment and by mastery of a given series. They found significant discrepancies between the two indications of achievement. Their findings are summarized in adapted form in Table 15-1.

A child who had completed the first grade books of reading series A presumably had thereby achieved to grade 1.0 in reading. Only one out of the five different reading achievement tests taken by the child agreed with the 1.0 reading achievement that had been inferred from actual performance on the reading series. An immediate implication derived from the Jenkins and Pany analysis is that perhaps allowance should be made for error about student performance. It is not clear, however, which of the many test results is the "correct" one. Moreover, the analysis points out that it is necessary to account for the sources of error in comparing one reading series against another; procedures to supplement the standardized tests seem the only sensible way out.

Figure 15-1 Dimensions of Responsibilities for Organization of IEPs for Gifted and Talented Pupils

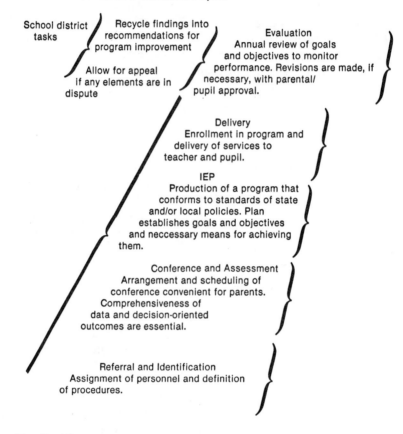

School district tasks

Recycle findings into recommendations for program improvement

Allow for appeal if any elements are in dispute

Evaluation
Annual review of goals and objectives to monitor performance. Revisions are made, if necessary, with parental/ pupil approval.

Delivery
Enrollment in program and delivery of services to teacher and pupil.

IEP
Production of a program that conforms to standards of state and/or local policies. Plan establishes goals and objectives and neccessary means for achieving them.

Conference and Assessment
Arrangement and scheduling of conference convenient for parents. Comprehensiveness of data and decision-oriented outcomes are essential.

Referral and Identification
Assignment of personnel and definition of procedures.

Note: Read figure across two pages

Another source of error can be in where and how the test is given. The conditions that existed during the test construction will not necessarily be present in the administration of tests. For example, test publishers have refined their test by use of trained test examiners under conditions of rapport in settings that are physically comfortable and attractive. Pupils are assumed to be motivated and familiar with the tasks.

Stoneman and Gibson (1978) investigated situational conditions upon test performance. They used two conditions of assessment: familiar classroom versus unfamiliar testing room and familiar examiner versus stranger. Children scored significantly higher when the test was given by the familiar examiner in the unfamiliar testing room, while the scores were lowest when

Figure 15-1 continued

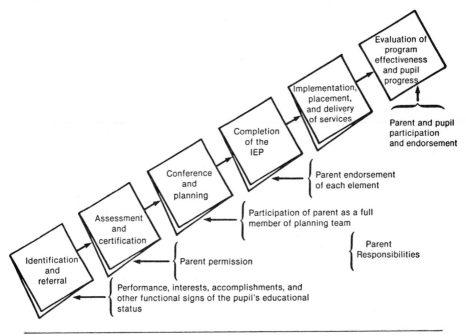

Table 15-1 Illustration of Discrepancies between Actual Performance and Assessed Performance*

	Grade Level Achievement According to Standardized Test Results				
	I	*II*	*III*	*IV*	*V*
Grade 1 reading series					
A	1.5	1.0	1.1	1.8	2.0
B	2.0	1.4	1.2	2.2	2.2
C	1.5	1.0	1.0	1.4	1.7
D	1.5	1.2	1.2	1.0	2.1
E	1.8	1.4	1.2	1.1	2.0
Grade 2 reading series					
A	2.8	2.5	1.2	2.2	2.2
B	3.3	1.9	1.0	3.0	3.0
C	2.2	2.1	1.0	2.7	2.3
D	3.1	2.5	1.4	2.9	3.5
E	2.2	2.4	1.1	2.5	2.5

*Adapted from Jenkins and Pany (1978).

the test was given by the stranger in the familiar setting. The other two situations produced about equal results; however, they were midway between the other two. The implication was that the same child performed better (e.g., higher scores) on the basis of the situation. The Stoneman and Gibson report is typical of many that illustrate how test performance is related to the testing situation. These findings do not destroy the credibility of standardized assessment, but they reflect the need to take these sources of error into account.

CONDITIONS FOR PREPARING IEPs

Present Status of Preparing IEPs

A report by Anderson, Barner, and Larson (1978) serves two purposes: an example of evaluation procedures applied to an ongoing school-sponsored program and a status summary on the preparation of IEPs. Anderson et al. examined the content of 400 IEPs that had been generated during one year by teachers with one year of experience. The IEPs were written in the context of the school district plan for Pub.L. 94-142. While the pupil population was not entirely gifted and talented, the report is relevant for its lessons about the procedure of preparing the document. Moreover, the pupils were enrolled in both regular and special settings. Findings of the study were as follows:

1. About 75 percent of the behavioral objectives were referenced to basic skills and 10 percent to affective aspects of behavior.
2. Specialists were held responsible for about 75 percent of the objectives while 25 percent were allocated to regular education teachers.
3. The accomplishment of about 75 percent of all objectives was to be evaluated by teacher-made tests and 25 percent by standardized tests.
4. Six percent of the IEPs lacked parent signatures.
5. The estimated time for accomplishment of an objective averaged about five months.
6. Typically, there was a one-to-one correspondence of goal to objective. (Anderson et al. speculated as to the adequacy of this correspondence.)
7. In general terms, the content of an IEP included the following elements: (a) summation of educational needs, (b) needed educational goals, (c) instructional objectives, and (d) recommended instructional and curriculum materials.
8. The content was found to be free of jargon and readable; the elements were internally consistent.

Anderson et al. judged that IEPs of high quality were predominant in the 400 they studied. They believed that there was a need, however, for training in the writing of goals and objectives, and in communicating with parents. They also felt that school districts should help specialists and teachers to elaborate more fully on objectives required for goal attainment, to introduce affective dimensions of behavior, and to use more fully the expertise of the regular class teacher.

A Frame of Reference for Preparing Prescriptions

An end product of the IEP process is a prescription. The prescription sets forth individualized goals and objectives, the procedures and timetable for reaching them, who will be involved in the process, and how it will be determined if the prescription is effective.

The first step in preparing an IEP is identifying a gifted and talented pupil. Identification, according to Kirk and Gallagher (1979), should involve two related matters. One is to spell out the reason that the learner came to the attention of school authorities for consideration as a gifted and talented person, i.e., what the child does or knows that caused teachers or parents to suspect giftedness or talent. The second is an appraisal of the pupil's actual performance compared with the performance of pupils of similar age, sex, and station in life.

Assessment involves the assembly of additional relevant information. Its outcome is to derive a hypothesis about future actions. At this point, on the basis of the identification process, it has already been decided that this is a gifted and talented pupil who is eligible for special education and services. The main question now is: What special education and services? The detailed analysis called assessment should result in specific information about what this particular pupil's special program and services should be.

Information should be grouped around correlates of school performance that require management. A first step under assessment is to assemble the known information about the physical, environmental, and psychological attributes of the pupil. A minimal listing of physical information includes (1) visual and auditory acuity, (2) perceptual abilities, (3) general health, (4) nutritional status, and (5) physical coordination. Environmental correlates include at least (1) adequacy of school experiences, (2) language of the family, (3) instances of positive experiences, (4) encouragement of the family, (5) extracurricular experiences and hobbies, and (6) peer relationships. Psychological correlates include at least (1) self-image and self-concept, (2) language skills, (3) cognitive/intellectual abilities (e.g., Bloom or Guilford), (4) attending skills, and (5) talent-related skills.

The second step of assessment is to form a hypothesis (or more than one) about the best program to enhance the pupil's development. The hypothesis serves as a tentative description of the learner and appropriate educational interventions.

The processes of identification and assessment flow into prescription. The central task in prescription is to transform the hypothesis, or hypotheses, into concrete recommendations for action.

The total IEP should be coherent, with no loose ends. It should have an orderly, rational sequence; every part should be plainly related to the other parts. The language should pose no problems to the ordinary parent, and the tone should be positive and constructive.

Managing and Maintaining the Conditions

Drawing upon the Pub.L. 94-142 model, Ballard and Zettel (1977) identified three principles for managing and maintaining the conditions for preparing an IEP. Although school officials are responsible for these principles, their implementation is a responsibility shared among the participants. Evaluation, also a mutual effort, is evidence that the principles are in operation.

The principle of *certain assurances* means that rights and protections are guaranteed to pupils and parents as overt, public policy.

The Pub.L. 94-142 model for the IEP places great emphasis upon *resource allocation.* One dimension is directed toward personnel development through in-service education of professional staff and faculty. The other dimension is that of pupil identification, which requires an activist, ongoing effort to locate eligible pupils.

The *detailed plan* principle requires the description of facilities, equipment, materials, and all else necessary to support the elements of special education and services. There is a division of opinion regarding the IEP and this element. Some believe that all services should be in place so that IEP recommendations can be implemented; others feel that recommendations should be stated, regardless of the availability of resources, so that needed resources can be identified. The key to resolving that difference of opinion seems to be that the lack of a necessary special education component or service is not an acceptable reason for the school district's failure to supply the required component or service. In short, the representatives of a school district may not with impunity say, "We don't have the particular kind of education required, so the gifted and talented pupil will have to do without it." This position was reinforced by a court decision that held a local school district responsible for furnishing special education for gifted and talented pupils from its own funds if the state did not supply the money to meet the need.

THE IEP AS PUBLIC POLICY

The IEP is an aspect of public policy. The policy is an open declaration by assorted sponsors to support and enforce given practices.

Higgins and Barresi (1979) list legislators, school board members, government officials, administrators, teachers, staff consultants, parents, and students as those who influence public policy about education. Their analysis reveals that individualized, appropriate education, including that for gifted and talented pupils, has come under the "sunshine" of public policy. They further observe that contemporary policy reflects a shift from the remote and general to the immediately applicable, targeted toward specific populations in local school systems. Consequently, each local school district is challenged to improve and innovate.

Higgins and Barresi found three types of public policy support. They did not advocate one over another. It is possible, however, to use them as a checklist to assess any local situation.

Type I: Commitment

The base, or foundation, from which programs, services, and practices emanate is commitment. Usually, policies are referenced to laws and/or court decrees. They are designed to ensure individual rights and protection, and they reflect educational philosophy regarding moral and legal obligations. Public policy, of course, can *mandate* services, or it can make such services a permissible activity.

Type II: Resource Distribution

Policy decisions are a matter of public record because any significant allocation of resources by a school board requires approval and appropriation. Resources can be funds, human, and material. This type of policy usually specifies accountability standards, organizational structure, and personnel assignments; it also translates philosophy into practices. Decisions at this level of policy reflect the status of services delivered to pupils and the level of support delivered to teachers.

Type III: Implementation

The policy of implementation is less formal than the previous two. Administrative guides and staff handbooks are the usual sources. The guidelines may be official or unofficial, but they do state the practices observed in operation. As a condition of quality, the practices would be referenced to Type I and Type II policies. Policy at this level directly affects gifted and talented pupils, their parents, and their teachers.

Public Policy and the Gifted and Talented

Higgins and Barresi found great variation in public policy regarding the gifted and talented. They reported that a complete examination of public policy for gifted and talented education at all levels of education, local, state, and federal, is long overdue. They cited the policy position of the Council for Exceptional Children that:

> our nation must be morally and ethically committed to providing exceptional children and youth with the programs they require to develop their potentials fully . . . educators should vigorously support programs for the gifted as consistent with their concept of the need for special assistance for all exceptional children.

The IEP, as used with gifted and talented pupils, operates within a context of endorsement and sanction. It is plain that teachers can and often do communicate with parents and their child without formal policy sanction. However, it is also apparent that policy sanction is a helpful resource, and one whose significance is growing.

Chapter 16

Specifying the Content of an Individualized Education Program

THE SCOPE OF THE INDIVIDUALIZED EDUCATION PROGRAM

The Individualized Education Program (IEP) has been increasingly accepted as a vehicle for the management of school and related education resources adapted to the needs and status of an individual learner. The IEP is *not* a lesson plan for day-to-day practice, but rather the map that provides guidance for day-to-day movements. Lesson plans, when needed, can be built to carry out the objectives stated in the IEP.

For gifted and talented children, the plan should have at least these five components: (1) current educational status, (2) annual goals and short-term performance objectives, (3) specification of services to be provided with reference to inclusion/retention with age peers, (4) projected estimates for duration of services, and (5) identification of appropriate criteria for at least annual review of objectives. The written IEP is often introduced by information about the pupil and how the pupil came to the attention of those who prepared the plan. At the end, it contains spaces for signatures, endorsements, or appeals because of disagreements.

Exhibit 16-1 outlines a design format for an IEP. The order of the parts can vary; for example, the description of current educational status may precede the description of the implementation. It is essential, however, that all elements be present.

There are three items of special note for gifted and talented pupils. IEPs for the gifted and talented are characterized by (1) references to the standard curriculum, (2) emphasis on affective as well as cognitive and skills dimensions, and (3) focus upon programs leading to goals/objectives rather than upon moving the child to a place/classroom to receive services.

Exhibit 16-1 Component Parts of the Individualized Education Program for Gifted and Talented Learners*

I. Identifying data
  A. Student name
  B. Present placement
  C. Responsible school district
  D. Referral for eligibility: by whom? by what criteria? when?
  E. Certified for eligibility: by whom? by what criteria? when?
  F. Evidence of parent permission for referral and certification
II. Participants
  A. Date of meeting
  B. Effective dates for the IEP: from _____ to _____
  C. Persons present: name? relationship?
  D. Signatures of persons present: name? accept, amend, reject, appeal?
III. Goals and objectives
  A. Curriculum areas (referenced to the curriculum in place within the school district; referenced to affective, cognitive, and/or skill behaviors)
  B. Time for completion (referenced to the school year)
  C. Responsible persons (names and relationship to learner)
  D. Evaluation (criteria, procedures, schedule and person(s) for determination if objectives are met)
IV. Implementation
  A. Participation
    1. Describe the extent to which the learner will participate in regular, or standard, educational programs (e.g., time per week).
    2. Describe the extent to which the learner will participate in modified programs.
    3. Describe justification for differential participation in light of goals/objectives.
  B. Services
    1. List any special instructional materials, equipment, media necessary to implement the goals/objectives.
    2. List any special transportation provisions necessary to implement the goals/objectives.

Exhibit 16-1 continued

3. List any special provisions for staff and faculty released time to implement the goals / objectives.
4. List any other special provisions necessary to implement goals and objectives.
C. Service management
   1. List by name(s) and signature(s) responsible faculty member(s).
   2. List by name and signature the administrator responsible for the plan.
   3. List by name and signature the district staff person responsible for the plan.
D. Program format or design
   1. List elements of program and effective dates for modified programs.
   2. List acceleration, enrichment options.
   3. List options for performance / talent furtherance.
V. Current educational status (assessment)
   A. Curriculum areas (identify status in grade level terms with reference to procedure, evaluator(s), and dates)
   B. Summative (list and describe the learner's performance in comparison to learners similar in age, sex, and socioeconomic status; possibly a chart or graph)
   C. Formative (interpret the learner's performance as priorities for affective, cognitive, and/or performance/talent dimensions; attend as appropriate to career education and physical education)
   D. Supplemental (list any relevant information that has a bearing on the learner's educational experience, e.g., motivation, attention, hobbies, clubs, etc. or instances of physical impairments, or parent insights or referral insights)
VI. Revisions (any amendments that altered any part of this plan; date and signature of parents; how amendments will be an improvement for the learner; justifications of any reduction in service)
VII. Compliance (sources and endorsements of the format by appropriate state agencies)

*Adapted from Torres (1977).

PREPARING GOALS AND OBJECTIVES FOR GIFTED AND TALENTED PUPILS

Goals and objectives should communicate. They should conform to acceptable criteria for clarity and precision. They should lead persons to necessary action and provide a realistic operational context for evaluation.

Bloom, Hastings, and Madaus (1971) speak of a goal as an aspiration of the school for its students, a declaration of a school's social mission, or the intentions of staff and faculty. Goals are general statements that identify direction, tone, and quality. Goals, consequently, serve as organizers for long-term emphasis. By contrast, objectives are specific descriptors of *pupil* performance that are evidence of goal attainment. Objectives can be placed into a step-by-step sequence toward a goal.

Preparing Goal Statements

Pennsylvania is one of the states that require local school districts to use the IEP in providing special education and services. Davis (1978) brought together and analyzed one Pennsylvania district's experience with IEPs for gifted and talented pupils.

Davis, when considering how best to develop objectives and goals for gifted and talented pupils, endorsed the use of a matrix similar to those presented earlier. His reference points were existing curricula such as language arts, social studies, fine arts, and physical education viewed in the light of cognitive and affective domains. The cognitive domain was referenced to evaluation, synthesis, analysis, problem solving, and research skills similar to those in the Bloom, Hastings, and Madaus (1971) model. The affective domain was referenced to self-adaptation and social adaptation. The goal section of the IEP, in Davis' view, should be directed toward these higher order skills. The Davis report is instructive as the translation of an existing curriculum and an existing framework, such as Bloom et al. (1971; see Chapter 1), into a resource base upon which to construct objectives and goals for IEPs. (See Chapter 8 to review the ideas of a Table of Specifications.)

Mager (1972) showed how a faculty could generate curriculum goals with a procedure termed goal analysis, which can be an alternative procedure. First, participants imagine the behavior or performances of someone who has achieved a goal or a close general approximation of it. Then each participant writes evidence of that performance on a separate card. Responses are then shared, and new and more precise statements are prepared. The new cards are sorted into common clusters from which goal statements can be generated.

Mager does not confine participants to educators. Participants could be any informed person who has expert judgment to share. The Mager method could be readily applied on the matrix foundation recommended by Davis.

The Attributes of Objectives

Bloom, Hastings, and Madaus (1971) paid tribute to Mager for popularizing the concept of the objective. An objective, in this sense, describes the desired or expected performance of a pupil after instruction. It has a future frame of reference. An objective is a precise statement that enables *any* reader to comprehend its meaning, including the pupil and parents. The objective does not tell the teacher how to carry out instruction, however.

According to Bloom et al., an educational objective has the three following elements: (1) the act or behavior to be demonstrated by the student, (2) the conditions under which the student will demonstrate the act, and (3) the criteria that will serve as evidence of performance. In actual practice, there are two variations. All three elements may be listed in one statement, which in technical language would be termed a performance objective, or the objective may be written to include only the elements of act and conditions with any statements about criteria deferred to a separate statement or evaluation. An example of a performance objective would be:

> The student will read five research articles that summarize identification procedures and will prepare a written report of five pages that will conform to the standards for publication of the American Psychological Association.

The goal under which this objective appeared might have been: The student will be able to use critical thinking in working out acceptable professional practices.

Evaluative criteria can also be expressed as percentage of accuracy or as conformity to known standards.

Matching Goal and Act

In the Forest Park Public Schools (1971) a guide was developed to help teachers match student behaviors to the global domains of Bloom. The acts of knowledge could include, for instance, matching, finding definitions, recalling items, and recognizing items. Examples of comprehension items would include paraphrasing, giving examples, and debating on a limited basis. Applications could include model building, repeating an experiment, and role playing (imitation level). Analysis could include listing attributes, outlining, comparing, constructing, and making deductions. Synthesis encompasses making an original plan or product, finding new uses or combinations, and identifying problems. Evaluation is made up of judging peer products and performances, evaluating one's own performance, and evaluating data according to specified criteria. The Forest Park Public Schools Guide is an illustration of translating the Bloom et al. (1971) procedure (see Chapter 1) into descriptors of acts applicable to gifted and talented pupils.

SERVICES

The adequacy of education and services can be judged by the reactions of parents, pupils, participating teachers, and school staff. This dimension of the IEP addresses the means by which goals and objectives are implemented or fulfilled.

Parental Evaluation of Recommendations

The gifted and talented child's family is placed in a partnership with the schools by the spirit and content of the IEP philosophy.

Brehm (1978) points to five questions parents should ask about the special education recommendations of school authorities. These questions were designed to help parents evaluate the efficacy of special education (e.g., practices either in addition to or modifications of regular education). In this sense, the Brehm questions can be especially helpful in the consideration of recommendations that might involve separating any child from other pupils in the education mainstream.

One question parents should ask, according to Brehm, is whether the proposed change in education program benefits the child and addresses the matter that brought the child to the attention of school authorities in the first place. For example, a child may be three grade levels above the next most advanced classmate in most school subjects. A simplistic recommendation to skip two or three grades without consultation with the child, without preparation of receiving teachers, and without an IEP ought to be a very suspect recommendation, indeed. If the criteria for effective acceleration were followed, however, the tactic of acceleration might be most helpful.

Brehm recommended that parents satisfy themselves that proposals consider social and emotional learning as well as academic learning goals. Moreover, school personnel should be familiar with out-of-school resources that might be helpful. The thrust recommended for parents is not a challenge to professional authority. Rather, the teacher, the other participating educators, and the gifted and talented child should be able to explain their perceptions of the need for the kind of special education and service being proposed.

A second high-priority question is an outgrowth of the first. Parents should ask what evidence justifies a particular recommendation. The educator should be able to demonstrate the probable effectiveness of a given recommendation. Sources could be testimony from other parents or from pupils currently enrolled. Research and evaluation reports in the literature could be helpful. Brehm recommended observation and visitation to programs. It would be particularly helpful if parents could observe gifted and talented children similar in age and development to their own.

Parents should, third, ask about possible negative effects. The program coordinator, the child's teacher, and the parent are advised to be especially conscious of any consequences of labeling. Parents should feel confident that any adaptations would not be accompanied by undue attention to the child. The special abilities of the child should simply be one element in the child's life, not the sole source of the child's self-image and self-esteem.

The fourth inquiry would concern emotional and social learning. Program standards of quality reveal that kind of program orientation. If so, they can be valuable sources of reassurance, and parents should ask to see the program's written standards of quality.

The fifth question suggested is directed toward the evaluation of recommendations. In evaluation, both general progress and the attainment of specifics should be scrutinized. Brehm attached great importance to assessment by the child's regular class teacher(s) as well as by any specialists who would have elements of information. Evaluation should be guided so as to modify recommendations to benefit the child. It should also help teachers clarify their expectations.

The Brehm questions are not referenced to legalistic constraints. Instead, her ideas are related to professional standards of practice and to respect for the competence of parents. Her recommendations illustrate a positive presumption about parents and the meaning of informed consent. (It is to be noted, however, that Brehm's standards would be required practices under Pub.L. 94-142 in those states in which provisions of this act apply to the gifted and talented.)

Coverage of Educational Services

Ballard and Zettel (1977) describe services as those provisions required to help the child benefit from education. Services are the means by which the goals/objectives for the learner are matched to the educational tasks to be taught to the learner. Categories include: transportation; diagnostic, assessment, and pupil evaluation services; identification services and procedures; support services; and instructional services.

Higgins and Barresi (1979) and Reynolds and Birch (1977) endorse the concept of services as a matching process rather than an exclusive focus upon a place to receive services. They consider services a reflection of public policy to support individualized education. As policy, the focus (e.g., goals) is as relevant as the location. According to their analysis, services are the means by which:

1. parents are to be involved in the activities to be undertaken.
2. teachers are able to fulfill goals/objectives. As personnel policies, it is necessary to consider the scheduling, selection of format, devising of content, and released time options for free and appropriate in-service training for professional development.
3. principals and other administrative staff are involved to support implementation of the IEP.
4. estimated costs of implementation can be determined so as to provide orderly budgeting.

Higgins and Barresi propose two parallel dimensions of services. One is a description of the frequency, scope, and activities to be undertaken by participants. The other is the selection of curriculum means of assessment of goals/objectives, equipment, and supplies.

Maximizing Services

The array of support services is great now, and it is growing. The State Board of Education of the Commonwealth of Pennsylvania (1976) allows the hardware dimensions of curriculum goals as part of instructional costs. Manchester (1977) described the extension of Pennsylvania's provisions for the IEP to the gifted and talented. Partridge (1976) observed that restricting inventories of "special" services to "special" settings has the effect of isolating programs and pupils.

Two strategies have emerged to prevent isolation of programs and to maximize access to support services. Both the Texas model (Partridge) and the Pennsylvania model allow the use and introduction of materials and equipment into regular class settings. For example, the Western Pennsylvania Special Education Regional Resource Center (1978) describes the potential benefits from participation of regular class teachers in the IEP process. In this way, pupils do not have to leave their classrooms to receive personalized services. The second and related strategy is the use of an IEP team who provide systematic consultation to the regular teacher in implementing service. The advantages to the specialists are that they, in turn, can benefit from consultation with teachers on procedures and receive feedback as to the suitability of specialized materials.

INSTRUCTIONAL DIMENSIONS

As has been stressed in this chapter, the IEP is *not* the same as a lesson plan. Rather, it is a long-term education program of major import for the pupil. The teacher's professional judgment and competence are in no way usurped by the policies associated with the IEP. The teacher chooses specific, day-to-day aptitude/intervention tactics associated with assessment, with instruction, and all else that directly concerns teaching.

Feldhusen and Treffinger (1977) have reported an investigation of the tactics used by teachers to implement the information generated by an IEP. They were able to identify four general guidelines that reflect existing practices. Their guidelines are instructive, since they are broadly applicable to instruction and can serve as criteria for translation of goals/objectives, deduced from assessment, into instructional procedures.

Defining the Elements

Feldhusen and Treffinger found that instructional objectives do, in fact, specify behaviors for pupil attainment. Objectives so stated can facilitate utilization of what was termed a Learning Activity Package (LAP), which consists of (1) introductory elements to motivate and orient students, (2) preteaching inventories to assess pupil status, (3) assembly of materials targeted to assessments and interest building, (4) use of discussion and other opportunities for student participation, and (5) continuing evaluation of student learning.

Awareness about New Possibilities

It is strongly urged that teachers be sensitive to new objectives that might arise out of introductory activities and/or the process of instruction. Gifted and talented children are drawn to teachers who respect ideas they spin off from current work.

Selecting Materials

Feldhusen and Treffinger also recommended the examination of inventories immediately available in the school district. They noted that materials need not have been originally developed specifically for the gifted and talented. These resources can be examined as to the behaviors required by the student. A match between the acts of an objective and the task demands of materials is required for material selection.

Evaluating Instruction

The emphasis of evaluation, as isolated by Feldhusen and Treffinger, is upon the utility of materials and methods to facilitate goals/objectives. For example, the time dimensions should be recorded and noted; durability and ease of operation should also be observed. They recommended that school districts encourage teachers to share with each other their experiences in developing their instructional materials.

Chapter 17

Assembling and Assessing Information

PREFERRED PRACTICES

The assessment of pupil performance is not an easy task. At the heart of the difficulty lies an uneasiness about "fairness." In more technical terms, professionals and parents both have reservations about whether conventional assessment has sufficient validity (e.g., accuracy) to predict the future, to forecast success in adulthood, and to summarize current status accurately. Certainly, thoughtful hesitation is justified. The day of unquestioned acceptance of pupil assessment procedures is past. Aside from fairness or validity concerns, long-standing public school assessment procedures have repeatedly been challenged by court decisions and legislation. Consequently, a new dimension of pupil assessment appears, namely, compliance with legislative and judicial interpretations and decrees.

Implications of rulings about the legality of testing in schools were reviewed by Tractenberg and Jacoby (1977). Their paper considered standardized achievement, intelligence, and aptitude test procedures, as well as teacher-made tests. The point of confrontation has been the provisions of the 14th Amendment of the U.S. Constitution that protect and affirm the Bill of Rights' guarantees regarding due process and equal protection. The contentions faced by the courts and legislatures have required them to balance purposes and interests. Schools plead that testing leads to a positive, differential treatment that fulfills worthy social purposes. Advocates object that testing leads to decisions about pupils that have deprived them of equal protection.

The legal system has been reluctant to interfere in areas of professional expertise and of local province. This reluctance has been eroded of late, however, by the nature and weight of evidence of misuse of testing. Tractenberg and Jacoby point to specific findings that prompted judges to intervene. The documented evidence included verification that (1) school districts evaded desegregation by assigning pupils to tracks or ability groups according to test scores; (2) aptitude tests, e.g., an estimate of what has been learned, are in reality similar to tests of achievement; (3) test scores influence teacher judgment, regardless of the pupil's performance; (4) enrollment in school may be denied, based solely upon test scores; and (5) classification of pupils by test scores per se are decisions based on factors such as sex, race, or socioeconomic status, which are irrelevant to innate ability.

Tractenberg and Jacoby isolated instances that are directly applicable to the education of gifted and talented pupils. They involve teacher-made tests, admission standards, school practice, and discrimination. For example, two school systems each sponsored a district-wide, specialized, segregated high school. In each, admission was based upon grade point averages and/or teacher-made entrance tests. The school district policy was to maintain a 50-50 balance between the sexes. In order to accomplish this, higher cutoff scores were set for female students than for male students. The courts, after study, found in favor of the female students. The districts were directed either to expand their programs or to employ similar cutoff scores.

In another instance, grade point average (admittedly the result of teacher-made tests) was supported as an admission criterion as long as it was uniformly applied. In a related case, a suit was brought against a district regarding teacher-made tests for graduation credit. One teacher used written examinations, while a teacher in a similar class used observation of skills. The courts refused to intervene, ruling that the dispute was one of style rather than discrimination.

Tractenberg and Jacoby concluded that the impact of legal decisions to date has been to make it necessary for schools to establish a solid, legally defensible justification for assessment and assignment practices. When testing leads to differential treatment, there must be compelling evidence and justification.

Tractenberg and Jacoby concluded that the implications of court decisions could be summarized as follows:

> school districts must exercise greater care and sensitivity in evaluating the educational potential and needs of students and in acting upon those evaluations. If they do not do so on their own initiative, the courts may be available to impose such a requirement. (p. 253)

It is obvious that there are legal sanctions in addition to moral and ethical obligations. Reynolds and Birch (1977) call attention to preferred practices of assessment that fulfill both legal sanction and ethical obligation. Adherence to their resumé can ensure sensitive and professionally sound assessment and evaluation. Their listing of practices is directed toward the teacher as the central figure in assessment. Their guidelines can be summarized as follows:

1. High-quality assessment includes assessment of both the learner and the program.

2. Screening procedures are undertaken for purposes of locating pupils who need further study.
3. Assessment is directed toward planning for the improvement of instruction.
4. Procedures are selected with care and precision for each learner so that known discrimination effects arising from physical impairment, sex, and economic status are eliminated.
5. Known sources of error with respect to physical impairment, sex, and economic status are kept in mind when interpretations and inferences are made from test results.
6. Parent permission for assessment is to be secured, and parents are to have access to all information consistent with their legal rights.
7. Dimensions of program assessment include physical facilities, materials, tactics of management of pupil behavior, methods, social-cultural differences, curriculum content, and tactics of evaluation.
8. Assessment, including specialized assessments, are conducted by the learner's teachers, who consult with specialists and consultants at their discretion. Assessment is to fit relevant educational purposes.

The essential contribution of assessment is to fulfill the processes of match, management, and maintenance identified in Unit III. The basic principle is that assessment must be directed toward individualized treatment that fulfills a worthy end for both learner and society.

UNDERSTANDING AND INTERPRETING DATA

The Individualized Education Program (IEP), as noted earlier, contains goals and objectives derived from assessment of the learner's current educational status. The integrity of the IEP is to be judged by the appropriateness of its match among goals and objectives × current status × evaluation (× means interaction in the scientific sense).

One major contribution of evaluation and assessment specialists during the 1960s was to identify four approaches to gathering and interpreting educational data about learners. These approaches, or options, are presented in Table 17-1. Types of testing and assessment procedures, according to this table can be norm- or criterion-referenced, and interpretations of results can be summative or formative. Hence, the four options. Unfortunately, both advocates and opponents of certain of these options have advanced such vigorous positions that it is easy to reach the mistaken conclusion that the four are mutually exclusive. This need not be the case. There is a "natural" fit among them; they are indeed complementary. The use of the options in a

Table 17-1 Options for Gathering and Interpreting Educational Data

	Assessment Procedures	
Interpretation Functions	Norm- Referenced	Criterion- Referenced
Summative	Pupil's performance is compared to standardized norms of a group. Typically, test is administered at end of learning. Test is used to sum up.	Content of summative procedures can suggest expectations. Criterion-referenced procedures can be useful to define mastery of previously specified learning tasks.
Formative	Results from norm references can alert teachers to the need for individualized education. Follow-up is required to individualize fully.	Pupil's performance is compared to known criterion of performance. Tests are useful in maintaining frequent checks of progress. Instruction is altered in light of pupil progress. Feedback to students is maximized.

coordinated manner allows for greater precision in matching a learner to task and to treatment.

Summative Approaches and Tactics

Bloom, Hastings, and Madaus (1971) emphasized that assessment is to be transformed into decisions. These decisions involve providing feedback to students, forecasting performance, selecting pupil evaluation procedures, evaluating program outcomes, and planning interventions.

Summative evaluation is an act of summation. Thus, it takes place at the end of some event or series of events. It is designed (1) to classify or grade pupils, (2) to enable teachers to judge instructional practices, and/or (3) to compare curricula against one another. Usually, summative evaluation occurs at the end of a course, unit, or school year. It is most frequently a comparison of a person's performance to the average performance of a group similar in age. Kirk and Gallagher (1979) equate summative evaluation with interindividual differences. Formal tests usually serve as a principal source for assessment, although teacher-made tests also play a part as a source of information.

The advantages of summative evaluation can be a sense of objectivity that offers students a sense of mastery and helps to identify the need for subsequent improvement. The disadvantage to students is that such feedback may come too late for remedial steps, since it occurs at the end of instruction.

Formative Evaluation and Tactics

Formative evaluation, according to Bloom et al., takes place during learning, rather than being deferred until learning (and instruction) is presumed to be completed. It is characterized by frequent assessment of pupil performance during the instructional phase. Its goal is to identify areas in which remediation is needed immediately so that teacher-pupil effort can be focused or refocused. It usually involves the comparison of pupils' performance to their own past performance. In the Kirk and Gallagher sense, it is equated with intraindividual differences. Bloom et al. further emphasize that formative evaluation takes place *during* instruction in addition to pre- and postinstruction. Formative equates with formulate. Its intent is to help check on and improve the formula, or plan, originally adopted for instruction.

The formative procedure originated with curriculum development. It was observed that continual trials and assessment during the development of a standardized reading series, for example, improved the final product. Continuing assessment was also found to be valid for instruction.

Typically, teachers conduct formative evaluation by observation, interview, and pupil reaction to instruction. Teachers usually devise specific assessments tailored to specific context and to a specific pupil.

Norm-Referenced Measurement

Norm-referenced test measurement, according to Popham (1976), is designed to determine a given pupil's performance in relation to the performance of pupils who took the test previously. The performance is represented by a source (e.g., total of points assigned by the examiner on the basis of correct answers) that is transformed into standardized reference descriptors* such as mean, median, standard deviation, percentile, or grade equivalent.

---

*An examiner's manual for a particular test offers further explanations of these terms. In general, the mean and median describe "averageness." A *mean* is the sum of scores divided by the number of scores. A *median* is found from examining the ranking of scores. The score at which 50 percent of all scores fall above and 50 percent below is the median. Standard deviations and percentiles allow more precise comparisons. A *standard deviation* is an indication of the spread of the score, using the mean as the reference point. Because of their mathematical properties, standard deviations describe a balance or proportion on either side of the mean. The third standard deviation below a mean includes about 3 percent of the scores, as does the third standard deviation above the mean. The second standard deviation below the mean represents about 13 percent of the pupils' scores, as does the second standard deviation above the mean. The one standard deviation range above and below the mean is a broad spectrum. A *percentile* is the rank of a score translated into an ordinal number, e.g., the 25th percentile, 75th percentile, and so forth. Percentiles range from zero to 100. The 50th percentile, or median, describes a score of which 50 percent of a comparison fall above or below that performance. The 97th percentile would mean a score exceeded by only 3 percent of the reference group. A *grade equivalent* simply is the average test score of pupils at a certain grade in school.

By means of these descriptors, the person's "raw" score can acquire a reference through which it may then be compared with either the performance of similar persons or the performance of potentially similar persons. For example, a standardized achievement test might serve both comparisons. A grade level equivalent would be determined and a comparison made with the performance of learners of the same age. That same "score" might be applied to the members of a Basic Scholars Program to assess the person's potential for an intended assignment or group placement. Typically, aptitude tests are comparisons of a performance score against the scores of competent performers.

The advocates of norm-referenced measurement, according to MacTurk and Neisworth (1978), argue that it has several advantages. One is that norm-referenced measurement affords a known reference. Given the ethically and professionally sound nature of test construction, a standardized test has known validity and reliability that are stated in the examiner's manual or in standard reference texts. Typically, a norm-referenced test has evolved through years of refinement that involved a national sample. The refinement has established the test's validity and reliability.*

---

*Validation is a statistical investigation that establishes two attributes of a measurement procedure. One procedure compares scores on the new test to scores on a recognized, existing test. A high positive correlation between the two scores is evidence that the new test is a valid approximation of the attribute. Another technique compares test scores between competent and naive persons. If the test is valid, competent persons should perform better. A variation of this technique is to assess how well the test scores predict future performance of successful versus nonsuccessful persons. The essence of validity is the extent to which a test predicts/measures that which it purports to measure.

Reliability, by contrast, is a question of two kinds of statistical consistency. The most common approach is to administer the test to the same persons over fixed periods of time (test-retest reliability). If the test is adequately constructed, the scores will be highly correlated. Another procedure is to compare scores of the same persons on odd-numbered items to scores on even-numbered items. If the two scores are positively correlated, the result is said to show internal consistency. Another and more complex procedure is to assess each item and its contribution to the total test score. Persons are classified as passing or failing the test. Their performance on each item is compared; an adequate item is one that is passed by the high group and failed by the low group. Reliability also generates the known error of measurement. Thus any obtained score is an estimate that the test manual describes.

When a test has undergone these procedures, there is a degree of confidence in the error of measurement, the stability of results, and the predictive nature of results. Those who advocate norm-referenced measurement, especially Hebb (1978), have observed that these procedures are as much an assessment of the environment as of pupils. Hebb acknowledged that this point has been overlooked. He deplored the uninformed interpretation that intelligence quotient (IQ) tests "explain" genetic attributes. He was critical of passive reactions to low performance and recommended that norm-referenced measurement should signal the need for intervention to modify environments.

Other advantages of norm-referenced measurement are that they indicate genuine and verified accomplishment of developmental landmarks and that the documentation of construction can

Criterion-Referenced Measurement

Rooted in program objectives, criterion-referenced measurements are devised by teachers to parallel instruction. They are nearly always coupled with the formative evaluation philosophy. Criterion-referenced procedures are also published commercially. An innovation by publishers of standardized reading series is an example. These publishers have produced tests that can be used to preassess student attainments as well as to demonstrate student mastery. These "tests" are so constructed that pupils can move along to higher levels without going through a unit if they can demonstrate sufficient mastery. Moreover, these tests are so keyed as to pinpoint particular needs for instruction. Popham (1976) observed that many school districts have developed criterion-referenced procedures that are tailored to their own special curriculum objectives. Popham defined the criterion-referenced measurement approach as:

> A criterion-referenced test permits us to determine whether or not an examinee can display a clearly defined set of behaviors. It is possible to reference an examinee's performance to a clearly defined set of behaviors so that we can say . . . whether a student does, or does not, possess a particular competency. (p. 593)

Criterion-referenced procedures yield a precise statement of what a pupil can or cannot do. The procedure also is a signal for personalized intervention.

The difficulty with criterion-referenced measurement is that, while such procedures can specify what a student can do, they may not provide enough information. These procedures do not offer information as to how well students should be doing. Moreover, there is no guarantee that criterion-referenced procedures possess predictive validity or are reliable measurements.

---

allow for appropriate variations in interpretation where results are impaired by known discrimination as regards sex, age, economic condition, physical impairment, and/or geographical residence. Moreover, these known sources of error can be reduced in subsequent editions. It was Hebb's contention that norm-referenced procedures are neither evil nor oppressive. He believed that examiners have not honored or followed the guidelines recommended by test producers. Additionally, he observed that users of tests have not exercised care in selecting tests according to validity or reliability criteria.

Popham (1976) observed that there are limitations to norm-referenced procedures. One objection is that the individual becomes obscured in group focus. MacTurk and Neisworth (1978) elaborated this view and advanced a second objection. They observed that these procedures are not program-specific. The behaviors assessed by a norm-referenced procedure may have little relationship to the objectives of a given program. A third objection, cited in both sources, is that these procedures can lead to complacency; favorable results can be interpreted as an indication that the education provided is "good enough."

Selecting Options

The weight of professional opinion and documented experience is that the four options of norm-referenced/summative, norm-referenced/formative, criterion-referenced/summative, and criterion-referenced/formative can coexist without undue trauma. Furthermore, there is great merit in using the four options selectively with respect to gifted and talented pupils.

The most common agreement, according to both Popham and MacTurk and Neisworth, is on the value of the criterion-referenced/formative option in individualized education. The norm-referenced/summative approach is the least favored, except as a global comparison for such purposes as cross-district comparison or state-wide assessments. It is the norm-referenced/formative and criterion-referenced/summative options that require care and precision. The task is to retain the descriptive power of the norm-referenced procedure and the sensitivity of the criterion-referenced procedure.

MacTurk and Neisworth provide an example of a valid utilization of these procedures for both program evaluation and individualized assessment. They described a preschool intervention based upon a criterion-referenced curriculum. The curriculum consisted of related domains of communication, self-care, motor skills, and problem solving. Instruction proceeded on the sequence suggested by each domain. A norm-referenced procedure was employed to assess pupil gains over the project period. The pupils showed progress in their movement through the criterion-reference curriculum, which was confirmed by norm-referenced procedures. Moreover, there was a significant relationship between the two measures. Consequently, both procedures could describe *what* the pupils could perform and *how well* they did compared with similar pupils. Popham advocates a variation of the comparative approach. He recommends a comparison of the performance of pupils not under criterion-referenced instruction with that of those under criterion-referenced instruction. This procedure affords helpful summative comparisons.

In everyday practice, teachers use all four options simultaneously; there is a summing up that leads to hypotheses concerning further help. Formative tests alert the teacher to select more pupil-sensitive procedures. As Popham observes, assessment of any style is to improve instruction. The goal is to proceed toward the design of an aptitude treatment intervention.

UNDERSTANDING APTITUDE/TREATMENT INTERACTION

Common Decisions

Teachers are sympathetic to instruction tailored to maximize pupil performance and their own efficient use of professional skills. Reynolds and Birch

(1977) point out common approaches used by teachers to translate assessment information into modifications of standard practice for individual pupils. These approaches, which are highly applicable to gifted and talented pupils, involve varying:

1. objectives. A common goal such as career education is retained; but specific objectives are individually altered. For example, participation in Junior Achievement could be an alternative to a unit in career planning.
2. the rate and duration of instruction. Acceleration is a well-tested way of enabling gifted and talented pupils to progress at their own various paces. Criterion-referenced procedures assist in this option.
3. the intensity of instruction, which can mean a remediation or expansion of skill areas. Independent study involves varying amounts of pupil-mentor interaction.
4. the sequence of selection. This is exemplified by advanced placement options based upon either norm- or criterion-referenced procedures.
5. instruction. Distinct tactics such as problem solving can be linked to distinct preferences or learning styles. Associated with this tactic is variation in the selection of instructional materials and equipment.

These notions remind teachers of the array of options at their command. Furthermore, as Reynolds and Birch suggest, these tactics remind teachers that achievement is a three-factor interaction. Achievement involves not only the two factors of teacher and pupil, but also environmental factors, such as materials, physical space, and school policies. It is this accounting of pupil behavior, teachers' inventory of skills, and educational resources that is essential in order to translate assessment data into an action design such as the IEP.

The Aptitude/Treatment Interaction Model

Aptitude/Treatment Interaction (ATI), as a concept, relates readily to what teachers do in clinical teaching, individually prescribed instruction, diagnostic instruction, precision teaching, and individually guided education. While the terms vary, the central focus is on the five tactics (or appropriate combinations) for adapting practice to a particular pupil or group of pupils. Reynolds and Birch cite the early work of Cronbach and Glaser (1965) and Cronbach and Snow (1975) to provide the technical verification for school practice.

The language of ATI may call for a modification of previous definitions of aptitude. For example, in this sense, aptitude is not an internal trait; it describes the ways a pupil learns best. Testing is meant to include, not to reject, pupils. Assessment includes both the pupil and the school environment. It is undertaken to improve instruction and learning for the pupil. Mastery is viewed as a consequence of effective interaction between aptitude and appropriately designed educational environments. Criterion-referenced procedures and formative evaluation are favored. Finally, grading practices are altered.

The chief value of the ATI model for gifted and talented pupils is that it reinforces the teacher's efforts to understand and relate the pupil's current educational status to the accomplishment of goals and objectives. It also emphasizes the affective and motivational aspects of learning and of teaching. It is founded upon an overt relationship between educational treatment and learning aptitudes that is confirmed by evidence obtained through measurement, observation, and interview. Confirmation data can be maintained by charting or other record-keeping.

The key idea is to establish the disordinal relationship between attribute and treatment. The notion of disordinal relationship means that a given aptitude will react more favorably to a given treatment than to another equally sound treatment. The essence, therefore, is to select treatments to match aptitudes. Often, the teacher must infer the descriptor of the pupil's aptitude.

For example, suppose one were teaching a unit on the diplomatic history of the United States. Suppose that past performance of pupils on tests reflected varying degrees of pupil mastery, independent of known intellectual aptitude. If there were a perfect ordinal relationship, then scholastic aptitude should have predicted performance, but it did not. Suppose, upon deeper reflection, one considered those pupils who, though alike on intelligence test results, varied on achievement test results.

All pupils should be like Philip. His fine mind soaks up information much like a sponge. His reports are well-organized models. Elizabeth has organized the group reports and has even scanned the pages of the text. If she had not been so distracted by her participation as a Vol-Teen for the Head Start Program, she might have had more time to study for the test on responsible citizenship. Andrew and Mike are both pain and pleasure. They appear indifferent in class; however, they always respond in class discussions, and they have constructive suggestions for strategies for projects. The difficulty is that they do not always follow through. John, on the other hand, constructed a teaching board of electric lights to indicate the pairing of terms to persons or events. Furthermore, if Andrew and Mike were not so busy reading *Advise and Consent,* they would be more attentive to the instruction at hand.

These learners are not really a threat to the teacher's competence. The discomfort really arises from a sense of personal and professional responsibility. The situation may be similar to that of the Drews model presented in Unit III. Aptitudes, or learning styles, such as conscientious, creative, social leader, and rebel emerge with their attendant strategies/treatments. It is these attributes (aptitudes) to which instruction is to be matched, and differential treatments of structure, guidance, participation, and extent of verbalism come to mind. These reflections and comparisons demonstrate the validity of the ATI model.

Aptitude Treatment Intervention and Grading

The assignment of letter grades is a common practice in American education. It is also one of the least satisfying aspects of teaching. The difficulty with grading, according to Bloom, Hastings, and Madaus (1971) is matching it to various styles of assessment. Reynolds and Birch (1977) speak of the need to match grading procedures to what they are intended to communicate. Both sources agree that grading is especially vexing in the education of gifted and talented pupils, although the difficulties may be more troublesome to teachers and parents than to pupils.

Decisions that must be made about grading are what to communicate, how to communicate, why to communicate, and with whom to communicate. These are general and urgent questions for gifted and talented programs. There are positive and realistic solutions, however. First, according to Reynolds and Birch, grading is an extension of evaluation/assessment and is intended to communicate pupil progress toward mastery of specific objectives. As such, grading ought to supply honest and useful information to both pupil and parents. Second, grading is a form of report on pupil performance in fulfillment of an IEP. In this instance, there should be sufficient documentation to describe accomplishments and to identify tactics for improvement. Third, grading ought to be criterion-referenced to an individual program rather than competitive with other students.

In situations of strict norm-referenced testing that relies on approximations of the "normal" curve, certain students are destined to be among the 3 percent receiving F, the 13 percent receiving D, and the 68 percent receiving C. Of course, there are also 13 percent who receive B and 3 percent who receive A. The irony is that, in a grouping of the gifted and talented for special purposes, an F grade could be A performance on the standard setting. In a criterion-referenced system, there is no need for students to be highly competitive, as they are pursuing individualized domains of learning.

College admissions offices and employers are not as grade bound as might be supposed. They are more interested in what persons can do and in the nature of the educational experience. For this reason, letters of reference may have more impact and influence than a summative grade point average.

An IEP furnishes the documentation of pupil performance and the way in which that performance was achieved. Letter grades are a summation of an individual's progress. Together, they communicate better than separately.

According to Bloom et al., another difficulty about grading lies in the computation. For example, in four marking periods, a student may have earned a D, C, C, and A for a cumulative final grade of C. If learning is an accumulation, as Bloom et al. contend, then an A would seem more accurate. This would apply especially to curriculum domains such as writing, mathematics, art, and music. Moreover, teachers disagree as to what grades represent. Some educators believe that an A is a norm of excellence restricted only to those persons who are superior to all other students, according to a fixed criterion. As such, their grades communicate an opinion of the *future* scientist, artist, writer, or teacher. Other educators believe that an A indicates mastery of the objectives that the pupil and the instructor agreed upon in advance. Under this procedure, the distribution of a given letter grade is not fixed. Also, under this system, there is documentation to show both student and teacher those areas where improvement is needed.

Educators who use criterion-referenced measurement may be challenged for assigning too many good grades, and professional peers may refer to such an educator as an easy mark. This discomfort can be allayed through reference to the IEP. Aptitude treatment intervention provides for varying objectives, rates, durations, intensity, sequence, and methods. Furthermore, the teacher's skills are challenged to the fullest. If guilt must be assuaged, contract learning that is founded upon the content of the IEP may be considered. In this system, the pupil and teacher formulate the goals to be attained under what circumstances, for what length of time, and by what criteria. Students can elect to pursue a particular level of mastery to be translated into a grade. The IEP and student documentation should be sufficient evidence that student performance qualifies as genuine accomplishment.

As a practical example of the ATI model, consider Table 17-2. The idea is that curriculum can be modified by advancing the pace of curriculum or expanding content and/or skills. (Educators will recognize that these are *not* either/or). The table summarizes relevant pupil attributes and relevant school attributes for the individualized selection of tactics.

PERFORMANCE ASSESSMENT

Scope

The IEP should have internal consistency. The work of Mager (1970) attracted attention among educators for its functional simplicity and its

Table 17-2 Selecting Tactics of Modifying the Standard Curriculum*

Aptitudes and Attributes	Curriculum Modification Tactics	
	Advancing	*Expanding*
Pupil	Acceleration when *pupil* 1. is motivated 2. has sufficient life experience to handle subject 3. demonstrates substantial achievement beyond age peers 4. shows ability to master faster learning rate 5. attains beyond reasonable expectations for the regular grade teacher 6. and family can be counseled as to the sources of financial aid 7. has access to advisory committee for resources 8. and family are involved in IEP	Enrichment when *pupil* 1. is motivated for product orientation 2. is prepared for the role of investigator 3. is committed to a task of complexity beyond that usual for age peers 4. has sufficient maturity to pursue a contract system 5. shows sufficient task commitment 6. has sufficient skills for conducting investigations
School	Acceleration when *school* 1. possesses criteria to assess mastery levels for advanced placement 2. has policies for acceleration throughout the entire school system 3. alerts teachers to account for pupils of younger ages in advanced classes 4. ties to a local institution of higher education 5. ties to local preschools for early admission to kindergarten 6. recruits competent volunteers 7. provides in-service training for teachers	Enrichment when *school* 1. curriculum is explicit in its grade level expectations 2. inventories schools and community for resources 3. inventories resources for project outlets 4. recognizes that learners can be producers, regardless of age 5. is tolerant and accustomed to exploration of ideas 6. is accustomed to flexible scheduling 7. provides in-service training for teachers

*Adapted from Sellin and Birch (1980).

comprehensiveness. Not only is it a practical example of the ATI philosophy, it is also another alternative for comprehensive assessment. Its elements involve (1) discrepancy assessment, (2) values assessment, (3) affective assessment, (4) behavioral assessment, (5) environmental assessment, and (6) evaluation.

Discrepancy Assessment

According to Mager, discrepancy assessment involves a perceived gap between a person's performance and a norm-referenced, or culture-referenced, expectation. Observations by informed parents and teachers give validity to the expectation measure. The gap is the discrepancy. In turn, discrepancies can be of two variations. It can be an absence or delay in behavior, but it can also be a positive attribute of behavior either in advance or in excess of the usual, or "normal." Screening, assessment, and observation verify the existence of a discrepancy. Tactics of identification are a source of documentation.

Values Assessment

The next step is to assign a judgment, a value, and a priority to the discrepancy. Assuming that the discrepancy is judged to be educationally important, there is a sense of urgency about management, match, and maintenance.

Affective Assessment

Affective factors account for motivation and are consistent with the dimensions of personality and performance identified in Chapter 3. Motivation is positive when a correct performance is rewarded and nonperformance is not satisfying. However, pupils may receive other messages from the environment. For example, if completing prescribed assignments is followed by more of the same assignments, this can be translated as performance is punishing. A pupil may expend great effort to meet a deadline, only to find there is neither recognition nor any other reward; the translation can be that performance has no significance. Finally, students may be able to charm their way out of assignments or even pass off half-completed work and find it judged acceptable; the translation can be that nonperformance is rewarding. These student learnings can be significant determinants of later performance and may account for the performance of underachieving gifted and talented pupils (Whitmore, 1980).

Behavioral Assessment

Behavioral assessment is directed to the skills and aptitude of the pupil and the tasks that are confronted by pupils. In the Mager sense, skill is the behavior of the student, and task is the behavior expected of the pupil. Skill may not be evident, even though it may be within the person's response pattern, for reasons that should be accounted for in assessment. For example, the learner may be expected to demonstrate comprehension (e.g., translation instruction into his or her own words). The skill may not be present because the learner has not been given sufficient practice, because a new emphasis upon remembering interferes with the old skill, or because the new requirement is too complex. Task assessment is analysis of what the person is expected to do. This procedure details the task's required behaviors, the sequence of behaviors, and specifications for adequate performance. The Table of Specifications procedure is an example of task assessment applicable to gifted and talented pupils.

Environmental Assessment

In one sense, affective assessment and task assessment are reflections of the environment. Reynolds and Birch (1977) offer a resumé of the dimensions of environmental assessment; so does Mager, who identified four sources of school environments: (1) practitioner, (2) physical environment, (3) instructional materials, and (4) administrative policies. Practitioner variables include the activities of the teacher, such as appropriate use of materials, clarity of expectations, promptness of feedback, and evidence of respect for student effort. Physical environment variables encompass size of facilities, adaptability of space to instruction, dimensions of physical comfort, and safety factors. Instructional materials involve clarity of sensory elements, relevance to goals, and availability of resources. Administrative policies include rewarding creative and competent staff, sensitive support for individualized education, tailored in-service training for staff, rational procedures for accountability, and encouragement for innovation.

Evaluation

The outcomes of the preceding assessments are oriented toward decision making. Evaluation of assessment data is the shifting of data into a plan to individualize instruction. In some instances, the purpose is fulfilled by notation for action in the IEP; in other instances, the purpose is fulfilled by the teacher's instructional plan. One cluster of decisions centers about variation (Reynolds & Birch, 1977). Examples of decisions that the Mager (1970, 1969) procedure identify can be summarized as follows:

- Affective dimensions identify the need for decisions to enable students to learn that performance is rewarding. There should be attractive activities without needless repetition, and opportunities for recognition and sharing of projects should be provided.

- Skill dimensions may require reintroduction and reemphasis of previous skills. A simpler solution or reduction of demands may be appropriate.

- Task dimensions may require analysis of specified expectations and sequencing. The use of performance objectives can assist in this clarification.

- Administrative policies must support the key role of the teacher.

Commentary

A number of ideas and proved alternatives have been presented for review by educators. It remains for individual educators and parents to adapt this information and the alternatives for a particular district.

The prototype for this unit presents the elements of a high-quality program for highly able learners. Exhibit 17-1 is a prototype of an IEP form for the Yourtowne Public Schools. It can be said to represent the collective decision of participants. The IEP form does *not* replace an accumulative record file or a complete case study. It was designed to be a summary.

In this instance, it was decided to limit the IEP to three parts, each of which is to serve a specified purpose. Part I documents pupil eligibility for the Basic Scholars Program and relates measurement/observation data to components. Part II sets forth pupil outcomes and associated strategies for implementation. Part III is intended to be at least an annual review of Parts I and II. This form also allows for comments and indicates those responsible for implementation.

Exhibit 17-1 Prototype of an IEP Form

YOURTOWNE PUBLIC SCHOOLS

School Year

Individualized Education Program
for the Basic Scholars Program

Pupil   Mentor

PART I: Identification and Certification

BSP Components

Relevant Sources	Basic Skills	Advancement	Interest	Talent	Human Services
General Measurements					
Specific Aptitudes Measurements					
Teacher Nominations					
Parent Nominations					
Other Nominations					
Other Scores					

Comments: _____

_____

Participants: _____

Supplementary Data: _____

Date: _____

Exhibit 17-1 continued

Pupil _____   School Year _____

PART II: Recommendations

Basic Scholar Component Outcomes	Curriculum Modifications	Suggested Topics	Resources	Responsible Person

Comments: _____

_____

Clarifying Data: _____

_____

Date: _____

Exhibit 17-1 continued

Pupil _____   School Year _____

PART III: Program Review, Revision, Follow-up
Change in: (Check as many as apply)
                              Nature of Recommended Change

	None	Drop	Add	Revise
Identification				
Program Component				
Outcomes				
Curriculum Modifications				
Suggested Tactics				
Resources				
Responsible Person				

Comments: _____

_____

Participants: _____

_____

Date: _____

Chapter 18

Understanding the Key Role of Teachers

For the individual teacher, there may be a gap between self-confidence and the confidence placed in the profession by parents, other professions, the courts, legislators, and other social institutions. The sweep of the 1960s and the 1970s was to shift emphasis from education as a social service institution to education as the result of the efforts of individual teachers. Teachers as a collective body have become more assertive in controlling their destinies and the educational welfare of their pupils. Efforts to reform and improve the individualization of education at district levels have been initiated by teachers. Consequently, recognition of the role of teachers in controlling public education is no reaction to a slogan; it is a reality. A significant effect of teachers' greater control over their own destinies shows in their clear perceptions of what they expect of themselves and of each other by way of professional competencies.

COMPETENCIES FOR INDIVIDUALIZED PROGRAMS

Haisley and Gilberts (1978) listed the competencies teachers said they valued for individualized programs. The summary list, it was suggested, could be used by teachers to inventory their own degree of mastery of key competencies. Actually, the Haisley and Gilberts inventory included a mix of relevant principles, skills, processes, and procedures for individualized programs.

Four principles of significance to educators emerge from Haisley and Gilberts' discussion. One is the principle of appropriate education, or the match between learner aptitude and educational intervention. A second principle is that of least restrictive environment, which relates to full educational opportunity and access to programs and services of suitable challenge and stimulation delivered in the context of regular education. A third principle is that of due process. The essence of this principle is securing

281

informed parental consent and endorsement for educational program and placement decisions; parents are regarded as full partners with equal status to participate, revise, and appeal. A fourth principle is nondiscriminatory identification and assessment, which requires the use of legitimate and multiple criteria to maximize efficiency and effectiveness in locating eligible pupils and arranging an appropriate education for them.

The skills discussed by Haisley and Gilberts can be grouped into six main clusters. There are *participation* skills, which a teacher uses when functioning as a member of the IEP team. These skills include the abilities to (1) compile information regarding the student's current educational status; (2) develop goals, objectives, and minimal criterion-referenced performance standards for the pupil; and (3) recommend helpful educational strategies. There are skills of *monitoring,* which involve appraisal of the IEP to ascertain that (1) procedural safeguards are followed with respect to the criteria of nondiscriminatory testing and (2) parents fully participate and are aware of their rights. A third set of skills can be described as *implementation.* These include (1) interpretation of evaluation results to parents and (2) evaluation of pupil progress. A fourth significant set of skills is needed for *consultation with parents.* Another set relates to *consultation with colleagues* to effect outcomes of the IEP. A related and final set involves the *management* of the recommendations of the IEP.

TEACHERS AS PARENT CONSULTANTS

A Sense of Trust between Home and School

Teachers can expect to serve as consultants to parents of gifted and talented learners because teachers are trusted professionals who will be perceived as valuable allies by parents. Teachers will be perceived as informed consultants regarding (1) identification, (2) home management, (3) educational management, and (4) referral to community resources. Educators would be well advised to prepare responses to these information and consultation needs of parents.

An Alliance for Helpful Assessment

The popular media have publicized the controversies about testing. Furthermore, the emergence of accountability has made testing a part of the public record. Given that parents have a legal right under the Buckley Amendment to inspect school records and to approve formal testing, parents can be expected to raise questions regarding testing.

Green (1975) advocated an alliance between parents and teachers to ensure that formal testing be properly used. His perspective was that of an educational psychologist with documented evidence that testing had been misused with minority group children. He described tests as helpful to the extent that procedures fulfill the following: (1) the learner's chances for intellectual and personal development are enhanced; (2) the learner's development of talents, abilities, and values are fostered; and (3) people in authority are assisted to make wise decisions. The destructive effects of testing have been shown to be: (1) interpretations that lead to a pupil's stagnation in one track; (2) restricted development of talents, abilities, and values through tracking; and (3) practices of interpretation that impose decisions.

Green advised parents and teachers to insist that (1) decisions about programming include the pupil's interests and preferences for educational content of challenge, (2) scores remain confidential and restricted on a "need to know" basis, (3) there be required in-service training for teachers and professional staff regarding testing and interpretations of tests, and (4) a parent-teacher advisory committee be established to oversee assessment practices in the schools. As a last resort, parents and teacher both should be prepared to seek legal redress.

The Parent-Teacher Conference

The conference between parent and teacher is a negotiation between participants who should be allies. There should be at least conferences to review pupil progress regarding the goals and objectives of the IEP, but ideally, there will be more frequent communication in order to share insights and ideas. Green inspired parents to have faith in the teacher. The teacher can respond accordingly if the purposes of the conference are acknowledged.

According to Rabbit (1978), the conference is undertaken in a spirit of teamwork. The conference has three main purposes: (1) giving information, (2) receiving information, and (3) finding solutions.

In giving information, it is the teacher's responsibility to be clear and comprehensible. The most frequent questions asked by parents, according to Rabbit's summary are (1) does my child behave and pay attention? (2) how is my child doing in schoolwork? and (3) how does my child get along with classmates? Ways of sharing information with parents include sharing examples of the child's work, sharing the grade book, sharing illustrative anecdotes, listening to tape recordings of the child during an actual lesson, listing and displaying examples of curriculum materials, discussing weekly assignments and lesson plans, and sharing the written rules or expectations governing the class. Rabbit reminded teachers to ask parents if this is the type of information they *really* want. Teachers can tailor giving to both their own agenda and the parent's agenda.

The willingness to receive information is proof that communication is a two-way street. Conferences require more than a monologue. Helpful information from parents relates to the child's interests, ambitions, home responsibilities, and relevant out-of-school experiences. Questions that may prompt parents to give information are what does your child think about school? what is a typical day? "Why" questions should be used only sparingly, since most persons perceive a why as a lawyer's challenge rather than a mere request for information.

Finding solutions calls for a mutual decision by parents, teachers, and, when appropriate, the gifted and talented pupil that an individualized program is necessary. Concrete steps include the following sequence: (1) listing positive attributes about the child, since success in one area can lead to success in other areas; (2) selecting one target goal so that neither the teacher, the parent(s), nor the pupil becomes overwhelmed; (3) listing all the possible ways the parent(s) and the teacher(s) can be helpful and selecting two or three for a first trial; and (4) scheduling a specific follow-up conference to review progress.

Rabbit emphasized that teachers should evaluate conferences. He suggested summing up outcomes by taking notes and sharing these notes with parents. He also emphasized home contact when things are going well to offset the feeling that conferences are usually sessions of doom. He also stressed the importance of written and verbal communications to acknowledge appreciation for parent interest and effort.

THE TEACHER AS A RESOURCE FOR QUALITY

Sato (1978) has affirmed the role of *all* teachers in maintaining high-quality services for the gifted and talented. He based these affirmations upon key assumptions. He also identified the steps that all teachers could take, together with specialists, in promoting high-quality education for gifted and talented pupils.

Assumptions

Teachers, according to Sato, touch and influence the quality of education for the gifted and talented in several ways. First, gifted and talented learners can be found in all age levels and in all socioeconomic groupings. Second, there are many ways in which gifted and talented pupils display superior performance. Third, superior performance is nurtured through informed adaptation of the curriculum to their individualized styles of learning.

Helping Skills

Sato identified skills that emphasize the central importance of teachers: (1) assessment and case study techniques, (2) practical guidance, (3) provision of learning opportunities at the higher level of cognition, (4) emphasis on affective as well as cognitive learnings, and (5) use of group procedures. It was emphasized also that teachers must keep informed of new developments in education.

Action Steps

Sufficient information is already available to teachers to indicate directions for professional improvement, such as increasing the skill of matching teaching strategies to individual attributes. Teachers can assert their need for preparation as a first step. This preparation would include (1) proficiency in criterion-referenced and norm-referenced assessment; (2) understanding of the interaction of affect and cognition (e.g., Bloom and/or Guilford); (3) the design of responsive, nurturing environments; (4) knowledge of program organization and resources; and (5) tactics of program evaluation. A second step would be to press for systematic identification of gifted and talented pupils. A third step would be to inventory and organize resources available to teachers for instruction and guidance. Finally, teachers should seek support for free and appropriate in-service education for themselves in order to serve pupils in an accountable manner.

Educational specialists for gifted and talented must understand the nature of consultation with their colleagues. The status of educators has been recognized as significant, especially as educators are able to identify their common core of practice as professionals.

TOWARD A COMMON CORE OF PRACTICE

Attributes of a Profession

The teaching profession has been characterized by specialization according to either content areas (e.g., science, physical education, remedial reading), or age levels (e.g., elementary, middle school). Teachers are separated from one another by these boundaries. As professionals, teachers have certain common attributes, but they do not have a common core of practice.

Stevens (1970) has identified the attributes of a profession and applied these standards to teaching. For example, professionals are characterized by a technical language system (beyond jargon) to communicate and summarize information. A profession is regulated by a code of ethics that governs decisions about conflict of interest and integrity. Moreover, a professional requires a license to practice, and conditions for licensure are regulated by state standards. A profession is also characterized by a period of formal training (and continuing training beyond preparation) with an identifiable content. Professions have also evolved professional associations that improve standards of services by disseminating knowledge, developing standards for preparation, and improving conditions of employment. These elements describe standards of practice, which is another attribute of a profession.

Stevens holds that a profession is characterized by an organized body of knowledge that is generated by a logical system of inquiry and is the basis for defining the unique elements of service delivered by the professional. It is the practitioner's preparation that results in a level of competence beyond that of the gifted amateur. Another attribute of the professional is furtherance of professional growth. This describes continuing education and scholarship; it also means a willingness to mentor future professionals in internships and practicum situations.

A Missing Element and a Promising Opportunity

The missing element in teaching as a profession is a common core of practice that describes the substance of education among *all* educators, regardless of either age or content specialization. There is general agreement that the IEP provides a context in which practices that should be common to all teachers can be understood. The learner's teacher is at the center of the IEP process. The teacher's role is like that of a chairperson of a board of directors who can draw upon the advice of members. The presence of a common core of practice could facilitate this role.

A Common Core

The absence of a common core does not mean that professionals in education have been unaware of the potential of the IEP. Reynolds (1980), on behalf of an ad hoc committee, has reviewed the implications of IEPs applied to the practice of education. He and his associates advanced a tentative listing of a common core of practice in which teachers should be prepared. That common core is summarized in condensed form in Table 18-1. The clusters are not discrete domains; they suggest appropriate groupings. Also, all have equal priority, i.e., they are not hierarchical.

Table 18-1 A Common Core of Practice

Descriptor	Dimensions of Practice	Recommendations for Implementation
Curriculum	Knowledge of the common goals and objectives through all grade levels and the interrelationships among content areas	Understanding of the sources of curriculum, including legal, cultural, and psychological; understanding of the process of curriculum design, adaptation, adoption, and revision
Basic skills	Knowledge of assessment and teaching tactics for literacy skills, life maintenance skills, and personal development skills; understanding of the interaction of curriculum content to foster these skills	Understanding and competency for literacy skills through fifth grade levels; understanding of life maintenance skills of health, consumerism, safety, and personal rights; responsible self-actualization
Professional values	Actions and judgments that reflect respect for individual pupil and parental rights and consideration for colleagues contained in professional ethics and / or legal sanctions	Knowledge of basic laws that regulate professional behavior as well as study of the codes of ethics of professional organizations
Interactions	Actions of collaboration, consultation, negotiation, joint planning, interviewing, conferring with staff, and allied forms of communication with colleagues, parents, specialists	Knowledge of how to perform these interactions as well as how to be consumer of consultation and referral services
Individualized teaching	Ability to match pupil aptitudes, interests, and current status to the content of instruction; ability to use norm-referenced and criterion-referenced measurement to define goals and objectives	Knowledge of the competencies associated with implementation of the IEP; knowledge of group tactics and simulation of one-to-one instruction; knowledge of cross-age tutoring and collaborative teaching; knowledge of how to structure practicum, internships, and externships to fulfill the teacher's needs for these skills
Pupil management	Ability to apply positive techniques to maintain positive pupil attention to school-related activities; ability to manage pupil distraction and crises	Knowledge of tasks of consultation to pupil as well as tactics of applied behavioral analysis; knowledge of the tactics of fostering self-realization
Exceptional conditions	Ability to manage the educationally significant attributes of individual difference; ability to express pupil needs in simple, direct, and technically accurate language appropriate for pupils, parents, colleagues, and other specialists	Knowledge and contact with professionals in allied discipline and social agencies; supervised contact with exceptional pupils to apply principles of individualized teaching and pupil management, including referral and consultation

The education of gifted and talented pupils would benefit if this core were adopted as a guide to continuing education, since it reinforces the central role of *all* educators in educational enterprise. To be sure, education of the gifted and talented is a specialization; however, it is a specialization of collaboration with others. Consider how helpful a common core of practice could be. First, it would not be restricted to graduate levels; it would be available to all first year teachers. Second, it would be a common preparation upon which to build specialization. Third, because of the dimensions of curriculum and basic skills, all persons in the educational community would have a common background. Fourth, the domains of interactions, pupil management, and individualized teaching would enhance the pursuit of high-quality standards of education and service. Under exceptional conditions, the teacher is the responsible and competent person in the life of the child, which places support services in the proper context. Fifth, professional values would encourage assertiveness upon the part of teachers to press for high educational quality. Finally, specialists in the education of the gifted and talented would encounter natural allies in the implementation of services, e.g., pupils, parents, colleagues, higher education resources, and community-based sources.

Summing Up

PROVIDING A RATIONALE FOR INDIVIDUALIZED EDUCATION PROGRAMS

There are sound precedents for the emergence of the Individualized Education Program (IEP). One was the enactment of Pub.L. 94-142, which has mandated the use of the IEP for all handicapped learners everywhere in this nation. Consequently, all school districts are familiar with its implementation. Secondly, the advent of criterion-referenced measurement as a supplement and complement has provided a means for nondiscriminatory assessment. The availability of procedures modeled after the Aptitude Treatment Intervention concepts has also been helpful.

As a service, the IEP is undertaken to fulfill useful goals, such as appropriate education, positive presumption, least restrictive environment, nondiscriminatory assessment, due process, and informed consent. The IEP serves program development goals. Review of IEPs identifies a census of each gifted and talented pupil, and documents needs for resources. Defining goals for the positive benefits of the IEP is one prior condition for implementation.

Another prior condition is advanced preparation of participants. An associated task is the structuring of both school responsibilities and the *informed* participation of parents. The structure is related to (1) identification, (2) assessment, (3) conference, (4) completion of the IEP, (5) implementation of the IEP, and (6) evaluation. An understanding of the limits of testing is another prior condition. Limits, as opposed to limitations, suggest that interpretations of testing should not extend beyond the boundaries intended by test makers. One example of limits is the mismatch that exists between the content of formal reading tests and the content of formal reading series.

The conditions for the use of IEP require attention to maintaining a balance between affective and cognitive outcomes, maintaining the relationship with the regular class teacner, and developing a frame of reference. This latter point refers to the value of the traditional use of educational diagnosis to guide practice. Preserving these conditions involves commitment to principles of (1) certain assurances, (2) detailing of resources, and (3) detailed resource plan.

Use of the IEP is a public policy in that endorsement is a positive sanction. Policies can be of one or more types of permissive commitment, resource distribution, and implementation.

SPECIFYING THE CONTENT OF AN INDIVIDUALIZED EDUCATION PROGRAM

The scope of an IEP can be said to include the following elements: (1) identifying data, (2) listing of participants, (3) goals and objectives, (4) implementation recommendations, (5) current educational status of the learner, (6) revisions as necessary, and (7) evidence of compliance to policy standards. Goals and objectives for the learner are similar in statement format to curriculum or program management statements. A goal describes a general aspiration, while an objective is intended for measurable performance. An objective has three elements: (1) the act to be performed by the learner, (2) the conditions under which the act will be performed, and (3) criteria for performance. The matching of goals to objectives follows the Table of Specifications procedures described in Chapter 8.

Parents are full partners in the IEP process. They can be expected to raise questions about recommendations of the following types: (1) balance of educational and social outcomes, (2) evidence to justify recommendations, (3) safeguards against labeling, (4) defining positive benefits for their child, and (5) procedures for evaluation of outcomes.

A positive result of an IEP can be the regular class teacher's access to consultation and resources designated for gifted and talented pupils, which are then available to all students in his or her class. Consultation can be helpful in selecting appropriate materials. The tactics of the Learning

Activity Package can be helpful in generating criteria consistent with the goals of the IEP.

ASSEMBLING AND ASSESSING INFORMATION

The section of the IEP entitled Current Educational Status is the basis for determination of goals and objectives. Courts and legislators have prescribed conditions for the use of norm-referenced and criterion-referenced texts. Of direct relevance has been the use of grade point average as a criterion for admission to gifted and talented programs. Teacher-made tests can be subject to examination. The difficulty has not been with tests *per se* but in their interpretations.

Dimensions of assessment cluster around measurement and the purpose of evaluation. Each of these clusters has its advocates. Measurement can be described as norm-referenced or as criterion-referenced; evaluation can be undertaken for summative or for formative purposes. These four approaches interact.

Assessment must translate into educationally rational variations of (1) objectives; (2) rate, duration, and intensity of instruction; (3) sequence, and (4) methods. The assembling of assessment data can be described as analyses of (1) discrepancies, (2) value judgments, (3) affect, (4) behavior, (5) environment, and (6) evaluation. A fundamental principle of assessment is that it is a balanced focus upon the learner *and* the environment of the learner. Recommendations are directed toward modification of either the learner, the environment, or both.

UNDERSTANDING THE KEY ROLE OF TEACHERS

The operation of Pub.L. 94-142 has been sufficient to generate documentation of two principles. One is the central role of the regular class teacher; the other is the identification of the teacher competencies required. These competencies cluster around the IEP, responsibilities as a parent consultant, and responsibilities as a consultant for other teachers. The specialist in education needs all these competencies, plus a knowledge of new techniques. Both the regular teacher and the specialist are expected to be partners on behalf of the gifted and talented pupil.

The teacher is a professional and the practice of individualized education has its own professional attributes. A special attribute is the teacher's willingness to continue his or her own education and the willingness to mentor future professionals. A common core of professional practice can be identified that should provide a framework of helpful alliances among members of the educational community.

Enrichment

PROVIDING A RATIONALE FOR INDIVIDUALIZED EDUCATION PROGRAMS

1. Examine your school district's policies for the IEP (either for handicapped learners or for gifted and talented learners). What type(s) of policy supports are evident? What provisions are made to assist regular class teachers? Share your findings.

2. Suppose you were being considered for the position of IEP coordinator within your school district, with emphasis upon the gifted and talented. Draft a letter of application that includes your qualifications to discharge the responsibilities of the position. Another alternative could be to draft a letter of nomination for a person you believe to be qualified to discharge the responsibilities of the position.

3. Prepare a script for a 15-minute radio presentation to publicize the IEP. Share your product with others.

SPECIFYING THE CONTENT OF AN INDIVIDUALIZED EDUCATION PROGRAM

4. Review the format of IEPs used in your district. What elements are present? What provisions are made for revisions? How is evaluation of goals and objectives conducted? Share your findings.

5. Interview three to five regular class teachers to learn about their experiences with an IEP. Perhaps others could interview principals, and others could interview parents. Identify sources of help in the improvement of education for learners.

6. Evaluate the three-page format for an IEP for gifted and talented learners in Exhibit 17-1. How would this IEP meet Pub.L. 94-142 standards? Share your product and seek ways to derive an improved format for your school.

ASSEMBLING AND ASSESSING INFORMATION

7. Consider a gifted and talented learner whom you know. Devise an IEP for this youngster. What sources of information would you prefer? What goals would, in your opinion, be of highest priority?

8. Review the section regarding grading. How does the content of this discussion match policies in your district? How does the content of this

discussion match the policies in college/university classes? How does examination of these sources affect your beliefs and practices regarding grading? Share your insights.

9. Suppose you were a member of a committee on academic standards and grading. Prepare a position statement of about 75 to 100 words regarding grading policies for gifted and talented pupils. Define criteria for grades of honors, satisfactory, and incomplete. Would these criteria be different for a more traditional grading system of A, B, C, etc.?

UNDERSTANDING THE KEY ROLE OF TEACHERS

10. As a responsible professional person, describe your beliefs about professionalism. What attributes are significant for you?

11. Design an interview to assess teacher priorities regarding the domains of competencies associated with Pub.L. 94-142. This interview could be four to five items per domain. Share your proposed instrument. What priorities emerge?

12. Prepare specifications for a 30-slide presentation regarding the common core of practice. How will you demonstrate that this core is indeed common to all educators?

Epilogue

Books about children are books about the world's future, especially when they deal, as this one does, with gifted and talented children. From birth through adulthood the gifted and talented have the potential to exceed their age peers in quickness to learn, in ability to learn at more and more advanced levels, and in ability to grasp complex concepts and help others understand and apply them. In short, they are both the thinkers *and* the thought leaders of the next generations.

Humankind, because of its wondrous ability to *think* its way through problems, has conquered predators and pestilence, developed arts and sciences, tamed the planet and its moon, and built a world society that balances personal, social and national rights (although that balance is still an uneasy one).

Viewed as a natural resource, gifted and talented children may well make up humankind's ultimate tangible asset. Those who plan and conduct the education of these young people carry a heavy responsibility, indeed. It is our wish that this book provide encouragement to parents, educators, and mentors to fulfill their aspirations of responsiveness.

References

Abeson, A., & Weintraub, F. Understanding the individualized educational plan. In S. Torres (Ed.), *A primer on individualized educational programs for handicapped children.* Reston, Virginia: Foundation for Exceptional Children, 1977.

Abeson, A., & Zettell, J. The end of a quiet revolution. *Exceptional Children,* 1977, *44,* 114–128.

Aldens, J. Family background factors and originality in children. *Gifted Child Quarterly,* 1973, *17,* 183–192.

Anderson, L., Barner, S. L., & Larson, H. J. Evaluation of written individualized education programs. *Exceptional Children,* 1978, 207–208.

Arieti, S. *Creativity: The magic synthesis.* New York: Basic Books, 1976.

Associated Press. He's a Froshboy. September 30, 1977.

Bachtold, L. Effects of learning environments on verbal creativity of gifted students. *Psychology in the Schools,* 1974, *11,* 226–229.

Ballard, J., & Zettell, J. Public Law 94-142 and section 504. *Exceptional Children,* 1977, *44,* 117–184.

Ballard, J., & Zettell, J. The managerial aspects of P.L. 94-142. *Exceptional Children,* 1978, *44,* 457–462.

Barbe, W. B. Evaluation of special classes for gifted children. *Exceptional Children,* 1955, *22,* 60–62.

Barbe, W. B. Family background of the gifted. *Journal of Educational Psychology,* 1956, *47,* 302–309.

Barbe, W. B. Homogeneous grouping for gifted children. *Educational Leadership,* 1965, *12,* 225–229.

Barbe, W. B., & Renzulli, J. S. (Eds.). *Psychology and education of the gifted.* New York: Irvington, 1975.

Bender, L. W. Can your catalogue stand the test of FTC guidelines? *Phi Delta Kappan,* 1975, *57,* 266–268.

Betts, E. A. *Foundations of reading instruction.* New York: American Book Company, 1946.

Birch, J. W., & Reynolds, M. C. The gifted. *Review of Educational Research,* 1963, *33*(1), 83–98.

Birch, J. W., & Johnstone, B. K. *Designing schools and schooling for the handicapped.* Springfield, Illinois: Charles C Thomas, 1975.

Bishop, W. E. Characteristics of teachers judged successful by intellectually gifted, high achieving high school students. In W. Dennis & M. Dennis (Eds.), *The intellectually gifted: An overview.* New York: Grune & Stratton, 1976.

Bloom, B. S. Affective outcomes of school learning. *Phi Delta Kappan,* 1977, *59,* 193–198.

Bloom, B. S. (Ed.). *Taxonomy of educational objectives: The classification of educational goals. Handbook 1. Cognitive domain.* New York: McKay, 1956.

Bloom, B., Hastings, J. T., & Madeus, G. F. *Handbook on formative and summative evaluation of student learning.* New York: McGraw-Hill, 1971.

Boyer, E. L. Closing the gap between home and school. *Christian Herald,* 1978, *101,* 22–32.

Brearly, M. and Hitchfied, E. *A Guide to Reading Piaget.* New York: Schocken Publishers, 1972.

Brehm, S. S. *Help for your child.* Englewood Cliffs, New Jersey: Prentice-Hall, 1978.

Brophy, J. E., & Everton, L. M. *Learning from teaching: A developmental perspective.* Boston: Allyn & Bacon, 1976.

Bruch, C. B. Children with intellectual superiority. In J. J. Gallagher (Ed.), *The application of child development research to exceptional children.* Reston, Virginia: Council for Exceptional Children, 1975.

Brumbaugh, F. N., & Roshco, B. *Your gifted child.* New York: Collier Books, 1959.

Bruner, J. S. *The process of education.* Cambridge: Harvard University Press, 1962.

Bureau of Special Education. *Mentally gifted children and youth.* Harrisburg, Pennsylvania: Pennsylvania State Department of Education, 1973.

Cammeron, W. A. Project evaluation. In N. H. Berger (Ed.), *Science career education for the physically handicapped.* Thomasville, Georgia: Thomas County Public Schools, 1978.

Chinn, P. C., Winn, J., & Walters, R. H. *Two-way talking with parents of special children.* St. Louis: C. V. Mosby, 1978.

Clark, C. Convergent and divergent thinking abilities of talented adolescents. *Journal of Educational Psychology,* 1965, *8,* 157–163.

Cole, R. W., & Dunn, R. A new lease on life for education of the handicapped: Ohio copes with P.L. 94-142. *Phi Delta Kappan,* 1977, *59,* 3–6.

Contanzo-Sorg, N. L. An implementation evaluation of a school system wide program for gifted students. Unpublished doctoral dissertation for the School of Education of the University of Pittsburgh. Pittsburgh, Pennsylvania, 1979.

Cooley, H., & Lohnes, W. *Evaluation research in education.* New York: Irvington Publishers, Halsted Press Division of John Wiley and Sons, 1976.

Correll, M. M. *Costs in teaching the gifted and talented.* Bloomington, Indiana: Phi Delta Kappan Educational Foundation, 1978.

Council for Exceptional Children. *Introducing PL 94-142.* Reston, Virginia: Council for Exceptional Children, 1976.

Council for Exceptional Children. Policies for the development of written individualized educational plans. *Exceptional Children,* 1977, *43,* 553–554.

Cox, R. L. Background characteristics of 456 gifted students. *Gifted Child Quarterly,* 1977, *21,* 261–266.

Davis, T. *IEP's for gifted students.* Doylestown, Pennsylvania: Bucks County Intermediate Unit No. 22, 1978.

Drews, E. The four faces of able adolescents. *Saturday Review,* 1963, *46,* 68–71. (Cited in Torrance, 1971)

Elardo, R. Behavior modification in an elementary school. *Phi Delta Kappan,* 1978, *59,* 334–338.

Ellis, J. R. *Career education for exceptionally gifted and talented students.* DeKalb, Illinois: Northern Illinois University in conjunction with the Illinois Division of Vocational and Adult Education, 1976.

Feldhusen, J. F., & Treffinger, D. J. *Teaching creative thinking and problem solving.* Dubuque, Iowa: Kendal/Hunt Publishing, 1977.

Fixx, J. F. *Games for the super-intelligent.* New York: Popular Library, 1972.

Fleigler, L. A., & Bish, C. E. The gifted and talented. *Review of Educational Research,* 1959, *29,* 408–450.

Flygare, T. Schools and the law. *Phi Delta Kappan,* 1979, *60,* 456–457.

Foley, J. J. Evaluation of learning in writing. In B. Bloom, J. T. Hastings, & G. F. Madeus, *Handbook on formative and summative evaluation of student learning.* New York: McGraw-Hill, 1971.

Forest Park Public Schools. *How to formulate objectives.* Forest Park, Illinois: Board of Education of Forest Park, 1971.

Frasier, M. M. The third dimension. *The Gifted Child Quarterly,* 1977, *21,* 207–213.

French, J. L. *Educating the gifted: A book of readings.* New York: Holt, 1959.

Frierson, E. C. The gifted. *Review of Educational Research,* 1969, *39,* 25–37.

Gage, N. L. (Ed.). *Handbook of research on teaching.* Chicago: Rand McNally & Company, 1963.

Gallagher, J. J. *Teaching the gifted child.* Boston: Allyn & Bacon, 1975.

Gallagher, J. J. *Organizational needs for quality special education.* In M. Reynolds (Ed.), *Futures of education for exceptional students.* Reston, Virginia: Council for Exceptional Children, 1978.

Gallagher, J. J., & Rogbe, W. The gifted. *Review of Educational Research,* 1966, *36*(1), 37–54.

Galton, F. *Hereditary genius.* New York: MacMillan, 1869.

Gardner, W. I. *Learning and behavioral characteristics of exceptional children and youth.* Boston: Allyn & Bacon, 1977.

Gear, C. H. Effects of training on teacher's accuracy in the identification of gifted children. *Gifted Child Quarterly,* 1978, *22,* 91–97.

Getzels, J. W. From art student to fine artist: Potential, problem finding, and performance. In H. A. Passow, 1979.

Getzels, J. W., & Jackson, P. W. The study of giftedness. Cooperative Research Monograph, U.S. Government Printing Office, 1960.

Glover, J., & Gary, A. I. Procedures to increase some aspects of creativity. *Journal of Applied Behavior Analysis,* 1976, *9,* 79–84.

Goldberg, M., & Passow, A. H. A study of the underachieving gifted. *Educational Leadership,* 1958, *16,* 121–125.

Green, R. L. Tips on educational testing: What parents and teachers should know. *Phi Delta Kappan,* 1975, *57,* 89–93.

Griggs, S. A., & Price, G. E. Learning styles of gifted junior high schools. *Phi Delta Kappan,* 1960, *55,* 361.

Gronbach, L. J., & Glasier, G. C. *Psychological tests and personal decisions* (2nd ed.). Urbana, Illinois: University of Illinois Press, 1965.

Gronbach, L. J., & Snow, R. E. *Aptitude and instructional methods.* New York: Irvington, 1975.

Gross, J. *Model state policy, legislations and state plan toward education of gifted and talented students.* Reston, Virginia: Council for Exceptional Children, 1980.

Grossman, H. J. *A manual on terminology and classification.* Washington, D.C.: American Association on Mental Deficiency, 1973.

Grost, A. *Genius in residence.* Englewood Cliffs, New Jersey: Prentice-Hall, 1970.

Groth, N. Mothers of the gifted. *Gifted Child Quarterly,* 1974, *19,* 217–222.

Guilford, J. P. Foreword in Meeker, 1969.

Guilford, J. P. Intellectual factors in productive thinking. In J. J. Aschner & C. E. Bish, *Productive thinking in education.* Washington, D.C.: National Education Association, 1965.

Guilford, J. P. Intelligence—1965 model. *American Psychologist,* 1966, *21,* 20–26.

Guilford, J. P. *The nature of human intelligence.* New York: McGraw-Hill, 1967.

Guilford, J. P. *Way beyond the I.Q.* Buffalo, New York: Creative Foundation, 1977.

Haisley, F. B., & Gilberts, R. D. Individual competencies needed to implement P.L. 94-142. *Journal of Teacher Education,* 1978, *24,* 30–33.

Hallahan, D. P., & Kauffman, J. M. *Exceptional children.* Englewood Cliffs, New Jersey: Prentice-Hall, 1978.

Hammermeister, K., & Mullins, J. *The hospital.* Pittsburgh, Pennsylvania: Division of Library Services, Western Pennsylvania School for the Deaf, 1977.

Haplin, G., Payne, D., & Ellett, C. In search of the creative personality among gifted groups. *Gifted Child Quarterly,* 1974, *17,* 31–34.

Harris, D. A. Bill of rights for the gifted. *Talents and Gifts,* 1976.

Harris, T. *I'm OK—You're OK.* New York: Harper & Row, 1969.

Havinghurst, R. *Human development and education.* New York: Longmans Green, 1953.

Hebb, D. D. Open letter: To a friend who thinks the IQ is a social evil. *American Psychologist,* 1978, *33,* 1143–1144.

Hedges, W. D. How to raise your school's ranking. . . *Phi Delta Kappan,* 1979, *60,* 377–378.

Hendrickson, B. Teacher burnout: How to recognize it: What to do about it. *Learning,* 1979, *7,* 36–39.

Higgins, S., & Barresi, J. The changing focus of public policy. *Exceptional Children,* 1979, *79,* 270–277.

Jacobs, J. C. Research studies reveal possible misconceptions of personality traits of the gifted. *Gifted Child Quarterly,* 1971, *15,* 195–200.

Jacobs, J. C. Teacher attitude toward gifted children. *Gifted Child Quarterly,* 1972, *16,* 23–26.

Jackson, J. L. In pursuit of equity, ethics, and excellence: The challenge to close the gap. *Phi Delta Kappan,* 1978,

James, M., & Jongword, O. *Born to win.* Reading, Massachusetts: Addison-Wesley, 1971.

Jenkins, J. R., & Pany, D. Standardized achievement tests: How useful for special education? *Exceptional Children,* 1978, *44,* 448–453.

Kagan, J. E. *Creativity and learning.* Boston: Houghton-Mifflin Company, 1967.

Kirk, S. A., & Gallagher, J. J. *Educating exceptional children* (3rd ed.). Boston: Houghton-Mifflin Company, 1979.

Krippner, S., & Blickenstaff, R. The development of self-concept as part of an arts workshop for the gifted. *Gifted Child Quarterly,* 1970, *14,* 163–166.

Kurtzman, K. School attitudes, peer acceptance, and personality of creative adolescents. *Exceptional Children,* 1967, *34,* 157–162.

Lanzo, L., & Vassar, W. Designing and implementing a program for the gifted and talented. *National Elementary Principal,* 1972, *51,* unnumbered pages.

Levinson, D., Darrow, C., Klem, E., Levinson, M., & McKee, B. Psychological development. In G. Rick, A. Thomas, & M. Roff (Eds.), *Life history research— Vol. 3.* Minneapolis, Minnesota: University of Minnesota Press, 1974.

Lewis, C. L., & Kanes, L. G. Gifted IEP's. *Journal of Education of the Gifted and Talented,* 1979, *2,* 61–69.

Lucito, L. J. Gifted children. In L. M. Dunn (Ed.), *Exceptional Children in the Schools.* New York: Holt, Rinehart, & Winston, 1963.

MacTurk, R. H., & Neisworth, J. T. Norm referenced and criterion based measured preschoolers. *Exceptional Children,* 1978, *45,* 34–39.

Mager, C. J. *Training teachers for the gifted and talented: A comparison of models.* Reston, Virginia: Council for Exceptional Children, 1975.

Mager, C. J. *Providing programs for the gifted handicapped.* Reston, Virginia: Council for Exceptional Children, 1977.

Mager, C. J. Developing multiple talents in exceptional children. *Teaching Exceptional Children,* 1979, *11,* 120–124.

Mager, R. *Goal analysis.* Belmont, California: Fearon, 1972.

Manchester, G. S. *Regulations for IEP for special education students.* Harrisburg, Pennsylvania: Bureau for Special and Compensatory Education, Department of Education, 1977.

Marland, S. P., Jr. Education of the gifted and talented. Report to the Congress by the U.S. Commissioner of Education. Washington, D.C.: U.S. Government Printing Office, 1971.

Martinson, R. *The identification of the gifted and talented.* Ventura, California: Office of the Ventura County Superintendent of Schools, 1974.

Mason, R. *Educational ideas in American education.* Boston: Allyn & Bacon, 1960.

Matthews, J., & Birch, J. W. The Lieter International Performance Scale: A suggested instrument for psychological testing of speech and hearing clinic cases. *Journal of Speech and Hearing Disorders,* December 1949.

Maul, P. *Alternatives in programming for gifted pupils.* Kalamazoo, Michigan: Kalamazoo Valley Intermediate School District, 1978.

McMahon, F. *Psychology the hybrid science.* Englewood Cliffs, New Jersey: Prentice-Hall, 1974.

Mead, M. Your world. *Redbook,* 1979, *52,* 27.

Meeker, M. M. *The structure of intellect: Its interpretation and uses.* Columbus, Ohio: Charles Merrill, 1969.

Mercer, J. In defense of racially and culturally non-discriminatory assessment. *School Psychology Digest,* 1979, *8*(1), 89–115.

Mercer, J. B., and Lewis, J. G. Using the System of Multi-Cultural Pluralistic Assessment. In A. Y. Baldwin, G. H. Gear, and L. J. Lucito (Eds.), *Educational Planning for the Gifted.* Reston, Virginia: Council for Exceptional Children, 1978.

Michener, J. A. *Chesapeake.* New York: Random House, 1978.

Milgrim, R. M., & Norman, A. Self concept as a function of intelligence and creativity in highly gifted children. *Psychology in the Schools,* 1976, *13,* 91–96.

Mordock, J. B. *The other children.* New York: Harper & Row, 1975.

Mortinger, G. J. Use of more specific instructions to modify several aspects of creative writing. *Directive Teacher,* 1979, 1, 7, and 23.

Muller, P. *Tasks of childhood.* New York: McGraw-Hill, 1969.

Mullins, J. M. Making language work better for handicapped people and everyone else. A paper presented at the Annual Convention of the Council for Exceptional Children, April 1979, Dallas, Texas. Pittsburgh, Pennsylvania, Special Education Program, University of Pittsburgh.

Mussen, P. H., Conger, J. J., & Kagan, J. *Child development and personality* (4th ed.). New York: Harper & Row, 1974.

Myers, E. Counseling the parents of sixth grade underachievers. *Journal of Education,* 1971, *154,* 50–53.

Nash, W. Effects of a school for the gifted in advertising the fourth grade slump in creativity. *Gifted Child Quarterly,* 1974, *18,* 168–170.

National/State Leadership Training Institute on the Gifted and Talented. *What about the gifted and talented?* Los Angeles, California, 1978.

Neisworth, J. T., Willoughby-Herb, S. J., Bagnato, S. J., Jr., Cartwright, C. A., & Laub, K. W. *Individualized education for preschool exceptional children.* Germantown, Maryland: Aspen Systems Corporation, 1980.

Newland, T. E. The mentally gifted. *Review of Educational Research,* 1941, *11,* 277–287.

Newland, T. E. The gifted. *Review of Educational Research,* 1953, *23,* 417–431.

Newland, T. E. *The blind learning aptitude test.* Report, USOE Grant No. OEG-3-6-061928-1558. Urbana, Illinois: University of Illinois, 1969.

Newland, T. E. *The gifted in socio-educational perspectives.* Englewood Cliffs, New Jersey: Prentice-Hall, 1976.

Oglivie, E. Creativity and curriculum structure. *Journal of Educational Research,* 1974, *16,* 126–132.

Olstad, D. The pursuit of excellence is not elitism. *Phi Delta Kappan,* 1978, *60,* 187–188, 229.

Parnes, S. J., Noller, R. B., & Biondi, D. M. *Guide to creative action.* New York: Charles Scribner's, 1977.

Partridge, D. L. A comprehensive special education program. In J. B. Jordan (Ed.),

Teacher please don't close the door. Reston, Virginia: Council for Exceptional Children, 1976.

Passow, A. H. Fostering creativity in the gifted child. *Exceptional Children,* 1977, *43,* 358–364.

Passow, A. H. (Ed.). The gifted and the talented: Their education and development. *The Seventy-Eighth Yearbook of the National Society for the Study of Education, Part I.* Chicago: University of Chicago Press, 1979.

Pegnato, C. W., & Birch, J. W. Locating gifted children in junior high schools: A comparison of models. *Exceptional Children,* 1959, *25,* 300–304.

Popham, W. J. Normative data for criterion referenced test? *Phi Delta Kappan,* 1976, *57,* 593–594.

Provus, M. *Discrepancy evaluation.* Berkeley, California: McCutchan Publishers, 1971.

Rabbit, J. A. The parent-teacher conference: Trauma or teamwork? *Phi Delta Kappan,* 1978, *59,* 471–472.

Radcliffe, S. A., & Hatch, W. R. *Advanced standing.* Washington, D.C.: U.S. Office of Education, 1961, Report Number OE-5414.

Raybin, R. Minimum essentials and accountability. *Phi Delta Kappan,* 1979, *60,* 374–375.

Rennels, M. R. Cerebral symmetry. *Phi Delta Kappan,* 1976, *57,* 471–472.

Renzulli, J. S. Identifying key features in programs for the gifted. In W. B. Barbe & J. S. Renzulli (Eds.), *Psychology and education of the gifted* (2nd ed.). New York: Halsted Press-John Wiley, 1975.

Renzulli, J. S. Two approaches to identification of gifted students. *Exceptional Children,* 1977, 513–518.

Renzulli, J. S. What makes giftedness? *Phi Delta Kappan,* 1978, *60,* 180–184, 261.

Renzulli, J. S. Issues and procedures in evaluating programs. In A. H. Passow, 1979.

Renzulli, J. S., & Gable, R. K. A factorial study of the attitudes of gifted students toward independent study. *The Gifted Child Quarterly,* 1976, *20,* 91–99.

Renzulli, J. S., & Smith, Linda H. *Individual Educational Program-Strength-A-Lyzer.* Mansfield, Colorado: Creative Learning Press, 1978.

Renzulli, J. S., & Smith, Linda H. Two approaches to identification of gifted students. *Exceptional Children,* 1977, *43,* 513–518.

Reynolds, M. C. *Delphi survey.* Reston, Virginia: Council for Exceptional Children, 1973.

Reynolds, M. C. (Ed.) *A common body of practice for teachers.* Washington, D.C.: American Association of Colleges of Teacher Education, 1980.

Reynolds, M., & Birch, J. W. Giftedness and talent: High rate of cognitive development. In *Teaching exceptional children in all America's schools.* Reston, Virginia: Council for Exceptional Children, 1977.

Rhodes, R. Prodigy. *Quest,* 1979, *2,* 22–26, 104–105.

Roweton, W. E. Indices of classroom creativity. *Child Study Journal,* 1975, *5,* 151–161

Rowland, & McGuire. The development of intelligent behavior. *Psychology in the Schools,* 1968, *5,* 47–52.

Sandborn, M. *Career education for gifted boys and girls.* Madison, Wisconsin:

Research and Guidance Laboratory for Superior Students, University of Wisconsin, 1976.

Sato, I. S. *The demands of giftedness and talent.* Los Angeles, California: National/ State Leadership Training Institute on the Gifted and Talented, 1978.

Sattler, J. M. *Assessment of children's intelligence.* Philadelphia: W. B. Saunders, 1974.

Seashore, H. G. The identification of the gifted. *Test Service Bulletin,* 1963, *55,* 1–6.

Sellin, D. F. Observations about trends in the education of exceptional children and youth. *School of Education Newsletter.* Pittsburgh, Pennsylvania: University of Pittsburgh, 1978.

Sellin, D. F., & Birch, J. W. *Educating gifted and talented learners.* Germantown, Maryland: Aspen Systems Corporation, 1980.

Sharpless, N. S. Preface to *Resource directory of handicapped scientists.* New York: Foundation for Science and the Handicapped, 1979.

Sheehy, G. *Passages.* New York: Bantam Books, 1976.

Sicgelman, M. Parent behavior correlates of personality traits related to creativity in sons and daughters. *Journal of Consulting and Clinical Psychology,* 1973, *40,* 43–47.

Sisk, D. Self concept and creativity. *Gifted Child Quarterly,* 1972, *16,* 229–233.

Solano, C. H. Precocity and adult failure: Shattering the myth. Paper presented at the Annual Convention of the National Association for Gifted Children, October 14, 1976, Kansas City.

Spencer-Pulaski, M. *Understanding Piaget.* New York: Harper & Row, 1979.

Stanley, J., George, W., & Solano, C. (Eds.). *The gifted and the creative.* Baltimore: Johns Hopkins University Press, 1977.

State Board of Education, Commonwealth of Pennsylvania. Specific provisions for gifted and talented school age persons, sections 13.21–12.13. In *Regulations of the State Board of Education.* Harrisburg, Pennsylvania: State Board of Education, 1976.

Stephens, B., and Simpkins, K. *Moral judgment in blind children.* Philadelphia, Pennsylvania: Temple University, 1974.

Stevens, G. D. Teaching as a profession. Paper presented before Convention of the Michigan Council for Exceptional Children, Grand Rapids, Michigan, 1970.

Stevenson, H. S. Learn. In Gallagher, J. J. (Ed.) *Applications of child development research to exceptional children.* Reston, Virginia: Council for Exceptional Children, 1975.

Stoneman, Z., & Gibson, S. Situation influences on assessment performance. 1978, *45,* 166–169.

Stufflebeam, O. Evaluation and decision making. In O. Stufflebeam, W. Foley, W. J. Gephart, E. Guba, R. Hammond, H. Merrian, & N. Provus (Eds.), *Educational evaluation in decision making.* Itasca, Illinois: Peacock, 1971.

Suchman, R. A. A model for the analysis of inquiry. In H. Klausmeier & C. W. Harris (Eds.), *Analysis of concept learning.* New York: Academic Press, 1966.

Suchman, J. P. Inquiry training. *Merrill-Palmer Quarterly,* 1961, *7,* 171–180.

Tannenbaum, A. J. Pre-Sputnik to post-Watergate concern about the gifted. In A. H Passow, 1979.

Tanner, T. A far out mind stretcher. *Phi Delta Kappan,* 1977, *58,* 603–605.

Taylor, I. A. Creative production in gifted young adults through sensory stimulation. *Gifted Child Quarterly,* 1970, *14,* 46–55.

Terman, L. M. et al. Genetic studies of genius. Stanford, California: Stanford University Press.
I. Terman, L. M. et al. The mental and physical traits of a thousand gifted children, 1925.
II. Cox, C. M. The early mental traits of three hundred geniuses, 1926.
III. Burks, B. S., Jensen, D., & Terman, L. M. The promise of youth, 1930.
IV. Terman, L. M., & Oden, M. H. The gifted child grows up, 1947.
V. Terman, L. M., & Oden, M. H. The gifted group at mid-life, 1959.

Thiel, R., & Thill, A. F. A structural analysis of family interaction patterns and the underachieving gifted child. *Gifted Child Quarterly,* 1977, *21,* 167–275.

Thinnes, T. Life at the top of the IQ scale can be difficult. *Kalamazoo Gazette,* May 28, 1978, A-14.

Thistlewhite, D. Effects of social recognition upon educational motivation of talented youth. *Journal of Educational Psychology,* 1959, *50,* 111–116.

Torrance, E. P. *Rewarding creative behavior.* Englewood Cliffs, New Jersey: Prentice-Hall, 1965.

Torrance, E. P. Curiosity of gifted children and performance on timed and untimed tests of creativity. *Gifted Child Quarterly,* 1969, *13,* 155–159.

Torrance, E. P. Psychology of gifted children and youth. In W. Cruickshank (Ed.), *Psychology of exceptional children and youth* (3rd ed.). Englewood Cliffs, New Jersey: Prentice-Hall, 1971.

Torrance, E. P. *Torrance tests and creative thinking.* Lexington, Massachusetts: Ginn, 1974.

Torrance, E. P. *Discovery and nurturance of giftedness in the culturally different.* Reston, Virginia: Council for Exceptional Children, 1977.

Torrance, E. P. Psychology of gifted children and youth. In W. M. Cruickshank (Ed.), *Psychology of exceptional children and youth* (4th ed.). Englewood Cliffs, New Jersey: Prentice-Hall, 1980.

Torres, S. (Ed.). *Appendix 2: Sample individualized education/plan form in a primer on individualized educational programs for handicapped children.* Reston, Virginia: Foundation for Exceptional Children, 1977.

Toynbee, A. Is America neglecting her creative minorities? In Taylor, 1964.

Tractenberg, P. L., & Jacoby, E. Pupil testing: A legal view. *Phi Delta Kappan,* 1977, *59,* 249–254.

Trezise, R. L. The gifted child: Back in the limelight. *Phi Delta Kappan,* 1976, *58,* 241–243.

Trezise, R. L. *Some suggested procedures for establishing a program for gifted and talented students.* Lansing, Michigan: Programs for the Gifted, Michigan Department of Education, 1978.

Uhler, S. A confederacy against the gifted. *Phi Delta Kappan,* 1977, *59,* 285–286.

United States Office of Education. *Education of the gifted and talented.* Washington, D.C.: U.S. Office of Education, Department of Health, Education and Welfare, 1971.

Ward, V. S. *The gifted student*. Charlottesville, Virginia: University of Virginia, 1962.

Warren, R. *Studying your community*. New York: Russell Sage Foundation, 1979.

Weiler, D. The alpha children. *Phi Delta Kappan,* 1978, *60,* 185–187.

Weiner, J. L., & O'Shea, H. E. Attitudes of university faculty, administrators, teachers, supervisors, and university students toward the gifted. *Exceptional Children,* 1963, *29,* 163–165.

Welch-Brown, J. Who are the handicapped scientists? *Science,* 1975, *100,* 546, 593.

Western Pennsylvania Special Education Regional Resource Center. IEP brings "goodies" to regular education. *Newsletter,* 1978, *11,* 1.

Whitmore, J. R. *Giftedness, conflict and underachievement*. Boston: Allyn & Bacon, 1980.

Wilson, B. G. Evaluation of learning in art education. In Bloom al.,1971.

Wilson, R. *Education for the gifted*. Chicago: National Society for the Study of Education, 1958.

Wolf, S., & Wolf, C. *Games without words*. Springfield, Illinois: Charles C Thomas, 1977.

Wolfensberger, W., & Glenn, L. *Program analysis of service systems*. Toronto, Canada: National Institute on Mental Retardation, 1975.

Woodrow, H. *Brightness and dullness in children*. Philadelphia: Lippincott, 1919.

Woods, E. L. The mentally gifted. *Review of Educational Research,* 1944, *14,* 224–230.

Wyne, M. D., & O'Connor, P. D. *Exceptional children: A developmental view*. Lexington, Massachusetts: D. C. Heath, 1977.

Wynn, R., DeYoung, C. A., & Lindsey-Wynn, J. *American Education* (8th ed.). New York: McGraw-Hill, 1977.

Young-Baldwin, A. Tests can underpredict: A case study. *Phi Delta Kappan,* 1977, *58,* 620–621.

Zivich, S. The spy in the rust-colored trenchcoat. *Reader's Digest,* 1979, *114,* 131, 259.

Index

A

Abilities. *See* Human Abilities
Abstraction
  application to new situations, 11
Acceleration
  development, 69
    social relationships, 69, 70
    values conflict, 70
Accommodation
  adaptation, 28
Accountability
  dimensions, 218-222
Achievers. *See also* Underachievers
  behavior, 94
Act
  matching to goal, 255, 256
Action Steps
  teacher quality, 285
Activities
  pupil, 235
Actors
  of innovation, 193, 194
Actual Performance. *See*
  Performance

Adaptation
  curriculum, 125, 167, 168, 170, 185
  human abilities as, 27, 49-51
  intelligence, 27-31
Adaptive Behavior. *See also*
  Behavior
  ability, 46-48
Adequacy
  federal definitions, 44
Adolescence. *See also* Childhood;
  Young Adulthood
  diversity, 98
  sequence of tasks, 61
Adolescents. *See* Adolescence
Adulthood. *See also* Middle
  Adulthood; Young Adulthood
  sequence of tasks, 62, 63
Advancement
  individualized education
    programs, 233
Advantages
  identification
    creativity, 115
    procedures, 112, 118
  nomination, 113

psychometric approaches, 116, 117
Affective Assessment
  performance, 274
Alliance
  teacher-parent, 282, 283
Alternatives
  generation, 197
  individualized education
    programs
      multiclass vs. district wide, 182
      regular class, 182
  programming, 99, 100
  selection, 197
American Association for the
  Advancement of Science, 97
American Association of School
  Administrators, 126
American Education. See Education
American Mensa Selection Agency,
  108
Analysis. See also Analytic Skills
  existing situation, 197
  preparing outcomes, 11, 12
  range of behavior, 6, 7
Analytic Skills. See also Analysis
  measurement, 13
Anticipation
  curriculum future, 183, 185-186
Applications
  abstraction to new situations, 11
  curriculum content, 130
  education, 216-218
  Guilford's model, 25, 26
  Piaget, 32, 33
  preparing outcomes, 9-11
  range of behavior, 6, 7
Appraisal
  curriculum structure, 128
Approaches
  case history, 119
    cost estimates, 120
    effectiveness, 119
    outcomes, 120
  psychometric, 116
Aptitude
  performance

description, 40
dimensions, 42
Aptitude/Treatment Interaction
  grading, 271, 272
  model, 269-271
  understanding, 268, 269
Art Education. See also Education
  Table of Specifications, 132
Assembling
  information, 261-263, 290
Assessed Performance. See
  Performance
Assessment. See also Behavioral
  Assessment
  information, 261-263, 290, 291
  needs policy, 159-160
  performance, 272-276
Assimilation
  adaptation, 28
Association
  evaluation behavior, 17
Assumptions
  teacher quality, 284
ATI. See Aptitude/Treatment
  Interaction
Attributes
  curriculum adaptations, 183, 185
  handicapped persons, 90, 91
  individualized education program
    objectives, 255
  Mensa person, 35-37
  personality, 72
  teachers, 183, 185-187, 285
Awareness
  individualized education program
    possibilities, 259

B

Backgrounds
  family, 67
  innovation, 193
Basic Scholars, 174
  individualized education
    programs, 231, 232

Basic Scholars Program. *See* Basic
Scholars
Behavior. *See also* Adaptive
Behavior
educational significance, 94
evaluation, 17
handicapped persons, 97, 98, 99
range of, 6
guidelines, 16-18
Table of Specifications, 134
Behavioral Assessment. *See also*
Assessment
performance, 274, 275
Behavior Type. *See also* Behavior
abstraction application, 11
analytic skills measurement, 13
evaluation, 17
Behaviors. *See* Behavior
Bill of Rights
education perspective, 139, 140
Bloom
performance, 5
Brady, Mathew, 131
Brainstorming
curriculum selection, 136-138
Budget
development, 206

C

CA. *See* Chronological Age
Case History
approach
cost estimates, 119
effectiveness, 118
outcomes, 119
perspective, 117
Child Who
survey, 157
Childhood. *See also* Early
Childhood
sequence of tasks, 60, 61
Choices. *See also* Options
opportunity, 86, 87
Chronological Age. *See also* Mental
Age

natural underachievement, 78
sequence of tasks, 58
Citizens' Needs Assessment
Committee, 154
Cognition
intelligence factors, 21, 22
range of behaviors, 6
Commitment
public policy, 250
Common Core of Practice. *See* Core
of Practice
Competencies
individualized education program
teachers, 281, 282
Components
individualized education
programs
advancement, 233
basic scholars, 231, 232
human services, 234, 235
special interests, 232, 233
talent development, 234
Composites
performance, 71-73
Comprehension
preparing outcomes, 8, 9
range of behavior, 6, 7
Concepts
intelligence as adaptation, 27
underachievement, 76, 77
Concerns
family, 67, 68
socialization, 68, 69
identification, 196
tests and testing, 243
Concrete Operations. *See also*
Formal Operations
Piaget, 31
Conditions
individualized education
programs, 240, 241, 248
learning, 145
Confederacy
development, 201, 224, 226
Confederacy for the Gifted and
Talented. *See* Confederacy

Conflict
  values, 70
Consensus
  advance, 215
Consequences
  prediction, 197
Considerations
  creativity
    identification, 115
  disabilities
    learning, 92-95
    physical, 90-92
  emotional impairment, 92-95
  funding, 209-211
  procedures
    identification, 112, 118
    nomination, 113
  psychometric approaches, 116, 117
  selection, 110, 111
Constraints
  program development, 164, 165
Consumer
  preferences, 139
Content
  individualized education
    programs, 251, 253, 289, 291
  intelligence factors, 21
  selection by brainstorming,
    136-138
  structure, 129, 130
Context
  educational quality, 223, 225
  program and budget development,
    206
Coordination of Secondary Schema
  sensory-motor period, 31
Core of Practice
  teacher, 285-288
Correlates
  performance, 73-75
Cost
  case history approach, 120
Council for Exceptional Children, 97
Coverage
  services, 257, 258
Covergent Thinking. See also

Divergent Thinking
  intelligence factors, 22, 23
Covert Underachievement. See
  Underachievement, 79
Creativity
  divergent thinking, 23
  identification, 115
  performance
    description, 40
    dimensions, 42
  psychological tests, 88
Criterion-Referenced Measurement.
  See also Measurement
  data, 267, 268
Culture
  opportunity, 83-86
Curriculum
  adaptation, 125, 167, 168, 170
  content
    selection, 136-138
  future, 183, 185-186
  goals
    common, 126, 127
    nature of, 125, 126
  matching, 168, 169, 171
  modification tactics, 273
  outcomes, 127, 128
    matrix, 130-136
  structure, 128
  use, 125

D

Data. See also Information
  interpretation, 263, 264
  measurement
    criterion-referenced, 267, 268
    non-referenced, 265, 266
Decisions
  aptitude/treatment interactions,
    268, 269
  matching, 148
Definition
  ability
    adaptive behavior, 46-48
    task commitment, 45, 46

educational context of quality, 177
gifted and talented
  adequacy, 44
  attributes, 43-46
  values, 43
instructional dimensions, 259
support systems, 202, 203
Demonstration
  role models, 42
Description
  education, 178
  gifted and talented persons, 39,
    50-52
  human abilities, 1-3
  language, 40
  needs assessment, 153
  quality education, 173
Development. *See also* Talent
  Development
  acceleration, 69
    social relationships, 69, 70
    values conflict, 70
  confederacy, 201
  programs, 189, 190, 224, 226
    budget, 206
    constraints, 164, 165
Diffusion
  outcomes, 198
Dimensions
  accountability, 218-222
  identification, 39
  organization responsibilities, 244
  performance, 42
Discrepancy Assessment
  performance, 274
District-Wide Alternatives. *See*
  Alternatives
Divergent Thinking. *See also*
  Covergent Thinking
  intelligence factors, 22, 23
Diversity
  adolescence, 98

E

Early Childhood. *See also*

Childhood
  sequence of tasks, 59, 60
Education. *See also* Art Education;
  Quality Education
  context of quality, 177
  curriculum
    goals, 126, 127
    outcomes, 127, 128
  description, 178
  excellence, 100, 101
  handicapped persons, 92-95
  programming, 161-164
  significant behaviors, 94
Educational Data. *See* Data
Educational Services. *See* Services
Effectiveness
  case history approach, 119
  identification procedures, 111
Efficiency
  case history approach, 119-120
  identification procedures, 111
Elements
  evaluation, 213, 214
  learning, 146, 147
  planning, 150, 151
  program and budget development,
    207
    funding, 209-211
    plan of work, 208, 211
  programming, 161-164
  support systems, 203, 204
Elimination
  handicapism, 95, 96
  trends, 97, 98
Emotional Impairment. *See also*
  Physical Disability
  educational considerations, 92-95
Entry Point Proposal. *See* Proposal
Environment
  nurture, 37
Environmental Assessment
  performance, 275
Estimates
  case history approach costs, 120
Evaluation
  accountability, 218

behavior, 17
instruction, 260
intelligence factors, 22
model, 215, 216
nature of, 213
parental recommendations, 256, 257
performance, 275, 276
planning matrix, 217
preparing outcomes, 16
range of behavior, 6, 7
role models, 42
tactics, 265
Examples
Piaget applications, 32, 33
EXCEL, 100
Excellence
education, 100, 101
Existing Situation
analysis, 197

Formal Operations. See also
Concrete Operations
Piaget, 31
Forms
individualized education
programs, 277-279
underachievement, 77, 80, 81
Foundation for Science and the
Handicapped, 97
Four Stages
Piaget, 31, 32
Framework
quality education, 181
Full Adulthood. See Adulthood
Funding
considerations, 209-211
support services, 206
Future
curriculum anticipation, 183, 185-186

F

Factors
intelligence, 20-25
Facts
curriculum content, 129
Family
backgrounds, 67
concerns, 67, 68
socialization, 68, 69
understanding, 65
Family Influences. See also Family;
Social Influences
outcomes, 66, 67
parental view, 65, 66
Features
innovation, 191, 192
Federal Definition. See Definition
Federal Trade Commission, 179
Fitzgerald, F. Scott, 41
Focus
needs assessment, 155, 156
policy, 158
pupil services, 156, 158

G

Gathering
data, 264
Generation
alternatives, 197
Goals
curriculum
common, 126, 127
nature of, 125, 126
individualized education
programs, 241, 242
preparation, 254
matching to act, 255, 256
orientation, 211, 212
Grading
aptitude/treatment interaction, 271, 272
Grost, Michael, 54
Guiding Concepts. See Concepts
Guilford
human abilities as operations, 18
model applications, 25, 26

H

Handicapism. *See also* Handicapped
  Persons
  elimination, 95, 96
  trends, 97, 98
Handicapped Persons. *See also*
  Handicapism; Physical
  Disabilities
  attributes, 90, 91
  behavior, 98, 99
  educational considerations, 92-95
Helping Skills
  teacher quality, 285
Hemingway, Ernest, 41
High-Quality Programs. *See* Quality
  Education; Programs
Human Abilities
  as adaptation, 27, 49-51
  as performance, 5, 6, 49-51
  description, 1-3
  operations, 5, 6, 18, 49-51
  opportunity, 83-86
  range of behaviors, 5
  social context, 53
  task commitment, 45, 46
  understanding, 1-3
Human Performance. *See*
  Performance
Human Service. *See also* Services
  individualized education
    programs, 234, 235
Hunter Family, 54

I

Identification
  concern, 196
  creativity, 115
  dimensions, 39
  gifted and talented, 167, 170
  leadership perspective, 109
  opportunity, 87-90
  personal sources, 114
  procedures, 110, 111
  advantages, 112
  effectiveness, 111
  limitations, 112
  underprediction, 121, 122
  value, 111-112
  psychometrics, 116, 117
  teacher, 122-123
IEP. *See* Individualized Education
  Programs
Impact
  quality programs, 213, 225, 227
Imperfect Understanding. *See also*
  Understanding
  Piaget, 30
Implementation
  alternatives, 197
  public policy, 249-250
Individual Order. *See also* Social
  Order
  needs, 177, 178
Individualized Education Programs,
  69
  case history tradition, 118
  components
    advancement, 233
    basic scholars, 231, 232
    human service, 234, 235
    special interest, 232, 233
    talent development, 234
  conditions, 240, 241
  content, 251-253, 289-291
  form, 277-279
  goals, 241, 242
  handicapism elimination, 96
  managing conditions, 248
  opportunity identification, 87
  options, 182
  organization responsibility,
    242-245
  outcomes, 241, 242
  preparation, 246-248
  prescriptions, 247-248
  public policy, 249-250
  pupil activities, 235
  rationale, 239, 240, 288, 289, 291
  staff responsibilities, 235-237

teacher competencies, 281, 282
use, 229-231
Influences
innovation, 193, 194
routes of, 194, 195
Information. *See also* Data
assembling and assessing,
261-263, 290, 291
Innovation
model, 196
organization for, 190-193
problem solving, 196
tactics, 193, 198, 199
teacher's role, 194-195
Instruction. *See also* Instructional
Dimensions
evaluation, 260
Instructional Dimensions. *See also*
Instruction
individualized education
programs, 259, 260
Integration
Piaget, 30
Intelligence
adaptation, 27-31
as factors, 20-25
human abilities, 5
psychological tests, 88
Intelligence Quotient. *See* IQ Test
Interpretation
data, 263, 264
Intervention
model, 166
Invariant Sequence
adaptation, 29
Piaget, 30
Invention of Mental Operations
sensory-motor period, 31
IQ Tests. *See also* Psychometrics
performance correlates, 73-75
vs. intelligence, 37

K

Knowledge
preparing outcomes, 8

range of behavior, 6, 7
Knowledge into Action
translation, 204-206

L

Language
describing performance, 40
opportunity, 83-86
socialization, 68
Leadership
identification, 109
Learner. *See* Pupil
Learning
conditions, 145
elements, 146, 147
style, 148, 149
TOMIC, 147, 148
Learning Disability. *See also*
Physical Disability
behavior, 94
educational considerations, 92-95
Lessons. *See* Outcomes
Levels
underachievement
covert, 79
natural, 77, 78
overt, 79, 80
Lewis, Sinclair, 41
Life
problems and rewards, 34
Limitations
identification
creativity, 115
procedures, 112
nomination procedures, 113
psychometric approaches, 116, 117
testing, 244-246

M

MA. *See* Mental Age
Maintaining
individualized education program
conditions, 248
match, 150, 153, 169, 171

Management
    goals, 211, 212
    matrix, 220, 221
    model, 222, 223
Managing
    individualized education program
        conditions, 248
    match, 150, 153, 169, 171
Match. *See also* Matching
    managing and maintaining, 150,
        153, 169, 171
    needs assessment, 153
Matching. *See also* Match
    curriculum, 168, 169, 171
    decisions, 148
    goal to act, 255, 256
    learner and curriculum, 139
    learning style, 148, 149
    outcomes, 144
Materials
    individualized education program
        selection, 259, 260
Matrix
    curriculum outcomes, 130-136
    management, 220, 221
    planning and educational
        evaluation, 217
Maximizing
    services, 258, 259
Mead, Margaret, 41
Meaning
    education, 177
Measurement. *See also*
    Psychometrics
    analytic skills, 13
Memory
    intelligence factors, 22
Mensa
    attributes, 35-37
    nurture, 37
    view from the top, 33, 34
Mensa Person. *See* Mensa
Mental Age. *See also* Chronological
    Age
    natural underachievement, 78
    sequence of tasks, 58

Mentally Gifted Minor
    parents, 142
MGM. *See* Mentally Gifted Minor
Middle Adulthood. *See also*
    Adulthood; Young Adulthood
    sequence of tasks, 62, 63
Model
    aptitude/treatment interaction,
        269-271
    educational intervention, 166
        programming priorities, 165,
        166
    evaluation, 215, 216
    Guilford, 25, 26
    innovation in programming, 196
    management, 222, 223
    TOMIC, 149, 150
Modification
    curriculum tactics, 273
Monitoring
    outcomes, 197
Motivation
    programming, 178, 197
    sources, 73
Multiclass Alternatives. *See*
    Alternatives

N

National Center on Educational
    Media and Materials for the
    Handicapped, 95
National Education Association, 126
National State Leadership Training
    Institute on the Gifted and
    Talented, 109, 181
Natural Underachievement, 77, 78.
    See also Underachievement
Nature
    education programming
        procedures, 164
    evaluation, 213, 214
    influence, 193
    learning, 145, 146
Needs. *See also* Needs Assessment
    individual vs. social order, 177,
        178

understanding, 105
Needs Assessment. *See also* Needs
  description, 153
  process, 154, 155
  products, 155-158
  proposals, 162
  translation, 158, 160
New Situations
  abstraction application, 11
Nomination
  procedures, 113
Norm-Referenced Measurement. *See also* Measurement
  data, 265, 266
Nurture
  Mensa, 37

O

Objectives
  curriculum, 128, 129
  individualized education program attributes, 255
Open System. *See also* Support System
  confederacy development, 201, 202
Operational Steps
  brainstorming, 137, 138
Operations. *See also* Concrete Operations; Formal Operations
  human abilities, 5, 6, 18, 49
  intelligence factors, 21-25
Opportunity
  identification trends, 87-90
  options and choices, 86, 87
  social context, 83
Options. *See also* Choices
  gathering data, 264
  opportunity, 86, 87
  quality education, 182
Organization
  individualized education programs
    responsibility dimensions, 242-245
  innovation, 190-193

Orientation
  goals, 211, 212
  socialization, 68
Originality
  divergent thinking, 23
Outcomes
  case history approach, 120-121
  curriculum, 127, 128
  matching learner and, 144
  matrix, 130-136
  diffusion, 198
  family influences, 66, 67
  monitoring, 197
  preparing
    analysis, 11, 12
    application, 9-11
    comprehension, 8, 9
    evaluation, 16
    knowledge, 8
    synthesis, 12-16
Overt Underachievement, 79, 80. *See also* Underachievement

P

Parents
  curriculum perspectives, 142-144
  family influences, 65, 66
  recommendation evaluation, 256, 257
  teacher
    alliance, 282, 283
    conference, 283, 284
People Organized to Save Humanity, 100
Performance
  actual vs. assessed, 245
  assessment, 272-276
  correlates, 73-75
  human abilities as, 5, 6, 49
  language describing, 40
  personal attributes, 72
  self-concept, 75, 76
  social context, 71
    composites, 71-73

Personal Sources
  identification procedures, 114
Personality
  gifted and talented persons, 41
  performance attributes, 72
Perspective
  case history, 118
  education bill of rights, 139, 140
  leadership identification, 109
  parents, 142-144
Physical Disability. *See also*
  Handicapped Persons
  considerations, 90-92
Piaget
  applications, 32, 33
  four stages, 31, 32
  intelligence as adaptation, 27-31
  principles, 27, 30
Plan of Work
  program development, 208, 209
Planning
  elements, 150, 151
  individualized education program
    rationale, 239, 240
  matrix, 217
Policy
  needs assessment, 159-160
Possibilities
  individualized education program
    awareness, 259
Poverty
  opportunity, 83-86
Practices
  identification, 123, 124
  needs assessment, 159-160
Prediction
  consequences, 197
Preferences
  consumers, 139
Preoperational Period
  Piaget, 31
Preparation
  individualized education
    programs, 246
    goals, 254
    prescriptions, 247, 248

outcomes
  analysis, 11, 12
  application, 9-11
  comprehension, 8, 9
  evaluation, 16
  knowledge, 8
  synthesis, 12-16
Prescriptions
  individualized education
    programs, 247, 248
Primary Circular Reaction
  sensory-motor period, 31
Principles
  curriculum content, 129
  intelligence as adaptation, 27
Priorities
  educational programming model,
    165, 166
  understanding, 105
Problem Solving
  innovation, 196
Problems
  gifted and talented persons, 34
  life, 34
Procedures. *See also* Processes
  curriculum content, 130
  education programming, 164
  identification, 110, 111
    advantages, 114, 115
    effectiveness, 111
    limitations, 116, 117
    underprediction, 121, 122
    value, 111-112
  nomination, 112, 113
  personal sources, 114
Processes. *See also* Procedures
  curriculum content, 130
  individualized education
    programs, 241, 242
  needs assessment, 154, 155
Products
  intelligence factors, 21
  needs assessment, 155-158
Programming. *See also* Programs
  alternatives, 99, 100
  education, 161-164

model, 165, 166
  innovation, 196
  motives, 178, 179
Programs. *See also* Programming
  development, 189, 190, 205, 224,
    225
    constraints, 164, 165
    elements, 207, 208
    funding consideration, 209-211
    plan of work, 208, 209
  impact, 213, 225, 227
  key features, 192
Proposals
  needs assessment, 161, 162
Provisions
  educational programming, 163,
    164
Psychological Tests. *See also* Tests
  intelligence and creativity, 88
Psychometrics. *See also* IQ Tests
  identification, 116-117
Public Policy
  individualized education
    programs, 249-250
Pupil and Task Match. *See* Match
Pupils
  activities, 235
  curriculum reactions, 140-142
  focus, 155
    policy, 158
    services, 156-158

Q

Quality
  educational context, 177, 223, 225
  substance of, 179-181
  teacher resource, 284
Quality Education. *See also*
  Education
  description, 173
  framework, 181
  impact, 213
Quality Programs. *See* Quality
  Education; Programs
Quality Teachers. *See* Teachers

R

Range
  behavior, 6
    guidelines, 16-18
    quality education options, 182
Range of Behaviors. *See* Range
Rationale
  individualized education
    programs, 239, 240, 288, 289,
      291
Reactions
  pupil, 140-142
Readiness
  Piaget, 30
Recommendations
  needs assessment
    parental, 256, 257
References, 295-304
Reflections
  pupils, 141
Reflexive Stage
  sensory-motor period, 31
Resource. *See also* Resource
  Distribution
  teacher, 284
Resource Distribution. *See also*
  Resource
  public policy, 249
Respect
  variations, 97
Responsibilities
  organization, 244-245
  staff, 235, 237
Rewards
  gifted and talented persons, 34
  life, 34
Role
  teacher, 281, 290, 292
    innovation, 194-195
Role Models
  performance dimensions, 42
Routes
  influence, 194, 195
Rules
  curriculum content, 129

S

School Careers. *See also* Pupils
  reflections, 141
Scope
  individualized education
    programs, 251-253
  performance assessment, 272, 273
Selection
  alternatives, 197
  considerations, 110, 111
  curriculum goals, 125, 126
  individualized education program
    materials, 259, 260
Self-Actualization
  orientation, 68
Self-Concept
  performance, 75, 76
Sensory-Motor Period
  Piaget, 31
Sequence. *See* Invariant Sequence
Sequence of Tasks, 57. *See also*
  Tasks
  adolescence, 61
  adulthood, 62, 63
    middle, 62, 63
    young, 62
  childhood, 59, 60
Services
  coverage, 257, 258
  maximizing, 258, 259
  needs assessment, 156-158
  parental recommendations, 256,
    257
Sex Role Identification
  socialization, 68
Simon, Diane, 106
Situations. *See* New Situations
Social Context. *See also* Society
  human abilities, 53
  opportunity, 83
  performance, 71
    composites, 71-73
Social Influences. *See* Influences;
  Society
Social Order

needs, 177, 178
Social Relationships
  accelerated development, 69, 70
Socialization
  family concerns, 68, 69
Society
  human abilities, 53
SOMPA, 87. *See also* Tests
  opportunity identification, 87
Sources
  motivation, 73
Special Interest
  individualized education
    programs, 232, 233
Staff
  responsibilities, 235-237
Stages
  knowledge into action translation,
    205
Starting Points
  innovation, 190, 191
Stating. *See also* Translation
  needs assessment
    proposals, 161
    recommendations, 160-161
Status
  individualized education
    programs preparation, 246, 247
Structure
  curriculum, 128
    content, 129
Style
  learning, 148, 149
Substance
  quality, 179-181
Support System. *See also* Open
  System
  definition, 202
  elements, 203, 204
  funding, 206
Survey
  Child Who, 157
Sustaining Beliefs
  innovation, 199
Synthesis
  preparing outcomes, 12-16
  range of behavior, 6, 7

T

Table of Specifications
  art education, 132
  curriculum
    outcomes, 130-136
    structure, 128
    writing, 134
Tactics
  curriculum modification, 273
  evaluation, 265
  gathering data, 264
  innovation, 193, 198, 199
Talent. *See also* Talent
  Development
  performance
    description, 40
    dimensions, 42
Talent Development. *See also*
  Development
  individualized education
    programs, 234
Task Commitment. *See also* Tasks
  ability, 45, 46
Tasks. *See also* Task Commitment
  needs assessment, 158-160
  sequence
    adolescence, 61
    adulthood, 62, 63
    childhood, 59, 60
    life's, 57
  socialization, 68
Teachers
  attributes, 183, 185-187
  core of practice, 285-288
  identification, 122-123
  individualized education program
    options, 182
  parent
    alliance, 282, 283
    conference, 283, 284
  quality resource, 284
  role, 281, 290, 292
    innovation, 194-195
  trust, 282, 283
Terms

curriculum content, 129
Tertiary Circular Response
  sensory-motor period, 31
Testing. *See also* Tests
  concerns, 244
Tests. *See also* Psychological Tests;
  Testing
  concerns, 243
Theme
  matching decisions, 148
Thinking. *See* Covergent Thinking
TOMIC
  learning, 147, 148
  model, 149, 150
TOS. *See* Table of Specifications
Tradition
  case history, 118
Transformations
  curriculum content, 130
Translation
  knowledge into action, 204-206
  needs assessment, 158-160
Trends
  eliminating handicapism, 96-97
  identification of opportunity,
    87-90
Trust
  teacher, 282, 283

U

Underachievers. *See also* Achievers;
  Underachievement
  behavior, 94
Underachievement
  concept of, 76, 77
  levels and forms, 77
Underprediction
  identification procedures, 121, 122
Understanding. *See also* Imperfect
  Understanding
  aptitude/treatment interaction,
    268, 269
  conditions of learning, 145
  consumer preferences, 139
  education programming, 161

family, 65
human abilities, 1-3
   adaptation as, 27, 49, 50
   operations, 49
   performance, 5, 49
   social context, 53
impact of quality programs, 213
individualized education
   programs, 229-231
needs, 105
   assessment task, 160
priorities, 105
sequence of tasks, 57
social influences, 65
teacher role, 281
testing limitations, 243-246
United States Office for
   Handicapped Persons, 97
Use
   curriculum, 125
   individualized education
     programs, 229-231
   needs assessment, 153

V

Values
   conflict, 70
   definition of gifted and talented,
     43
   identification procedures, 111-112
Values Assessment
   performance, 274
Variations
   respect for, 97-98
View from the Top
   Mensa Society, 33, 34

W

Writing
   Table of Specifications, 134

Y

Young Adulthood. *See also*
   Adulthood; Middle Adulthood
   sequence of tasks, 62